Guide to
STUDENT
PHONE
2011

7
DAY
BOOK

Guide to
STUDENT MONEY 2011

16th edition

GWENDA THOMAS

Guide to Student Money 2011

This 16th edition published in 2010 by Trotman Publishing an imprint of Crimson Publishing, Westminster House, Kew Road, Richmond TW9 2ND

© Gwenda Thomas & Trotman Publishing 2009, 2010

© Gwenda Thomas and Trotman & Co 1992, 1994, 1996, 1998, 1999, 2000, 2001, 2002, 2003, 2004, 2005, 2006, 2007, 2008

Previously published as *Students' Money Matters*

Author Gwenda Thomas

The *Guide to Student Money* is based on a survey conducted among students throughout the UK by Trotman Publishing.

Developed from an original idea by Andrew Fiennes Trotman.

British Library Cataloguing in Publication Data
A catalogue record for this book is available from the British Library.

ISBN 978-1-84455-236-8

Typeset by RefineCatch Ltd, Bungay, Suffolk

Printed and bound by TJ International Ltd, Padstow, Cornwall

Contents

Berlin
Mathematical
School

Freie Universität Berlin

Berlin: an excellent place to study mathematics

The Berlin Mathematical School (BMS) is a joint graduate school of the three mathematics departments at the universities in Berlin: Freie Universität (FU), Humboldt-Universität (HU) and Technische Universität (TU). It combines the broad expertise in mathematics at the three departments into an excellent environment for postgraduate studies.

The BMS PhD programme consists of two phases. In three to four semesters, Phase I leads from a Bachelor's degree level to an oral qualifying exam. The study programme for Phase I covers a broad mathematical background and the specialization required for high-level research.

Phase II (four to six semesters) is dedicated to thesis research. For entry straight into Phase II, applicants are expected to have a Master's degree or equivalent, or must pass the BMS qualifying exam and meet the regular admission requirements of the Berlin universities' PhD programmes.

Berlin is home to research groups in the following areas:

1. Analysis, geometry, and mathematical physics
2. Algebraic and arithmetic geometry, number theory
3. Probability, statistics, and financial mathematics
4. Discrete mathematics and optimization
5. Visualization and geometry processing
6. Numerical mathematics and scientific computing
7. Mathematical modelling and applied analysis.

At least half of the Phase I and all Phase II students at BMS receive **financial support** – either from one of the projects or from the BMS itself.

The BMS offers a wide range of support for its students ranging from the visa application process, housing, and child care, all the way to applying for post-doc positions. In addition the BMS offers mentoring programmes, conference funds, summer schools, support for students with children, transferable skill trainings as well as German language courses for international students, and a 'Buddy' programme for new students. Moreover, students have access to all facilities at each of the three universities. Lounges at FU, HU, and TU serve as social meeting places.

Students testimonial

'As a BMS student I have an opportunity to work with world-class scientists in my field. Through BMS lectures, I can develop my knowledge in many new disciplines in mathematics and science. BMS gives me the opportunity to join not only different math research groups, but due to its connections to MATHEON, also DFG research projects. However, BMS is something more than an excellent graduate school, it is almost like a big, international family with mathematical roots.'

Agnieszka Miedlar, Phase II Student

For further details please visit the Berlin Mathematical School website at www.math-berlin.de or call us on +49 30 314 78651.

Introduction

When I first compiled *Students' Money Matters*, now the *Guide to Student Money*, back in 1992 (this is its 16th edition), student loans were being introduced for the first time and I felt there was a need for such a publication.

I opened the book then by saying: 'When it comes to money, there is no doubt that for most UK students going on to higher education things are tough and are likely to get tougher.' I was right. But I had no idea then just how tough the going was to get and how sweeping the changes would be over the next 18 years. If this book was needed then (and it certainly was popular), it is even more essential today with the introduction of top-up fees and probably worse to come. Unless your family has a bottomless purse or you have a private income, getting through university financially is going to tax your ingenuity to the full.

But don't let this put you off university. It is still the great experience it always was. Students will have fun. The social scene is as active as ever. This year's *Student Money* survey assures us of that. Students are resourceful by nature, and most are managing to get by financially. Certainly they are leaving university with massive debts to pay off – but remember, as a graduate with a good degree you are likely to earn considerably more during your lifetime than you would do otherwise. Currently, there is a blip in this happy story. It's estimated that starting salaries for graduates are not increasing in 2010 for the second year in a row; they are stuck at a median figure of around £25,000. However, on a more positive note, graduate vacancies are not falling as rapidly as first predicted by the Association of Graduate Recruiters (AGR) *Graduate Recruitment Survey 2010 – Winter Review*. With luck, the credit crunch will be a distant memory by the time you graduate and the picture will have changed totally. But it's the financial hurdle of the next three to four years that you have to get over first, and this is where the *Guide to Student Money* can help.

How this guide can help you

In this new edition of the *Guide to Student Money*, we investigate the means and methods by which students can support themselves while studying for a degree, Higher National Diploma (HND) or other higher education (HE) qualification. The book is aimed primarily at students starting in HE this academic year (2010–2011) and beyond. *Student Money* does not set out to argue the rights and wrongs of the financial situation students find themselves in; neither does it tell you what to do. Our aim is to give helpful information and advice and to point out the pros and cons to be considered when seeking loans, overdrafts, work experience, a job, a roof over your head, etc. It is for you to weigh up the evidence and information and make your own decision – because what's right for you could be totally wrong for somebody else. However, it does include comments from employers, university tutors, careers advisers and, most importantly, students. As you might expect, the undergraduates with whom we discussed students' financial situation were very forthright in their views. These comments have been included, uncensored. There is nothing more valuable or illuminating than a report from the battlefield.

Here's how the book is organised.

▶ Chapter 1, 'That's the way the money goes', looks in detail at how students spend their money. An important section gives information on how much it is likely to cost you to live as a student in different parts of the country, plus detailed budgets from several students so you can get a picture of your likely expenses. There is information on the cost of university accommodation and a number of actual students' budgets showing exactly where the money goes.

▶ Chapter 2: now you know how much you are going to need, the second chapter, 'Fees and funding', takes a good look at where the money is likely to come from. Topics covered include top-up fees, loans to cover fees, maintenance loans, grants and bursaries.

▶ Chapter 3: so the funding is out there, but how are you going to get hold of it? This chapter looks at applying for loans and grants, means-testing, paying back your debts, additional hardship funds and why some parents have never had it so good.

▶ Chapter 4: not all nations in the UK follow the same funding system as outlined in previous chapters. Here, we look at the differences in the funding package for those in the devolved parts of the UK – Scotland, Wales and Northern Ireland.

▶ Chapter 5 provides advice for students who fall into special categories (such as part-time students, those on healthcare courses, students from overseas, students with children, etc). The financial and social implications of studying for part or all of your degree abroad are discussed.

- ▶ Chapter 6 deals with working and earning money during your course. A high proportion of students work during vacations, and a growing number work during term time. What do they do? How much do they earn?

- ▶ Chapter 7 takes time out with a gap year and provides full information on organisations to contact. There is a special section on the student travel scene.

- ▶ Chapter 8 highlights one possible source of additional finance – sponsorship – going through how to apply and what you should look out for.

- ▶ Chapter 9 focuses on other sources of funding such as scholarships, trusts, charities and professional institutions and has tips on how to approach different funding bodies.

- ▶ Chapter 10 examines funding for postgraduates.

- ▶ Chapter 11: 'Budget like a bastard' was the advice given by a first-year student at Northumbria University in our student research. With that in mind, the final chapter of the *Guide to Student Money* gives you all the information you need to budget without it becoming a burden. It also includes useful information on how the banks can help you with overdrafts, loans and freebies and explains why the bank is the student's friend.

How to use this book

To produce the *Guide to Student Money*, we drew up a list of all the questions we thought you, as a student, would want to ask about financing your studies. We then set about finding the answers. As a result, the book is written largely in the form of a dialogue.

The answers given have been kept as short, simple and direct as possible. We've cut through all the red tape and official jargon. Where we felt that you might want to dig deeper into a topic, alternative reference material has been suggested, along with appropriate organisations you can contact.

Occasionally, you will find that information has been repeated. This is to help you, the reader, find what you need to find quickly rather than having to flick from one section to another.

The book is written in a logical order – you will probably find the next question at any stage is the one you would want to ask. However, it is a reference book, and readers need to be able to dip into it, seeking answers to questions as they arise. To help you find the section you require quickly there is a contents list, which covers the main points addressed, and an index. Each chapter opens with a list of the main topics covered. If your exact question is not there, turn to the section covering that topic and you will probably find the answer. In the unlikely event you don't find the answer, do contact us – we are always interested in hearing of any omissions. Throughout the book, you will also find useful nuggets of information such as thrift tips from current students.

Money, and more particularly the lack of it, can be a depressing subject. We hope you'll find the *Guide to Student Money* an illuminating, helpful and amusing read, and that the information in the book will make your time at university or college less worrying and a lot more fun.

In the last edition, we asked for your comments, criticisms and suggestions for the next edition. These are included here along with updated facts and figures taken from new surveys of the student scene, in particular the *NatWest Student Living Index Survey* and our own *Guide to Student Money* research undertaken among some 140 student contacts. But nothing is static, least of all the pecuniary plight of students, so please keep those comments coming. It is only by being vigilant and keeping in touch with 'campus correspondents' that we can pass on the right information to those who follow.

Our thanks for helping to prepare this book must go to all those students who were an invaluable source of so much of the information – and also to the employers and financial and HE institutions who have given vital assistance in researching the material.

Gwenda Thomas

CHAPTER 1

That's the way the money goes

How much is it going to cost you to be a student? This chapter answers questions on:

- ▶ So how much will it cost you? (page 2)
- ▶ What makes so many of you do it? (page 3)
- ▶ Fees: will I have to pay them? (page 4)
- ▶ Your living expenses (page 4)
- ▶ Student budgets around the country (page 33)
- ▶ Typical student budgets (page 35)

So how much will it cost you?

Take a deep breath. How does £14,088 a year – and a staggering £15,090 a year if you are studying in London – sound horrifying? Well, that is how much the National Union of Students (NUS) estimated students needed last year, and that was just for a 39-week academic year. Multiply those figures by three or four, depending on the length of your course, and you'll have some idea of what your university degree could cost – £40,000–£50,000 and more.

Facts and figures

Will you be able to afford university?

► 65% of students were surprised at how much they spent at university.

► 5% only were not surprised.

► 30% did not comment.

Source: *Guide to Student Money* survey

You might be able to do it for less. As you'll see from the budgets at the end of this chapter, the students we interviewed were having to manage on what they could get through grants, loans, bursaries, sponsorships, parents and their own hard work and endeavour, and it wasn't anywhere near £14,000. Making ends meet while also enjoying yourself **is** possible: there are over a million students in our universities to prove it. So don't let the headline figures scare you off university. It won't be easy, but it can be done and it will be fun.

Where does the money go? Around a quarter goes on fees, books, course equipment and travel (see this and the next chapter); the rest on your living expenses – accommodation, food, socialising, clothes, general expenses and having a good time.

Many factors can affect your financial situation. Some students are luckier – or perhaps more determined – than others in:

► raising additional finance
► managing to work as well as study
► choosing to study in cheaper parts of the country
► finding/receiving additional bursary funding
► living at home
► choosing a generous university
► being excellent money managers.

While others:

► find that money slips through their fingers like water
► are great socialisers and imbibers

- ► take courses for which they have to buy expensive equipment or books, or to travel
- ► have expensive tastes and hanker after all the good things in life
- ► have a wide range of hobbies and interests
- ► study in expensive areas such as London.

Obviously, you should not pick your course on the basis of where it is cheapest to live, but it is as well to know what costs you are likely to face. This chapter looks at what it is likely to cost you to gain HE qualifications. But first …

What makes so many of you do it?

Last year, around 639,860 people applied for HE courses in the UK, a record number of students, and it looks as if the figure will be higher this year. What is the great attraction? Why did they want to forfeit the chance of having money in their pockets to become near-penniless students and pile on the debt?

These students taking part in the *Guide to Student Money* survey had no doubts.

'I want to get a job I enjoy.'

'To improve my job prospects with the hope of getting a varied career. I'm not a nine to five person.'

'I wanted to continue learning; university was the obvious path.'

If we asked everyone now studying in universities and colleges across Britain, we'd get thousands of different answers. Most would be positive, but not all.

'I don't rate uni at all. I wish the government would encourage people to do something they are good at and not waste money and time pushing people into a place they don't want.'

Law and Japanese student, Oxford Brookes

Many, however, would say 'money' – or the potential for earning it. And there is no doubt that a degree can help increase your earning power. Graduates can expect to earn on average 20–25% more than those who don't continue their formal education beyond A level over a lifetime, and much more if they study medicine or engineering, according to a report published by Universities UK. But whatever your reason for studying, it will be hard going financially for the next few years. How are you going to manage?

Fees: will I have to pay them?

Yes, unless you're a Scottish student or EU student studying in Scotland (more of that in Chapter 4).

Most students who started their course in or after 1998 have had to pay something towards the cost of it. But in 2006 the maximum tuition fee per annum was hiked up to £3,000. With year-on-year 'inflationary' rises, this year it will be £3,290. If you are a non-EU student, your fees are going to cost you a great deal more than this, wherever you study (see also Chapter 5).

Will the government take the cap off fees, as many universities want? There is talk of fees of £7,000 p.a. or worse from next year. But it is still just talk. As the *Guide* was published, no decisions on fee changes had been announced. If you have already started your course, you won't be affected by any of these changes.

Your living expenses

These have to be paid for largely by you. Maintenance grants and bursaries are being given by the government and universities so there is some help available, especially for low-income families (see Chapter 2 for full details; information on Scotland, Wales and Northern Ireland can also be found in Chapter 4). Managing is not going to be easy, but it shouldn't be impossible. However, wherever your money comes from, it's you who will have to eke it out and make ends meet. So here are the facts.

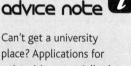

advice note

Can't get a university place? Applications for universities, especially the new universities, were up by nearly 25,227 (that's 5.5%) this year according to UCAS, and a record number of students – 160,000 – were turned away. If all of them are trying for a place again, the university scramble could be worse this year. If you are denied a place, think gap year (Chapter 7) – and try again next year.

Accommodation: the major demand on your finances

Accommodation will probably soak up half your income. If it's full board in university accommodation, you are looking at over three-quarters of your total income.

Finding the right place to live is important, especially in your first year. It can affect your whole attitude to your college, your course, your study, the town or city where you are staying, making the right friends and whether you actually do well. If it's half an hour's walk or a bus ride across town to get to the library, you may think twice about going there. If you're stuck in a bedsit with a grumpy landlord and no other students around you, the weekends could be very long and lonely. Halls are generally thought to be the best option for first years, but they aren't right for everyone.

'It is impossible to get a decent night's sleep because of noisy students returning after a night out.'

First-year Arts student, Robert Gordon University

'Occasionally you'll hear people running along the corridor at two in the morning. But mostly people are considerate.'

Modern Languages student, Cambridge

Most institutions give first-year students first refusal on halls of residence and most students jump at the chance. It gives you a circle of ready-made friends and a great social life. But for some students, living with a hundred or so other people, sharing bathrooms, meal times, TV programmes, problems, passions – even bedrooms – can mean unbearable strain. Others thrive on the camaraderie.

Criticising mixed halls, one student told us:

'Coping with an ex-boyfriend over cornflakes and coffee at 8 a.m. is something not to be endured.'

Where can I get information and help?

College prospectuses will generally give you information about halls of residence, though these may not be altogether bias-free. Students' unions may also have a view – ask if they have an alternative prospectus or students' union handbook. If it has to be accommodation in the private sector, ask for the university-approved accommodation list. Above all, check out the accommodation for yourself if you can when you make your first visit. Look at:

- cost
- whether rooms are shared
- eating arrangements – full board, half board, kitchen/self-catered
- facilities provided
- distance from college
- transport availability – and frequency and cost
- shops.

The college accommodation office is responsible for placing students in halls of residence and will send you details once you've accepted a place. It will also help you to find rented accommodation.

Accommodation in halls of residence

Costs vary significantly between different types of accommodation and different universities, with much higher costs in the London colleges in particular. Be aware that the number of meals per day, the number of days per week that meals are served and the number of weeks in the academic year can vary between institutions. Some establishments offer accommodation other than the norm, such as en-suite, up-to-the minute facilities or out-of-town accommodation.

When comparing self-catered university halls of residence with the rented sector, remember that gas and electricity are probably (but not always) included in the cost of college accommodation. This is unlikely to be the case in the rented sector.

cash crisis

Students in the South East but studying outside the London area are thought to be suffering particularly badly, as they are being asked to pay London-equivalent rents while not qualifying for the larger student loans available to students who study in the capital.

Will I have to share a room?

Possibly. In some colleges, especially the older establishments, you may have to share a room for one or two terms. If you do have to share, you will probably be sent a questionnaire designed to find out what sort of person you are and the kind of person you could live with. Some typical questions are listed below.

► Would you want to share with a smoker (where it's still allowed)?

► Are you an early riser?

► Do you like to go to bed late and get up late?

► Are you a party person?

► What kind of music do you like – is there any kind you can't stand?

Honesty is the only way to harmony. Even if you are easy-going about smoking, do you really want to sleep in a smoky atmosphere? And, although your intentions may be very laudable at the moment, how are you going to feel about your room-mate stomping around at eight in the morning when you've been out partying until two?

'Halls are great, except you don't get to pick who you live with; sharing a flat with six other people can be a nightmare, especially when food goes missing and the kitchen becomes a garbage site.'

First-year Management Studies student, Middlesex

'I'd never shared a room with anyone before and didn't really like the idea. At first it was strange, but after a couple of weeks you got used to it. Having someone around most of the time is fun.'

First-year Economics student, St Andrews

'I thought I wouldn't like sharing a room, but actually it's nice to have someone to come home to.'

First-year Modern Languages student, Durham

'I don't get on with my hall mates, I want to move.'

First-year, Ancient and Medieval History, Lampeter

'I strongly believe the London weighting should be further increased. My loan has never done more than barely cover my accommodation and that has made everything really, really stressful. If I hadn't found a job I don't know what I would have done.'

Third-year Mathematics student, University College London (UCL)
(Job: football statistician; pay: £15 p.h.)

How much is uni going to cost me?

Most of the figures given in this section on what students are likely to have to pay are based on the *NatWest Student Living Index Survey*, August 2009, which was carried out among students in 20 major university towns throughout the UK (excluding London) and research undertaken by the *Guide to Student Money*, which homed in on a smaller number of universities and students. Both revealed some interesting facts … as you will discover.

Action

Check out the length and terms of your accommodation contract. A recent survey of university students found that more and more landlords were asking students to sign 52-week contracts for accommodation.

it's a fact

Have you found yougo yet? It's a student-only social network site developed by UCAS (http://yougo.co.uk) dedicated to helping young people thinking about a move into HE to get in touch. The idea behind the site is to connect, online, current Year 12, S5 or equivalent students with those considering similar courses or universities, so they can 'meet' and chat before they arrive on campus. As a member you'd have the opportunity to 'make friends' with current students so you'd know what to expect when you arrive.

If you are renting in the private sector, remember that a deposit may have to be paid upfront – a month's rent is the norm, but it could be more, and this will be kept against loss or damage until you vacate the premises.

This means they are paying rent during the Christmas, Easter and three-month summer vacations when they are likely to be at home – something you don't have to do in university accommodation.

Another problem we encountered was that students such as medics who have to undertake a placement away from their university may find they are paying for somewhere to live on that placement for a couple of months while still paying for the accommodation in their university town.

From one who knows:

'If your landlord won't fix something, take a photograph of the problem so you have evidence that it's not your fault. With this in hand, the landlord will find it difficult to play the trick of docking your deposit when you leave. Our curtain railing has come down and the landlord won't fix it. But he won't pull a fast one on us.'

Law student, Northampton

How Much is Accommodation Going to Cost?

Average outside London: £74.18 per week; in London, if you find somewhere under £100 a week you are doing well.

While on average students throughout the country, excluding London, are paying £74 per week, Oxford with average rents at £84.65 p.w. and Brighton at £86.53 p.w. were worryingly high. You could pay less if you're living outside the centre, but you would then have travel costs. The cheapest places to rent in England according to the *NatWest Student*

Living Index Survey were Leicester at £65.89 and Cardiff in Wales at £67.85. But Northern Ireland beats them all with an average of £46.09, according to the Northern Ireland Housing Executive. Don't forget that on top of rent you may have utilities (gas, electricity, water) to pay for. The *Student Living Index Survey* estimates these cost around £21.11 a week, which is something you probably won't have to pay in university accommodation. Full details of rents in different parts of the country are shown in Table 37 on page 136.

Possible problems when renting student accommodation

'Exploding shower, broken-down washing machine, dangerous housemates.'
Third-year Entertainment Crafts student, Cleveland

'Entertaining unwanted visitors – cockroaches from the café downstairs.'
First-year Modern European Studies student, Thames Valley

'Difficulty with housemate, leak in house, noise.'
First-year Legal Practice Course (LPC) student,
University of the West of England (UWE)

'Lodgings miles from anywhere. Buses stopped at 7p.m. so late study and going out meant paying for a taxi home.'
Second-year Engineering student, Brunel

'I'm living with my landlord and a horde of mice. They eat everything – the mice, that is!'
Third-year Mental Philosophy student, Edinburgh

'An ex-prisoner broke into the flat – he was living there, unbeknown to us, for four days.'
Fourth-year Archaeology student, Lampeter

'A mouse chewed through the kitchen wiring and we lost the use of our oven and boiler. Agent said: "Mice don't eat wires, they eat cheese."'
Fourth-year Medicine student, St George's

'Landlords hate spending money. Learn some basic DIY and plumbing and you'll be fine.'
Second-year DPhil in Education student, Oxford

'Typing in fingerless gloves and arctic wear was a good solution. At least the rent was cheap.'
First-year Classics Master's student, Oxford

'Heating non-existent! We all wear gloves and thick socks around the house and jumpers in bed. But the mice are quite content.'
Third-year Creative Imaging student, Huddersfield

'My previous landlord wouldn't give me a contract and refused to return my deposit.'
Second-year Journalism student, Lancaster

'Fleas in my bedroom.'
Third-year Modern Languages with English student, St Andrews

advice note ℹ️

Landlords who don't give deposits back should be a thing of the past in England and Wales. A tenancy scheme has been introduced. Check www.direct.gov.uk/en/TenancyDeposit/index.htm for full details before handing over your deposit, and check that your landlord is adhering to the new law. Of course, if you trash the place, you can't expect to see your money back – it works both ways. Scotland is still debating the issue, and Northern Ireland has three government-approved schemes; check which your landlord is using before you hand the money over.

'Too few appliances in kitchen, e.g. one oven for 10 people.'

Second-year Human
Geography student, Lancaster

'Only one small common room for 600 students, and only nine washing machines.'

First-year History student, Manchester

'Two dogs and the landlord, not the best of housemates.'

Third-year Biochemistry student, St Andrews

'The gas man called the house a "death-trap".'

Third year English and
Social Anthropology student, St Andrews

But it's not all complaints:

'Our landlord is very sweet; he bought us a huge packet of biscuits for Christmas.'

Second-year Psychology student,
Queen's University Belfast

'Our landlord is ace. When the security system started beeping at 1a.m., he came out to fix it.'

Second-year Law student, Reading

Alice's story

Problem: my bedspring broke. Sleep was impossible. Exams were looming. I needed rest but my landlady was very slow to get things done. Strategy was called for. I invited the landlady over and got her to sit on the bed while we talked. I asked her if she was comfortable, and she had to agree she was not. I then asked her if she would like to sleep on the bed – every night. A new bed arrived within four days.

Should I take out insurance?

That's something only you can really decide. A recent survey completed by Endsleigh shows that, on average, students now take £4,200 worth of belongings to university, and this is not going unnoticed by thieves. These possessions are often highly valuable and portable – for example laptops, iPods and mobiles. If you lost them, how would you replace them?

Insurance is another drain on your resources, but it could be money well spent and save a lot of heartache. Endsleigh receives some £350,000 worth of claims from students during their first month at uni, which is fairly substantial. If you are living in halls, you may find there is a comprehensive policy covering all students and that this is included in your rent bill. If you are living in rented accommodation, the landlord of the house or flat you rent should have the premises covered by insurance for fire and structural damage, but this is unlikely to cover your personal possessions. Students tend to keep open house, and because people are coming and going all the time security is often lax. If you do have a lot of expensive possessions it might be worthwhile considering taking out your own insurance, especially if you carry expensive belongings around. Ask yourself: what would it cost me to replace my iPod, stereo, TV, DVD player, camera, designer watch, PC, course books, whatever? Compare that with an outlay of, say, £30 a year. Rates for personal insurance depend on where you live. It costs more if you live in a big city than a sleepy rural town. In a crime hotspot, rates can be prohibitive.

'Everybody round here hires a TV, so if it walks it's covered by the TV rental company. The same goes for washing machines and all other appliances.'
First-year student, Liverpool

'We had a microwave and sofa cushions stolen! But mainly it's computers, TVs, stereos.'
Third-year Genetics student, Birmingham

You can also take out insurance to cover the fees you have paid just in case you are ill – or worse – and can't complete your year.

NatWest's Essential Contents Insurance seems ideal for the student living in rented accommodation because it offers 'pick and mix' cover for the things that are valuable to you, such as laptops, iPods and mobile phones, which means that you don't pay for cover you don't need. It can include cover for walk-in theft (though not for money). You can even cover downloads that you have purchased and stored on home entertainment equipment or mobile. The cost varies according to what you choose to insure, and there is a lot of detail you should look into before deciding, but it sounds like a good deal.

Endsleigh, who specialise in helping students, offer student possessions insurance starting at £16 for £3,000 worth of cover in halls of residence and £28 for £3,000 of cover off-campus in a 'good' area. They also offer a multitude of different cover options to add on to your contents cover. These include electrical items cover (which would include your laptop and iPod outside of your home), mobile phone cover for just £39 a year (which will also cover BlackBerries and iPhones), non-electrical item cover, legal cover and tuition fee and rent protection, to cover you in case you need to drop out of university due to illness or your financially supporting parent is made redundant.

Do you make music? Whether you play in an orchestra or for a rock band, whether it's part of your course or you do it for pleasure or to make extra money, if you lost that valuable guitar, violin, double bass or cello you'd be stuck. Insurance rates vary depending on whether you are in the UK or travelling in Europe and what kind of instrument you have. Endsleigh offers flexible cover against theft and accidental damage for any musical instrument, subject to a minimum premium of £20. Cover is available for orchestral instruments (such as violins or double basses) and non-orchestral instruments.

There is a choice of where cover can operate: UK only; UK and up to 30 days in the EU; and anywhere in the world. Shop around to get the best cover before making a decision.

Are you covered by your parents' insurance?

If you are, that is obviously the cheapest form of cover, but don't assume that your possessions are covered by your parents' home insurance once you go to uni. Some standard home insurance polices specifically exclude students – I wonder why? Get your parents to check the small print.

Where to live?

How to decide where to live

The *Guide to Student Money* survey asked students how they decided on their accommodation and whether they would recommend that method. It would seem there are four main ways for students to find accommodation – the university itself, the internet, letting agencies and word of mouth.

By far the most popular way of finding accommodation is through your university, which is hardly surprising, and these days it is mostly through the university website. Most students found this very satisfactory:

'Comprehensive list, easily searchable by size and price.'
Third-year Literature student, Aberdeen

'Accommodation very close to the university and reasonably priced.'
First-year Pharmacology student, Aberdeen

'University sent me a brochure – I wanted to be in halls for the first year.'
Photography student, Falmouth

'The student message board site. A good way for students to get in touch with each other.'
Fourth-year English student, St Andrews

But others were not so contented:

'Still recommended by the university ... despite us and many others asking that the accommodation should be removed.'
Third-year Journalism and Media and Cultural Studies student, UWE

'They are not efficient and don't appreciate the seriousness of problems.'
Fourth-year Maths student, St Andrews

The second most favoured option was the internet, although the response was more mixed:

'Better deal.'
Fourth-year Biomedical Sciences plus Physiology student, Aberdeen

'Less effort.'
Second-year Chemistry student, Aberdeen

'Awful.'
First-year Zoology student, Aberdeen

Letting agencies are also popular with students:

'More options.'
Second-year, Music Systems Engineering student, UWE

'Easier than going directly through landlords as landlords can be difficult.'
Second-year English and Creative Writing student, Falmouth

'Fast – no hassle.'
Second-year Biology student, Aberdeen

'In St Andrews you need to try all options and this is one of the main ones.'
Second-year Medicine student, St Andrews

The most satisfactory method, however, seems to be recommendation through a friend:

'You can get a good report of the house and landlord.'
Third-year Real Estate student, UWE

'It's good to have a recommendation.'
Third-year Music student, Dartington

'Less interest (competition) from others.'
Third-year Contemporary Crafts student, UWE

'Information is passed on about landlord.'
Third-year Biblical Studies and Theology student, St Andrews

'Honest advice.'
Second-year Photography student, Falmouth

In some places there are also accommodation fairs, which offer a wide range of choice, according to a first-year Textile student at Falmouth.

To give you some more ideas about where to live, we asked students what they thought.

Living in halls: Rachel's story

Rachel is a first year at St Andrews, studying French. She chose halls because she thought it would help her meet people and make friends quickly – which she has. She decided on full catering because she felt it would be nice to have people to eat with and everything provided. As she says: 'There would be less to worry about.'

Rachel certainly isn't roughing it. She has her own en-suite room. 'It is small but warm and cosy, which is important in Scotland,' she says. However, it comes at a price – around £6,000 a year. St Andrews is an old university and a single room is a luxury. Many rooms are large but shared.

Rachel's room is on a mixed corridor with 12 other student rooms and they share a fully equipped kitchen. Full catering means three meals a day Monday to Friday but just breakfast and lunch at the weekends, not the evening meal.

'We generally cook all together at weekends, it's cheaper,' she says. 'And with an Italian neighbour in charge of the cooking, it's fantastic. We all help chopping this and that and washing up, but she is the chef. Her lasagne is phenomenal and her pasta bake is just amazing. Some restaurants will give you 30% off on a Sunday night, though, so occasionally we eat out.

'There's a great social life at St Andrews. I'll go out about twice a week. It starts with a few friends, but the town is so small you are always bumping into people you know who tag along, so by the end it's a large group. There is one nightclub and a number of bars. But much of the entertainment we make ourselves.'

Additional food costs Rachel about £20 a week and her social life around £15 a week.

Rachel studies mostly in the library twice a week; it is open until midnight most nights in term time and only ten minutes' walk away. 'Noise can be a problem in halls,' she says. 'That's one of the reasons I am hoping to move into a flat next year. Fortunately, most people around me have a good taste in music, but it's not much fun being woken up at two in the morning by someone who has been celebrating passing an exam when you still have exams to take the next day.' However, with rent in St Andrews, which can reach around £125 each a week, Rachel does not think it will be a cheap year.

'Living in St Andrews is like living in a bubble; everything is there and you don't need anything or want to go outside, so you don't.'

Sharing a flat: Matt's story

Matt is a third-year Forensic Science student at Nottingham Trent. His is a story of contrasts. Two years ago, he had a bad experience. He moved into a newly converted flat in what had been a telephone exchange. 'You could say there were eight of us living in that flat – three boys, four girls and a ghost. The building had a chequered history. Extraordinary things went on there – including a suicide. I can't say I actually saw an apparition, but I certainly heard a lot of creaks, bangs and strange laughter.'

The flat had a kitchen with a large dining area plus a TV and seven large bedrooms with en-suite bathrooms. There were no bills to worry about: all the utilities were included in the rent which, at £84.99 a week, wasn't exorbitant for Nottingham. It sounded perfect! But it wasn't a happy household. 'Things went missing,' says Matt, 'including my champagne. There was no togetherness. We each catered for ourselves, which is an expensive way to live. My food bill alone was £25 a week. If only people could have been bothered to put their dirty dishes in the dishwasher it would have helped.' Matt's advice: 'Get the whole sharing thing sorted before you move in and don't air your grievances on Facebook: it just makes things worse.'

The next year, he moved into another new block of student flats built on top of TK Maxx in the centre of Nottingham. He was eight floors up and had a fantastic view right across the city. He shared with four other students, all male. The accommodation was similar to his previous flat and they all had en-suite bedrooms.

'This is the best accommodation I have had,' Matt assured us at the time. Why? 'We are five blokes sharing. The flat is tidy, we all get on, there are no arguments, nothing goes missing and there's a good atmosphere. If we are all in, then we will cook together – Tesco is just round the corner. Weekly food bill: £15–£20. Rent is £89 a week: £4 more than last year, but worth every penny. What's more, the rent included a travelcard for the buses.'

But then we caught up with Matt this year: he has just moved into a house and now says: 'No, this is the best accommodation I have had so far.' Why?

'I'm living with three girls so it's very civilised and I have a massive room, large enough to swing a cat in – if I had one.'

Sharing a house: Luke's story

Luke is a second-year Sports Science student at Exeter University

Students visiting Luke and his six housemates should enter with caution. There's a massive pile of shoes just by the front door. 'I started it,' he says. 'When you have a room on the third floor and you're downstairs, you don't want to be running up two flights when you want to pop out to the off licence.' So he started leaving his shoes by the front door. The idea caught on and the pile just grew.

The house is large – seven bedrooms – which Luke shares with three other boys, who are all studying Sports Science, and three girls, taking Childhood and Youth Studies. There's a sizeable kitchen where they eat, a sitting room, two bathrooms and a small patio garden. Do they all get on? 'We all met in halls,' Luke says, 'and yes, it works pretty well. We have a rota for cleaning up the kitchen – a day each a week. Then we'll all blitz the rest of the house when the mess gets too much. The garden looks after itself.'

He adds: 'The bedrooms all have double beds – which is unusual, most rooms have single beds – and mine is sufficiently large to accommodate my computers, my guitars and sports gear. That's unusual too.

'We don't have a kitty. When something runs out we kind of know whose turn it is to restock.

'We four boys cook together,' says Luke. 'Being into sport we need protein. So we tend to eat well – nothing fancy though – mince or chicken in a pan with a dollop of curry sauce. We take it in turns to cook. Occasionally, I'll do a roast. Worth staying in for! Food bill: around £10 each a week.

'At £80 a week each, the rent is reasonable for Exeter. This is one of the better houses and we are only a five-minute walk from campus. To secure the place, we had to put down a hefty deposit – £360 each this year and another £400 each for next year because we have decided to stay on.

'We haven't had a party yet, but people continually drop in. Generally we drink here before we go out and hit the clubs – it's cheaper that way. It's two litres of cider for just £3, not bad. We tend to go out two to three times a week. Several of us play guitar, so when we come home we'll have a session – that's one of the big advantages a house has over halls, you can make as much noise as you like – well almost!'

Thrift Tips

'Book travel in advance. I travelled from Durham to London for £10.'
Second-year Modern History student, Durham

'Work as a TV extra or catalogue model.'
Third-year Psychology student, Wolverhampton

'Sell your work.'
Third-year Visual Studies student, Norwich School of Art and Design

'Use your hobby – I photographed a family on holiday and pocketed €100.'
Wolverhampton student

Living at home: Aysha's story

If Aysha Tezgel manages her future clients' finances as well as she is managing her own at university, she will go far. Aysha is 22 and in her final year at City University's Cass Business School, where she is studying Banking and International Finance with German.

When she started her degree, she was determined to have a good time while at university but without getting into debt. 'I chose a university so I could live at home,' she says. 'This was not really a problem. The Cass Business School has an excellent reputation.

'I also have generous parents who said I could live at home rent-free. So I had no worries about bills and shopping. Even my laundry was done, so I could concentrate on my studies.' With end-of-year results in the 70s and 80s, that approach certainly paid off. Her major expense was her monthly travelcard, which even with her student discount was £120. 'Again, my parents often paid for it.'

In that first year, she also received a partial maintenance grant and a university bursary of £1,000. But it was only when the Worshipful Company of Needlemakers came up trumps with a £1,000 scholarship (given through the university) that Aysha knew that she was going to make ends meet, at least for her first year.

During two gap years, Aysha had saved more than enough to cover her fees, but still decided to take out a fee loan and leave her own money happily earning interest. 'My rainy day fund,' she calls it. She also took out a £1,000 student loan, which was a great help during the long summer vacation. 'I need £4,000–£5,000 for living expenses to cover travel, books, food, drink, clothing and other day-to-day expenses. If I were to live by myself, even in halls, I would need at least £12,000–£13,000.'

Things were much the same during her second year. But now, in her third year, Aysha's family is, like so many others, feeling the effects of the credit crunch, and she cannot rely on her parents for so much help.

Ever resourceful, Aysha has taken two part-time jobs. She works for a professor at the Business School and a bank consultancy firm and earns about £300 a month. You might think in your final year that is the last thing you would want to do. But both jobs are very closely related to her course and will count as valuable experience on her CV. 'So I haven't had to touch my rainy day fund yet,' she says.

Aysha doesn't feel she has missed out on the social life by living at home. When something good is going on – a party, clubbing, whatever – she just beds down with one of her many friends.

'I'm still glad I am living at home because I need the support of my family more than ever in the final year, with the burden of a 10,000-word dissertation plus eight exams and eight pieces of coursework.

'The major drawback of living at home? The commuting, especially when you have a 9a.m. lecture.'

More and more students are choosing universities where they can continue to live at home because it is cheaper. In fact, 72% of our student contacts said they knew of someone who had decided to study in their own home town for financial reasons. As you will see in the next chapter, the amount of loan you can borrow if you live at home is smaller, but then this means less debt. For some students, this idea would be unthinkable: going to university is all about gaining independence. But if that results in you having to abandon your course because of debt, then you could be back where you started – at home! It's worth thinking about.

Do I have to pay council tax?

Students are largely exempt from paying council tax. Certainly, if you live in a hall of residence, college accommodation, student house or somewhere in which all the residents are students, you will be exempt. If you live in a house where there are already two adults, your presence does not add to the bill. If you live in a house with one adult, that person will not lose their 25% single occupancy discount providing they can supply proof that you are a student.

However, things are never quite that simple, as Leeds Metropolitan University Welfare Officer Paul Hubert pointed out to us. 'Frequently,' he said, 'students in external accommodation do not spot the problems coming and these can prove intractable.'

Some examples are as follows.

▶   A full-time student moves into a house shared with non-students and housemates expect them to contribute to the council tax bill.

▶   A flatmate drops out of their course during the summer and fails to claim benefit.

▶   A part-time student thought they would be exempt.

▶   The student/postgrad is writing up work and is refused student status by local authorities.

If in doubt, go to your university welfare officer – they are usually on the ball.

Thrift Tips for Drinkers

'Make your own beer – it's fun, cheap and tasty.'
Third-year Digital Media student, Wolverhampton

'Organise parties at home and get others to bring the drink.'
Second-year Journalism, Film and Media student, Cardiff

'Drink cider rather than beer – it's cheaper and takes less to get you drunk.'
Fourth-year Biochemistry student, Oxford

'Become teetotal.'
Third-year Design student, Wolverhampton

Impossible? Try the next tip.

'Learn to drink slowly.'
Third-year English student, Wolverhampton

Other living expenses

While your accommodation will probably take at least half of your available resources, how are you going to spend the rest?

Food

Average: £23.26 eating in and £15.83 eating out per week.

Once you have a roof over your head, the next major expense is food, and here the *NatWest Student Living Index Survey* showed that costs were fairly similar throughout the country with an average weekly food bill of £39.09, just a couple of pounds up on last year. However, when we started to look at individual areas within the UK, the picture changed. The hungriest students, with an average weekly spend of £44.50, were in Liverpool, followed by Newcastle, where students had an average weekly spend of £43.88. The biggest eaters in Scotland were at Dundee, with an average weekly spend of £43.12. For frugal living go to York, where students' average spend is £32.74 (£19.23 in the supermarket and another £13.51 on eating out).

(We have no figures for London or Northern Ireland.)

Socialising/entertainment

Going out – average: £17.61 per week. Alcohol – average: £26.18 per week.

Facts and Figures

Biggest social spenders and their weekly spend:

- Leeds: £57.61
- Portsmouth: £50.06
- Dundee: £49.37
- Nottingham: £47.61
- Cardiff: £46.64
- Manchester: £46.53
- Glasgow: £46.39
- Cambridge: £46.05
- Oxford: £45.16
- Brighton: £43.98

Source: *NatWest Student Living Index Survey* 2009

The *Student Living Index Survey* didn't assess how good a 'good time' students were having or how often they went out, but on average students spend £43.79 per week on clubbing, pubbing, gigs, cinema and drinking. The biggest spenders, with bills of around £57.61 per week, were to be found in Leeds, followed by students in Portsmouth, who had a weekly bill of £50.06.

If you look at alcohol consumption alone the top prize still goes to Leeds, with an average weekly spend of £32.78. The most abstemious students can be found in Edinburgh, with an average weekly alcohol bill of £18.38. They also tend to be the big stay-at-homes, with a rather meagre average weekly spend of £11.24 a week on going out.

After rent, the students who responded to our own *Guide to Student Money* survey put food as their highest expenditure with socialising as their second highest expenditure.

Thrift Tips for Hungry Students

Students told us:

'Give dinner parties and charge.'
Second-year Industrial Relations and Modern History student, St Andrews

'Make your own sandwiches for lunch and sell them to friends.'
First-year Medicine student, Cambridge

'Get to like pasta!'
Fourth-year Psychology student, Paisley

'If each of your friends brings a potato, carrot or leek, you've got a great stew for next to nothing.'
First-year Music student, Huddersfield

Books and course materials

Average: £9.50 a week.

All students said they spent more on books in the autumn term and in their first year than at any other time. Some reported that they'd then taken to using libraries instead of buying as books were so expensive. It is difficult to give a meaningful average figure for books because what you need to buy depends on your course and how well stocked your college library is in your subject. It's worth checking this out before

It's a fact

What are students drinking?

- ► Most popular alcoholic drink: Cider
- ► Most popular non-alcoholic drink: Water
- ► Cheapest alcoholic drink: Beer
- ► Cheapest non-alcoholic drink (excluding water): Tea

What to Cook

The *Guide to Student Money* survey asked students for easy-to-cook recipe ideas and they came up with some good ones. For sophistication we went for frozen grapes with dark chocolate, for originality nettle soup – but our hot favourite has to be melted Snickers on toast!

'Pasta and pesto! Cheese on toast is a classic too.'
Fourth-year student, Aberdeen

'Tinned tomatoes, tin of chickpeas, spoon of curry paste and some fresh spinach, served with rice. Mega-cheap and tasty.'
Second-year student, Falmouth

'Baked beans, chips, and fried vegetables with frankfurters are my favourites and cheapest dishes.'
Aberdeen student

'Frozen grapes with dark chocolate.'
Second-year student, St Andrews

'See what's on offer then google those ingredients and see what you get.'
Second-year student, St Andrews

'Grilled cheese and tomato on tortillas for a yummy snack.'
First-year student, St Andrews

'Minced beef, carrot, parsnip, onion, tomato in a big pan, cook up and add whatever else you can find and it's guaranteed to taste awesome.'
Second-year student, UWE

'Nettle soup. Pick a bunch of nettles, fry an onion, garlic, any veggies and a potato and stock, then whizz up, adding enough stock to bring to correct consistency.'
Third-year student, St Andrews

'Melted Snickers on toast.'
First-year student, Lancaster

starting your course if you can. As a very general guide, the average figure in the *NatWest Student Living Index Survey* was £9.50 a week.

More and more students told us they were using the library.

Book check

Your university or college may have a second-hand bookshop. Find out before you start buying: books are very expensive. Check out your college library, too. Is it well stocked in books on your subject? Is it close to where you study and where you live? Try the internet – there are many sites for buying and selling textbooks.

It's a Fact

Great news, guys – it looks as if you are going to be outnumbered yet again! Of university applications received by the January 2010 deadline, 324,554 were made by females and just 246,002 by males. Have a good year!

Source: UCAS

Rebecca tells us she spends £30 a week on equipment. She is currently on an MA in Photography at University College Falmouth, and says equipment is her greatest expense after rent and food.

Photocopying, library costs and fines, etc.

Average: £4.03 per week.

Many universities provide a photocopying card, which can ease your costs. For those on courses where study covers topics in a wide range of books, the cost can be considerable. On average, £4.03 a week was spent on photocopying and library costs. Many of our student contacts said most of their copying costs went on ink and paper for their own printers.

Field trips

Up to £700 per trip.

Geography, biology, astrophysics, computer science, music, sustainable development, medicine, education, ancient and medieval history – the list goes on. All these courses included field trips. Costs last year ranged from £2–£3 to £700. Of the 140 students contacted by the *Guide to Student Money* last year, 16 mentioned field trips as an expense. Interestingly, they were all studying different subjects.

The actual cost will depend on the course you are taking, so an average would be meaningless. We found one student at Oxford who gave a range of £4 to £700. Keep field trips in mind when checking out your degree.

'Geology is becoming very expensive. I have two compulsory field trips a year costing £150 each.'

Third-year student, Durham

Mobile phones

Average: £9.99 per week.

Most students today have a mobile. New deals have brought bills down, as our research shows, and more and more students rely on their mobiles rather than pay for a landline. Highest spenders according to the *NatWest Student Living Index Survey* were students in Cambridge, with average weekly bills of £12.18, and the lowest Nottingham, with a weekly bill of £8.79.

Internet

It would seem this is no longer a major expense for students. Many find it is included in their rent.

Clothing

Average: £18.38 a week.

Thrift Tips for Cutting the Cost of Your Phone Bill

Certain 08 numbers (0844, 0845, 0870 and 0871, for example) masquerade as costing the same as local calls but may not be as cheap as you think, and may not be covered by any cost-saving phone deal you have in place either. Many mobile phone packages exclude free phone numbers such as 0800 and 0808, so you pay the going rate for calling these. To find the cheapest way to phone an 08 number, log on to www. saynoto0870.com. They might give you an alternative local number, or show how your call can be routed in a different way.

A broadband connection can mean a monthly bill of around £20, but in most houses this would be shared between perhaps four or five students. Look for the special offers, and if you are hoping to hop from one offer to another make sure there are no tie-in clauses in the contract.

Average student spend on clothes is up on last year's £16.62. Do students feel we are coming out of the recession? The change is very apparent when we look at the best-dressed universities in the *NatWest Student Living Index Survey*. Last year, Nottingham was top of the league, with an average spend of £23.86. This year it's Cambridge, with a weekly average of £25.10. The university least bothered sartorially this year was Edinburgh, with a weekly bill of £11.16.

Best-dressed regions

England was very close to the average with weekly bills of £18.88, while the rest of the mainland was below average – Scotland at £16.65 and Wales at £15.95. Table 1 shows the best-dressed universities.

Table 1 Best-dressed universities (of 20 looked at)

University	Average spend per week
Cambridge	£25.10
Oxford	£22.87
Birmingham	£21.25
Liverpool	£21.01
Dundee	£20.35
Leicester	£20.29

Source: *NatWest Student Living Index Survey* (London and Northern Ireland were not included)

Travel during term time

Average: £11.01 per week

To survive, it seems you need to be fit. Students said that walking was their main way of getting about. For many, however, travel was still a significant cost. This year, London – which usually has the highest bills – was not part of the *NatWest Student Living Index Survey*. In the rest of the country, it was the students in Birmingham who seemed to have the highest weekly term-time travel bills at £18.00, while at the other end of the scale students in Cardiff had weekly bills of around £4.73. Our average figure of £11.01 includes taxis. Average termly spend among the students *Student Money* contacted was £70, with another £32 a term to go home.

Check with your local authority to see if you are entitled to financial help with transport. Scottish students can claim extra for travel as a grant if costs exceed £159 a year.

About a fifth of students are thought to own a car or motorcycle. This estimate includes many mature students, who tend to drive longer distances than younger students during term. While petrol is an obvious cost, we felt that an average was not helpful. Cycling seems to be much less popular than it was a few years ago. Students complained that cycling was dangerous, and another gripe was having their bicycles stolen – even being mugged for a mountain bike. Students cited pollution and traffic congestion as problems.

The *Guide to Student Money* discovered that 35% of students had some form of transport. Of these, 62% had cars and 36% bicycles.

Travel check

▶ The frequency of university and local bus services: a huge number of students complained about the infrequency and unreliability of bus services and the fact that they didn't run at night.

'... and when the buses do come they are often so full they don't stop. It's quite common to be late for lectures.'

Second-year International Tourism and
Management student,
Robert Gordon University

▶ The last bus: a number of students complained that in many cities, bus services finish early with no regular service after 10.30p.m. – a major problem for sociable students in outlying districts. Check on this when choosing accommodation; you don't want to find out that ...

'... the last bus was at 7p.m. Even a modest social life was impossible.'

Law student, Bristol

'... student bus prices end on Saturday night, through Sunday into Monday morning. The price is then increased by over 500%.'

Student, Falmouth

Facts and Figures

▶ Students spend around half their money on accommodation.

▶ The number of students taking up university places in autumn 2009 was up by 5.5% on the previous year, making a grand total of 431,854 (UCAS figures).

▶ 7.4% of students in the UK drop out of their course (Higher Education Statistics Agency, 'HESA').

▶ The NUS believes a major cause of dropping out is financial hardship (NUS Student Hardship Survey).

▶ Other reasons include exam failure, ill health and switching courses.

▶ Britain has one of the lowest university drop-out rates for degrees on the global completion table.

▶ Transport in St Andrews was highly criticised.

'There isn't a train station in St Andrews.'

'Buses delayed and fail to turn up.'

▶ Another Scottish city didn't fare any better.

'Public transport in Aberdeen in abysmal, I refuse to use it.'

▶ And for those who resort to their own transport, parking was seen as a problem.

'They lock the gates of the car park. If I leave my car on campus to go out with friends, I can't get it out again.'

Student, UWE

'Very difficult to park and public transport is not the best.'

Student, St Andrews

▶ The area at night: an increasing number of both male and female students in many more universities said it was dangerous to walk alone at night. They included students from Huddersfield, Staffordshire, London and many more. Many also said taxis were expensive.

'Late night in London is often dangerous. Many confrontations!'

First-year Music student, City University

'Walking at night. Irregular buses. Someone destroyed my bike.'

Second-year Pharmacology student, Oxford

'Walking through an estate at night.'

First-year Medicine student, St George's, London

'Taxis can cost £4 for a three-minute journey after midnight.'

Third-year English student, St Andrews

'You need a car in Bradford; walking even in the early evening is dangerous.'

Second-year Technology and Management student, Bradford

▶ But there were more positive comments.

'Taxis are in good supply in Bangor and a journey across town is cheap.'

Second-year Psychology student, Bangor

Megabus, Megatrain and Student Rail and Coach Cards

Before you do anything, check out Megatrain and Megabus travel. With or without a card, they could be the cheapest option. Travel is available to many of the UK's largest towns and cities for as little as £1 each way plus 50p booking fees – rather less than to cross London on the tube. See www.megatrain.com or www.megabus.com.

Regular train and coach services offer student reductions, provided you buy their special student cards, which last for a year. One longish journey will more than cover the initial outlay, which is:

16–25 Railcard: £26 for one-year card
£65 for three-year card
(January 2010)
Reduction: one-third off all rail fares.
Travel restrictions: check with station for full details.
Check internet for any reductions

16–26 Coachcard: £10 for one-year card
£25 for three-year card
(January 2010)
Reduction: up to 30%.

Travel between home and college

How much will it cost to get to your college from your family home and back again during the year? The average spent on longer trips was £20.38 per week. If you live in Exeter and decide to study in Glasgow, getting there is going to be a major expense and you won't be popping home very often. But if home is Birmingham and you study somewhere close at hand like Manchester, it's relatively cheap and you might go home weekly, which over time would tot up. So an average isn't really meaningful.

Plan your trips home and book early – there are some fantastic bargains on trains and coaches (see below). Coaches are generally cheaper than trains, but they take longer and the amount of luggage you can take with you is usually limited. The most popular means of transport for students is the train. However, many students told the *Guide to Student Money* that their parents might give them a lift at the beginning and end of the year when they have a lot of luggage. If you do have to stagger home with your luggage using public transport, remember your costs may need to include taxi fares.

See Table 2 for some comparative travel costs from London. Prices are based on return fare prices in February 2010 using a 16–25 Railcard or Coachcard discount.

Table 2 Comparative travel costs from London

Typical fares	Train	Train	Coach
	Advance single. Two singles need to be purchased. Limited number of tickets	Off-Peak Super Return	Mostly off-peak booked in advance. £1 booking fee charged
London to:			
Edinburgh	From £7.90 × 2	£71.50	£35.80
Newcastle	From £11.15 × 2	£69.05	£37.20
Manchester	From £5.30 × 2	£43.70	£24.00
Nottingham	From £6.60 × 2	£33.20	£24.40
Birmingham	From £3.30 × 2	£27.65	£19.70
Cardiff	From £7.60 × 2	£40.05	£27.10
Bristol	From £6.60 × 2	£32.20	£21.50
Exeter	From £7.90 × 2	£42.70	£33.70

Many tickets have special conditions and advance booking conditions vary. With some rail tickets, it is cheaper to buy singles. Train companies operating on the same route have different fares. Check with National Rail Enquiries on 0845 748 4950 and ask for a full list of options for the journey you are making. See also www.moneysavingexpert.com, and don't get taken for a ride.

Coach prices: travel on Friday is generally more expensive; reductions are available if you book in advance. For National Express enquiries, call 0871 781 8181.

It's a fact

Check out National Express Funfares on the web before you book. Travel for just £1 each way to selected city centres. Different destinations are selected each month. Visit www.nationalexpress.com.

Travel restrictions: some journeys cost slightly more at certain times.

Can I afford to run a car?

If your only income is the standard funding for students, most rational people would say no. But since so many students do seem to have cars they must be managing it somehow. A recent survey by Reaction UK suggested that nearly half of all students own or use a car. Travel from your home to your university will probably be cheaper by car, but you may also find yourself going home many more times during term, acting as chauffeur to the party or taking trips at weekends. And don't underestimate the maintenance bills: they can be astronomical, especially for an old car. Then there's the road tax, currently £125 p.a.

(£68.75 half-yearly) for cars under 1549cc and £190 p.a. (£104.50 half-yearly) for the rest for cars registered before March 2001. If your car was manufactured after March 2001 you'll be charged according to its CO_2 emissions. There are 13 different bands, and costs range from zero for cars with very low CO_2 emissions to £405 a year (£222.75 half-yearly) for a mighty 4×4 gas-guzzler. Add to that your MOT and AA or RAC membership (which makes sense if your car has a tendency to break down) and include your biggest outlay of all – insurance for third party, fire and theft (the cover favoured by most young people) – and the cost is starting to escalate.

How much to insure my wheels?

Two wheels or four, it's not going to be cheap or easy.

Four wheels

Students lucky enough to have a car may find they don't have much luck getting insurance, especially if they are first-time drivers and aged under 21. Try Endsleigh Insurance (an insurance provider originally set up by the NUS). Worried that many students who ran cars couldn't afford the cost of cover, the NUS asked Endsleigh in 1997 to try to find a way to reduce motor insurance premiums for students – which they did, by up to 30%.

A word of caution: think twice about 'fronting': that's the old trick of mum taking out the insurance and naming the student as second driver. If there's a claim and it's discovered that the student is really the main driver, you could find the insurance company won't pay up.

Insurance costs vary, depending not just on who you are, but on where you live. Big city drivers pay a higher premium than, say, those in the country. In London, the costs are prohibitive. Endsleigh warns: 'Insurance premiums are based on the address where the car resides for the majority of the year. Therefore, if you are living away from home while studying you must provide the address where you live for the majority of the year.' So even if it would be cheaper to take out insurance from, say, your parents' home address, think before you do it. Giving false information could lead to claims not being paid.

Two wheels

You might think a bike is much easier to insure. But any student intending to take a bicycle to university must think in terms of having it pinched, or at least borrowed without permission. Insurance companies certainly do.

advice note *i*

► Restrictions on cards can change, so always check what is being offered and when you can travel.

► Look for special reductions: occasionally, the rail or coach companies will have special promotions such as half-price student cards or half-price fares. They may also give discounts on things like CDs or subscriptions to magazines. Check out www.gobycoach.com. Special internet-only promotions are sometimes available.

Thrift Tip

Want to save £760?

Then stop smoking! On average, students spent £14.63 a week on cigarettes according to the *NatWest Student Living Index Survey*. Multiply that by 52 (it's not just a termly habit) and you start to realise just how much is going up in smoke. Reading had the worst offenders with an average weekly smoking bill of £18.36 (we are talking a staggering £954 a year here), followed closely by Portsmouth with an average weekly bill of £17.42. As the survey would also include many who didn't smoke at all, we think these weekly figures are very modest.

Insurance advice: a good padlock and detachable wheel or saddle should be your first form of insurance. Consider exchanging that expensive mountain bike for something that looks as if it's come off the tip.

Who to try: Endsleigh offers cover for bikes and fixed accessories up to £1,500 against accidental damage and theft anywhere in the UK and up to 30 days' cover in Europe. Premiums depend on the value of your bike and where in the country you live, ranging from £27 for bikes worth up to £149 in a fairly theft-free area. Also try the banks – some offer fairly good deals.

Remember that around half of all UK-registered bikes are scooters – which are easily stolen. Some insurers exclude theft cover unless the bike is garaged

So Where is the Cheapest Place to Study?

The NatWest research this year is very clear about where the cheapest places to study are: top of the list is Manchester with a bill of £174.48 for general living expenses and rents of £73.57, followed closely by Birmingham, with a weekly bill of £174.14 for general expenses plus average rents of £74.16. This makes a grand weekly total of £245.30 for Birmingham and £248.05 for Manchester. However, the lowest average rents were found in Leicester at £65.89. The most expensive place to study (excluding London) was Oxford, with a weekly bill of £323.03.

This is not the end of the story, as you will see if you turn to Chapter 6, page 136.

at night. Immobilisers don't always stop thieves either, as a bike or scooter can be bundled into even a small car. Endsleigh provides insurance for scooters and small motorbikes. A lot of their enquiries in this area come from students with bikes under 250cc. They offer comprehensive insurance, third party, fire and theft cover and third party only.

Student budgets around the country

The budgets in Table 3 are based on research carried out in August 2009 for the *NatWest Student Living Index Survey*. For students living in university accommodation, utilities (gas/electricity/water) are generally included.

Table 3 Average student's budget per week

	England	Scotland	Wales	Oxbridge
Alcohol (consumed at home or while out)	£26.18	£24.94	£30.03	£24.02
Supermarket food shopping	£22.86	£24.97	£24.66	£23.67
Buying clothes	£18.88	£16.65	£15.94	£23.98
Going out (cinema/clubs/gigs)	£17.25	£16.83	£16.61	£21.58
Eating out (incl. cafés, restaurants, canteen food, etc.)	£15.63	£17.23	£14.62	£18.39
Cigarettes	£15.19	£14.91	£9.08	£15.39
Utility bills	£20.60	£23.34	£20.86	£25.39
Transport costs for longer trips	£19.87	£21.15	£29.30	£13.70
Day-to-day travel (incl. taxis)	£11.06	£12.10	£4.73	£10.29
Telephone/mobile phone bills	£10.04	£10.27	£8.32	£11.33
Books and course materials	£9.63	£9.30	£8.45	£8.00
CDs, DVDs and videos	£9.38	£9.54	£7.07	£8.71
Laundry/dry cleaning	£4.38	£4.50	£3.13	£4.55
Photocopying/library costs, fines, etc.	£3.91	£4.91	£3.35	£3.50
Rent	£77.88*	£74.59	£67.85	£83.10

*Oxbridge and London excluded
Source: *NatWest Student Living Index Survey* 2008

How much will you need to survive each year as a student?

£6,000 a year? £7,000? £8,000? £9,000? £10,000?

Thrift Tips

'Rent out any extra room space.'
First-year Contemporary Photographic Practice student, Northumbria

'Visit car boot sales to sell, buy and sell again.'
Fourth-year Environmental Science student, Stirling

'Offer to walk the neighbours' dogs for a couple of quid an hour.'
First-year American Studies and Computing student, Wolverhampton

*'Never be afraid to ask if there is a discount for students. I found my NUS
card reduced my swimming sessions from £1.95 to 75p.'*
Computer student, London University

*'A lot of websites pay you to fill out questionnaires to receive text
message advertising. You can also sign up for offers on sites such as www.
britishfreebies.com and find yourself with enough free samples of shampoo
for the year.'*
Sheffield Hallam student

'Try www.moneysavingexpert.com for all kinds of savings.'
Third-year Media and Print Journalism student, Huddersfield

Students from a number of universities also suggested www.student
beans.co.uk for great discounts.

'Coach A level and GCSE students.'
Third-year Medicine student, Oxford

Don't shop on an empty stomach – it's disastrous.
Shop just before closing and get the bargains.
Watch out for special coach company offers.
Check that water rates are included in your rent.
Look for special student nights at clubs, theatres and cinemas.
*Students' union shops buy in bulk so they can give good discounts. Beer,
stationery, dry cleaning and even holidays could be part of their cost-
cutting service.*

'Always take the sugar in coffee shops or bars.'
Second-year English with Creative Writing student, Falmouth

The NUS estimated that for the last academic year (2009–2010), students would need £15,090 if living in London and £14,088 in other parts of the country for the 39-week academic year. You'd be lucky if you had that. In fact, based on what you are likely to receive in funding, the NUS suggested an average shortfall in funds of £5,632 for a student in London and £6,196 for a student elsewhere. And that was last year. In reality, you're going to have to survive on what you can get and what you can earn. How much is that likely to be? See the next chapter!

A level students thinking of giving university **cash crisis** a miss because of debt should remember that, on average, graduates can expect to earn 20–25% more than people who finish their education with A levels, which could amount to £160,000 over a lifetime and much more if you are taking medicine – a cool £340,315 (Universities UK report, 2007). However, government research put the figure even higher, at around 45%.

Typical student budgets

Four students show where their money goes, and where it comes from.

Matt's budget

Third-year Forensic Science student, Nottingham Trent

It was the murder of a local girl in his home town of Croydon that made Matt decide on his choice of subject. 'Forensics played an important part in solving the case.'

This year, he lives in a large, four-bedroom house with three other students. Where his money goes is shown in Table 4 and his income is shown in Table 5.

Matt says: 'My advice to all new students is to watch the first two weeks. Freshers week is the killer; many students spend over a grand. The first term at university is expensive – and it can be the undoing of some students, condemning them to three years of anxiety and debt. By the end of my first term here I was down to having just £7 a week for food. I've done better

Table 4 Matt's outgoings per year

Outgoings	Per week	Per year	Comments
Rent	£50	£2,400	
Utilities			
Gas	£11.50 per month	£103.50	No problem, one of the girls organises the payment.
Electricity	£9.25 per month	£83.25	
Water	£10 per quarter	£40	
Mobile	£21 per month	£252	Contract includes all calls.
TV/internet	£8 per month	£121	Share internet connection.
Food in	£17.50	£630	Occasionally we cook together, but mostly I cater for myself – more expensive than sharing. I get Asda to deliver.
Food out (approx.)	£18.75	£675	Takeaways.
Laundry	£0	£0	Washing machine provided.
Toiletries	£10 per term	£30	
Socialising, entertainment and music	£40	£2,080	I've really cut back on the drinking and tend to go for high-energy drinks. Out twice a week – clubs, pubs, etc.
Sport			
Travel (in town)	£0	£0	Annual travelcard means you can go anywhere in Nottingham; these are given out for free.
Travel home		£90	£20 return on a coach to Croydon in Surrey.
Books		£0	Use the library.
Vices		£0	Quit smoking and saved £416 p.a.
Clothes		£100	Hoodie/T-shirt.
Gifts		£20	Mostly over Christmas.
Holidays		£0	Can't afford them.
Fees		£3,225	
Total		**£9,849.75**	

Table 5 Matt's income per year

Income	Per year	Comments
Fee loan	£3,225	
Student loan	£2,100	
Parents	£2,400	They are not expected to contribute, but they do.
Grant	£2,100	From the government.
Jobs	£0	None around.
Overdraft	£1,250	Interest-free overdraft from the bank. Could get another £500 but haven't had to ask yet.
Total	**£11,075**	

since, and it looks as if I'm going to end the year with funds. People seem to be cutting back. We do go out, but there is more drinking at home. Not sure if that's the effect of the credit crunch or just because I'm happier.'

Stories abound of students spending £3,000 just on socialising, though funnily enough you never seem to meet anyone who has actually spent this much. But overspending there certainly is, especially during freshers week, and once you get badly into debt it's very difficult to get out of it.

Beth's budget

Second-year Geography student, St Andrews

Beth is 19. She lives in a university house with three other girls – the same girls she shared with last year, just in a different house that is slightly closer to the university and with nicer facilities. Each has their own bedroom and there are two bathrooms plus a shower and a kitchen/diner, and this year there is also a common room. It is self-catering. It takes about 10–15 minutes to walk to lectures in the main university quad or to the shops.

The figures given in Tables 6 and 7 are for Beth's first term.

Beth says: 'It's a relief to find I can manage my finances. Last year, it was difficult moving into a house with five people you didn't know. We were

Table 6 Beth's outgoings for her first term

Outgoings	Per term	Per year	Comments
Rent	£800	£2,400	Utilities are included, which is good value.
Food in	£100	£300	I'm vegetarian. I cook in bulk and freeze it. We each cater for ourselves. We tried eating together because it's cheaper but it didn't work out; we were never all around at the same time and some of us had a lot to learn about cooking.
Food out	£30	£90	Mainly 'bring a dish and bottle' parties and ceilidhs. You should taste my blue cheese canapés and cranberry sauce – yum.
Toiletries	£20	£60	Shampoo etc.
Laundry	£20	£60	£1.80 for a wash, £1 for a dry once a week.
Phone	£20	£60	Top-up. I do have a landline in my room, which my parents pay for and use.
Computer	£14	£42	Extra leads.
Entertainment/ cinema	£10	£30	Mostly DVDs and special late-night showings.
Socialising	£40	£120	We make much of our own entertainment in St Andrews.
Giving parties	£30	£90 approx.	Occasional parties with bonfire on the beach.
Club membership	£70	£210	I joined five clubs: trampolining – £12; canoeing – £15; Christian Union – £3; Amnesty International – £2; Gym membership – £30.
Travel (term-time)	£60	£180	Visiting my sister at Edinburgh Uni.
Fare home	£50	£150	Return to Greater London on the train.
Vices		£0	Don't have any.
Books	£60	£180	Wait and buy from last year's students at half price.
Field trips	£10	£30	Edinburgh/Dundee.
Clothes	£50	£150	Biggest outlay: Athletics hoodie – £30.
Gifts	£120	£120	Well, it's Christmas!
Fees	£607 approx.	£1,820	Low because it's Scotland.
Total		**£6,092**	

Table 7 Beth's income for her first term

Income	Per term	Per year	Comments
Fee loan	£607 approx.	£1,820	To pay for fees.
Maintenance loan	£1,348 approx.	£4,045	Full maintenance loan less grant.
Maintenance grant	£905	£2,715	
Bursary	£0		Not given in Scotland.
Parents	£188	£564	£75 a month while at uni.
Grandparents	£800	£2,500	
Overdraft	£0		Free overdraft facility of £1,200 from the bank, but haven't used it yet.
Savings	£800	£800	I'm a great baby-sitter.
Total		**£12,444**	

such different personalities. People would eat and just leave the dirty dishes for someone else to wash up. And cleaning the house was a tussle. This year is much easier, we can shout at each other about the cleaning or the noise because we know we'll make up afterwards. Occasionally we have parties for things like Hallowe'en, which involves buying wood for a bonfire on the beach and some drinks, which all adds up to about £10 per person; we've had three in the first semester.

'The best advice I received when I arrived was don't take any money to the freshers fairs,' she adds, 'otherwise you'll join every club. As it was, I joined five – those third years are very persuasive.'

Luke's budget

Second-year Sports Science student, Exeter

Luke is 20 and lives in a large house with six other students – three boys who are also studying Sports Science and three girls. They are all good friends, having met while living in halls last year. They each have their own room: his is right at the top of the house and sufficiently large to accommodate his guitars and sports gear. There is a large kitchen, two bathrooms, a sitting room with a TV and a garden which is paved over.

Luke's advice: 'Save as much as you can before you come. The first term is very expensive – you go out more than at any other time and spend more than you think. I learned the hard way. Try to get a job and get it organised before you come to uni, because when you get there you'll find all the jobs have gone.'

Tables 8 and 9 show Luke's outgoings and income.

Table 8 Luke's outgoings per year

Outgoings	Per week	Per year	Comments
Rent	£80	£3,840	48-week contract.
Utilities – gas, electricity, water		£320	£80 a quarter approx.
Deposits		£360/ £400	One was for this year and the other for next year. We're staying on. It will be repaid less any damage.
Food (general)	£10	£330	We boys cook and eat together – much cheaper. You should try my roast.
Food (personal)	£10	£330	Crisps, protein-enriched drinks.
Food (eating out)		£115	Chinese/pizza every two weeks, £7 each. Use vouchers that come through the door.
Toiletries		£30	Mouthwash, shampoo, etc. Mum stocks me up in the holidays.
Laundry	£0	£0	Have a washing machine. Mum provides soap.
Phone		£420	£35 a month – mum pays.
Entertainment/ socialising	£0	£990	Mostly alcohol and clubs. Cost of a night depends on how much we drink before we go. Term time only. Detox body during the holidays.
Club membership		£100	Cricket – £75; snow sports – £25.
Gym membership		£235	
Travel (term-time)	£0	£0	Walk.
Fare home	0	£210 approx.	£20–£70 return depending on train or coach.
Vices	£2	£66	Kebab after a night out.
Books		£0	Use library.
Photocopying		£60	£20 per term ink for my printer.
Clothes		£90	T-shirts.
Equipment		£30	Lecture notes.
Gifts		£60	Birthdays mainly.
Holidays		£20	Few days in Wales with friends.
Fees		£3,225	
Total		**£11,231**	

Table 9 Luke's income per year

Income	Per year	Comments
Fee loan	£3,225	
Maintenance loan	£3,900	
Maintenance grant	£800	
Bursary	£0	Nothing yet.
Parents	£1,650	£25 a week from mum – she had been saving for my uni years. £25 a week from dad.
Deposits	£760	Paid by parents; will give back when returned.
Phone bill	£420	Paid by mum.
Gym membership	£235	Paid by mum.
Overdraft	£80	Free overdraft facility from the bank of £1,250.
Total	**£11,070**	

Alex's budget

First-year History and Politics student, Lancaster

Alex is 18 and lives in self-catered university halls. He is housed in a block on the university campus which is divided into eight flats with eight students in each. Each student has an en-suite room and shares a very large kitchen which will seat all eight of them – possibly more – and is equipped with two of everything – two ovens, fridges, freezers, microwaves, hobs, kettles, etc. He chose to live in a mixed flat so there are four girls and four boys. This is not always the case; he knows of one flat with seven boys and one girl. He says their flat seems to work very well – no fighting over the equipment. He chose self-catering because he thought it would be cheaper and says it would be cheaper still if they all ate together, but he tends to eat with his girlfriend who lives in another block.

Asked what advice he would give to new students, Alex says: 'Save as much as you can before you come. It's going to cost a lot more than you think. If you take your course fees and rent and then think half as much again, you should be somewhere near the truth. And don't go out too much.' Alex limits himself to going out twice a week.

Tables 10 and 11 show how Alex managed in his first term.

Table 10 Alex's outgoings in first term

Outgoings	Per term	Comments
Rent	£1,200	That includes everything – heating, lighting, but not food.
Food in	£300	
Food out	£33	University Air Squadron – full meal £1.50, twice a week.
Toiletries	£0	Mum stocked me up with shedloads.
Laundry	£0	Take it home to mum.
Phone	£60	£20 a month.
Entertainment/ socialising	£275	Alcohol and clubs, cinema on campus £2. Go out twice a week approx.
Swimming club membership	£25	Covers the whole year.
Gym membership	£30 per year	Covers the whole year.
Travel term-time	£440	Petrol for car – £40 per week. Uni buses into town are free. Occasional taxi home is £10.
Fare home	£10	By car – it's only 40 miles.
Car insurance	£333.30	£1,000 a year.
Tax	£41 approx.	£125 a year.
Up-keep of car	£0	Dad's a mechanic.
Vices	£50	Energy drinks.
Books	£100	Get them cheap on the internet.
Clothes	£100	Mum buys them mostly.
Equipment	£10	Stationery.
Gifts	£100	
Holidays	£150 so far	Amsterdam – uni trip. Not sure how much I'll spend while I'm there.
Fees	£1,075	£3,225 a year.
Total	**£4332.30**	

Table 11 Alex's income in first term

Income	Per term	Comments
Fees	£1,075	Paid from compensation for car crash, received when 18 months old and held in a trust.
Bursary	£1,000	Given for excellent A levels – four A grades.
Parents	£1,200	They pay my rent.
Overdraft	£0	
Job	£300	University Air Squadron, 10 days at £30 a day. Will help future career as a pilot.
Travel expenses	£308	Petrol paid for by Air Squadron – 50 miles a week at 28p per mile.
Total	**£3,883**	

As Alex says on page 41: think rent + fees + half as much again. It's not going to be cheap.

CHAPTER 2

Fees and funding

This chapter answers questions on the main sources of finance for students embarking on higher education in 2010–2011.

Note: the information in this chapter is based on the funding package for students starting university in the UK in 2010–2011. Any variations in Scotland, Wales and Northern Ireland can be found in Chapter 4 Devolutionary differences; additional help for special categories of students is covered in Chapter 5.

Fees: how things are now

The arguments are over – top-up fees, or as they are officially called 'variable fees', are here to stay for most students in most areas of the country and already inflation is hiking them up still further. But now there is talk of taking the cap off how much universities can charge UK students for fees. The government is likely to make a decision some time soon: it may well have done so by the time this book is published. Figures of £7,000 p.a. and more have been bandied about. However, that is not for this year and whatever is decided on fees will not be retrospective, so students who are already at university will stick with the current fee arrangement – an increase of around 2.5% each year. If you think you are already paying too much in fees, it's certainly less than what is to come.

Is your course value for money?

Our *Guide to Student Money* survey asked students what they thought: 67% said their course was worth what they pay, which means around 33% do not.

Those that think it isn't said:

'Very expensive when worked out as the price per lecture.'
Second-year Maths student, Lancaster

'It's a crazy amount of money, and we still have to buy everything else ourselves e.g. books, trips, etc.'
First-year Film student, Falmouth

'Only four weeks' worth of classes in two years, yet you pay for two years' tuition.'
Second-year, Museum and Gallery Studies student, St Andrews

'It costs £9,000 and you only get two days of teaching.'
First-year, LPC student, UWE

'We have to pay to print out lecture notes. If we are paying over £3,000 for tuition, the lecturers should print them out themselves.'
First-year Animal Science student, UWE

Those that think their course is good value for money said:

'There is a lot of support and resources.'
First-year Law with European Legal Studies student, Aberdeen

'I'm getting good-quality education, and I'm studying something I'm passionate about.'
Fourth-year French Language and Linguistics student, Aberdeen

'The facilities are bloody amazing. As are the tutors. We seem to have a lot of contact with them too.'
First-year Photography student, Falmouth

'I should end up qualified [to practise] at the end, unlike a number of courses I looked at.'
First-year Geography and Planning student, UWE

'The university is world-class, the lecturers know what they are teaching and there is plenty to learn about.'
Third-year Chemistry student, St Andrews

While student debt is rising at an unprecedented rate, and will continue to do so, some ingenious ways have been introduced to help alleviate some of the financial anxieties while you are actually studying. So it's not all doom and gloom.

Student funding: the main points

Fees

► Universities can charge different (variable) fees for courses, but most do charge the maximum.
► The maximum a UK student starting a first degree in 2010–2011 can be expected to pay in fees is £3,290 p.a.
► From this year, Welsh-domiciled students studying in Wales no longer receive a fee grant so they pay the same fees as England (see page 98).

- ► Scottish students studying in Scotland do not pay fees at all (see page 94).
- ► Students can take out a loan to cover their fees which they will pay back gradually once they have graduated.
- ► Payback for loans will begin in the April after you graduate if you are earning over £15,000.
- ► There will be no help with fees for low-income families.

Remember, not every student **cash crisis** gets everything. How much support you can receive will depend on three factors:

- ► where you live
- ► family income
- ► where you choose to study.

Maintenance

- ► Maintenance grants of up to £2,906 are available for students, depending on family income on a sliding scale up to around £50,000. There is a big grant increase for Welsh students this year – see page 99.
- ► Bursaries are available from universities, especially for students from low-income families.
- ► Main source of maintenance income is the student loan, available to all students, based on a family income of max. £4,950 (£6,928 in London).

Looking at the Detail

Devolutionary differences

Since devolution, Scotland, Wales and Northern Ireland have gradually introduced many changes to the student funding package. So if you come from or are planning to study in Scotland, Wales or Northern Ireland, start by reading this chapter followed by Chapter 3, which covers the general principles on applying for funding, and then turn to Chapter 4, where all the differences from the English system are outlined. You may be in for a pleasant surprise.

Am I a special case?

If you fall into any of the categories listed below, check out Chapter 5:

- ► Courses with a difference (page 108)
- ► Students from abroad (page 109)
- ► Studying abroad (page 124)
- ► Part-time students (page 114)
- ► Healthcare courses (page 115)
- ► Attending a private higher education institution (page 114)
- ► Specialist courses (page 118)
- ► Additional help for special groups (page 120).

▶ Part of the loan is means-tested on family income and on the amount of maintenance grant students receive.

▶ Non-repayable Special Support Grants of up to £2,906 are available for students receiving government support – largely lone parents/disabled students.

Fees: what you pay

How much will I have to pay towards my fees?

Your university will set a price for each course up to a maximum of £3,290 p.a. Fees are flexible, but most universities charge the full amount for most courses. In 2009–2010, we found three universities charging lower fees. However, this year they have all succumbed and will charge full fees to new entrants in 2010–2011 – so much for the idea of 'variable' fees.

Who will pay my fees?

You. There will be no help from your local authority (LA*) for fees and your parents will not be asked to contribute. What's more, family income will have no bearing on what you pay. Universities can charge what they like for a course up to the maximum of £3,290 p.a., and what they ask is what you must pay, but you may take out a loan to cover these fees. What follows outlines your options, and Table 12 at the end of this section summarises them for you.

Will every student pay the same fees?

Unless you come from outside the EU, students on the same course at the same university will pay the same fees – they are not means-tested – but course fees can vary even in a university. Your university will decide what fees it is going to charge.

Remember: Scottish students studying in Scotland do not pay fees at all, while non-Scottish students who study in Scotland do but at a different rate to students in England, Wales and Northern Ireland.

Do fees ever go up?

Yes, every year. When the top-up fee programme was first mentioned, the government said that fees would not go up before 2010, but the original

---

*LA stands for local authority in England and Wales. When the term LA is used in this book, please read Student Awards Agency for Scotland (SAAS for Scotland) and Education and Library Board for Northern Ireland (ELB).

top-up fee of £3,000 p.a. has been given an annual inflationary lift, so it is now £3,290 p.a. When top-up fees were introduced in 2006, a review was promised in 2010.

What will happen next? There is plenty of speculation in the media. Polls suggest that most university vice-chancellors would recommend £5,000, but some want to remove the cap altogether and have the freedom to set their own fees, similar to the US system where fees at Ivy League universities can top £20,000. While this is only speculation at the moment, there will certainly be changes in 2011; and they won't be for the better, or cheaper. However, if you are starting your degree this year, you will be saved from even greater debt.

How am I going to pay my fees?

Where is a student going to find £9,870 or, at worst, £13,160 for fees?

They won't, at least not while they are studying. One of the better aspects of the current funding system is the fee loan, which all students can take out. And you don't have to start paying it back until you have graduated and are earning at least £15,000 (see page 83 for full details). So nobody has to pay fees upfront; there will be no getting slung out of uni for not having the money to pay them and no juggling your finances between eating and studying as in the past. You just keep piling on the debt.

Where will the loan come from?

From the Student Loans Company (SLC).

How do I get my loan for fees?

You apply to Student Finance England (www.direct.gov.uk/studentfinance) at the same time as applying for your maintenance loan and a grant. It is all done on the same form and handled together. Student Finance will then process your application and pass it on to the SLC, who will pay out the money. The form is available from www.direct.gov.uk/studentfinance to fill in or download, or by calling 0845 300 5090. For more information on applying for finance see Chapter 3, page 68. For the rest of the UK, see Chapter 4.

How much can I borrow?

Whatever your course costs, up to £3,290 p.a.

Is it means-tested?

No.

What will happen to the money I borrow for fees?

It will be paid direct to your university.

Who can get a fee loan?

UK first-degree students, EU students and those taking a Postgraduate Certificate in Education (PGCE).

Is taking out a loan for fees a good idea?

Yes. The big plus of the funding system is that, because students can take out a loan to cover their fees, they (or their parents) will not have to pay fees before they start university or while they are studying. So all your maintenance loan, any bursary and maintenance grant you receive, anything your parents give you and everything you earn will all go towards living costs. You should have fewer money worries than your predecessors during your time at university, but your debt will undoubtedly be greater when you graduate.

If my parents want to pay my fees, can they do so?

There is nothing to stop parents paying your fees. These have to be paid at the start of each year. Most universities allow fees to be paid in tranches, but you will need to talk to your particular institution. Some universities will give a discount if fees are paid in full upfront.

Who gets help with fees?

Nobody, unless you:

▶ started your course in 2005 or before
▶ are a 2005–2006 gap-year student who had an exemption
▶ are a Scottish student studying in Scotland (see page 94).

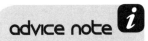

advice note

If your parents want to pay your fees but will have to borrow to pay them, it's worth remembering that the loan offered by the SLC is probably the cheapest money you can borrow, so it might be an idea to come to a family arrangement – you take out the loan for your fees and they pay it off for you.

What happens if I drop out of my course?
Will I have to pay fees?

Probably, but there are no hard and fast rules. If you drop out before
1 December you may be all right as your fees won't have been paid out
before that date. But generally it will be a matter of discussing it with your
university – after all, they have gone to the expense of providing a place
for you.

I want to change my course: what happens
about my fees?

Again, it will be a matter of discussion with your university. If you are changing
to another course in the same university, fees may not be a problem, but if you
are moving to another university it might be more difficult.

advice note

If a fee debt of £9,870+
(£13,160+ for a four-year
course) fills you with
horror, and well it might,
don't abandon your degree
aspirations – yet. There are
some excellent bursary
deals on offer and many
students, especially those
from low-income families,
may find that while
studying they are better off
than their predecessors who
went without top-up fees.

Will I be able to get a loan for fees
for any course I take at college?

No. Courses for which fee loans will be
given include: full-time (including sandwich)
degree, Higher National Certificate (HNC),
HND, PGCE, school-centred initial teacher
training or equivalent courses undertaken at
a UK university, publicly funded college or
comparable institution.

Courses for which loans are not available
include: school-level courses such as A levels
or Scottish Highers, BTEC and SCOTVEC
National Awards and City & Guilds courses
for those over 19, postgraduate courses (except
teacher training), all part-time courses* (except
initial teacher training courses), some correspondence and all Open University
courses.

*See page 114 for details of grants for part-time courses.

What can I do to raise funds to pay my fees if I am unable to get a loan?

1. Talk to your LA.
2. Talk to the college where you want to take the course.
3. Apply for a Career Development Loan – see page 63.
4. Apply to professional bodies, trusts, foundations, benevolent funds – see Chapter 9.

Table 12 Fast facts on finance (for students starting their course 2010–2011)

Fees	Max. £3,290 p.a.
Fee loan	Up to £3,290 p.a.
Student loans	£6,928 in London, £4,950 elsewhere, £3,838 living at home (less in your final year); 28% is means-tested on parents' income and maintenance grant received if you have been assessed for such a grant.
Maintenance grant	£2,906 for low-income families (less in Scotland, more in Wales and Northern Ireland). Means-tested according to family income.
University bursaries	At least £329 p.a. for those on full maintenance grant (most give more).
Access to Learning Fund (Contingency Fund – Wales; Hardship Funds – Scotland; Support Funds – Northern Ireland)	Discretionary distribution; given largely to help with rent and other financial hardships.
Part-time students	Increased levels of fee grants to max. £1,230 plus course grant of £265 – slightly more for fees in Wales.
Salary payback threshold for fee and maintenance loans	£15,000

Maintenance: grants, bursaries and loans

There are three elements to students' maintenance:

▶ maintenance grants

▶ university bursaries

▶ student loans.

This year, for the first time, the maintenance package students receive in England has not increased. Even though some costs may have increased you will have to make do with the same amount students received last year.

Maintenance grants

What are they and will I get one?

Maintenance grants are largely given to lower-income families. Whether you get anything will depend on your family's income. If it's £25,000 or below you will receive the full amount of £2,906. If it's over £50,020 you will receive nothing. Between those figures, what is given is on a sliding scale, as shown in Table 13.

Table 13 Maintenance grants for new students in England: who will receive what in 2010–2011

Family income	Grant
£25,000 or less	£2,906
£30,000	£1,906
£35,450	£1,106
£40,000	£711
£45,000	£381
£50,020	£50
More than £50,020	£0

Maintenance grants are not new: they have been creeping into the funding system since the year 2000. What is new, though, is the amount – up to £2,906 – and the number of students who will receive them. This is not government generosity, however, but because students no longer receive help with fees.

Maintenance grants are means-tested according to your or your family's income up to £50,020, but note this is only in England and Wales. In the rest of the UK, the family income cut-off point is much lower – see Chapter 4.

It's a Fact

There is no upper age limit for receiving grants and fee loans. But to qualify for a maintenance loan you have to be under 60.

How many students will receive a maintenance grant?

This year, in England, around a third of students are expected to receive a full grant and around a third a partial grant.

When will I get my grant?

It will be paid in three instalments, one at the start of each term.

Who calculates how much I will get?

Student Finance England, based on the information you supply on your application form.

University bursaries

Universities have always offered bursaries to good students, but never on the scale that they are doing now. The government stipulated that to charge the maximum fee – currently £3,290 p.a. – universities must sign up to an Access Agreement, which stipulates that students receiving the full £2,906 maintenance grant (i.e. those from low-income families) must be given a further non-repayable bursary of at least £329, making a grand total of £3,235 combined maintenance grant and bursary (which until this year was the same amount as the full fees) – but your university bursary could be more.

Some universities stick to the guidelines. Others are far more generous; some use bursaries as an incentive to attract students. Many offer bursaries on a sliding scale to all those receiving a proportion of the maintenance grant. The average bursary given by universities in 2009–2010 was £800 p.a. for those receiving the maximum maintenance grant. This could be given in kind, for example in the form of reduced accommodation costs. Even students who don't actually fall into the low-income category are cashing in. Examples are given on page 56. For up-to-date information, check out the bursary map website: http://bursarymap.direct.gov.uk.

Shop around. There are some fantastic bursary deals about, and every university has a different approach. Finding a university giving generous bursaries could be more cost-effective than trying to find a low-cost course, and probably better educational value too.

Where will the money for bursaries come from?

In 2006–2007 and 2007–2008 (the latest figures available), £335 million was spent on bursaries and outreach. This represents about 25% of fee income. In addition, many universities are heavily endowed by generous benefactors and have always offered scholarships, awards and bursaries to selected students.

Where can I find out about university bursaries and scholarships, and what's being offered?

University prospectuses and websites are a good starting point and should provide plenty of information. Table 14 gives some examples as well. You can also try:

► www.direct.gov.uk/studentfinance

► www.ucas.com.

Many students are missing out on bursaries just because they didn't ask. Check with your university if you are entitled to a bursary even if you are not from a low-income family. They are not necessarily given out automatically.

cash crisis

There is also more information on university awards and scholarships, including sports bursaries, music scholarships, location scholarships and awards for students from abroad, in Chapter 9 of this book.

To compare and contrast what universities are offering, take a look at *University Scholarships, Awards & Bursaries*, published by Trotman. As well as giving full information about the bursaries now offered by

Table 14 Some examples of bursaries being offered by universities to students in 2010–2011

University of Westminster, London	Bursary of £400 given to all students receiving a maintenance grant.	
University of York	**Family income**	**Bursary**
	Up to £25,000	£1,436
	£25,001–£35,910	£718
	£35,911–£41,040	£360
	Over £41,040	None
University of Manchester	All home students from households with income of less than £25,000 eligible for a bursary of up to £1,250 p.a. Advantage scholarships of £3,000 for students who gain three A grades at A level and family income is £25,000 or less. Success scholarships of £1,250 for students who gain three As at A level regardless of family income.	
University of Oxford	**Family income**	**Bursary**
	Up to £17,999	£3,225 + £875 (first year only)
	£18,000–£25,000	£3,225
	£25,001–£49,999	£200–£3,255
Warwick University	£1,500 given to all students if household income under £36,000.	
Newcastle University	**Family income**	**Bursary**
	Up to £25,000	£1,500
	£25,001–£32,284	£750
	Achievement bursaries also given.	
University of Chichester (offered 2009–2010)	**Family income**	**Bursary**
	Under £25,000	£1,077
	£25,001–£29,999	£821–£1,026
	£30,000–£34,999	£564–£820
	£35,000–£39,999	£308–£563
	£40,000–£49,999	£256

universities to students from low-income families, it lists over 100 institutions offering scholarships, awards and bursaries. Many are for people studying specific subjects, or are travel awards. Subjects vary from the more usual Engineering, History, Geography, Languages, Law and the sciences to the more specialised, such as Cultural Criticism Studies, Paper Science, Rural Studies, Retail and Textiles.

The NUS is calling for a national bursary scheme after a government survey showed a third of students based their HE decisions on the amount of financial support available.

cash crisis

Getting a bursary: Sam's story

Sam Wakeford, 22, has completed two years of an Archaeology and Anthropology degree at Trinity Hall, Cambridge. He was elected for this year (2009–2010) to one of six full-time sabbatical posts in Cambridge University Students' Union, and will return to do the third year of his degree in October 2010.

As an independent student with no family home, funding was extremely important to him when choosing a university.

'Cambridge was always very clear about what financial support was on offer,' says Sam, 'and they are particularly supportive to students in my situation, which was extremely reassuring. I was given the full Cambridge Bursary in each of my first two years (£3,100 then £3,150), and I'll receive it again (now £3,400) when I do my third year. Because I don't have a home anywhere else, they also let me live in college all year round.

'I was determined to go to university, bursary or no bursary,' he adds, 'but the bursary means that in every year of my degree I don't have to work during term time, and I can also afford to attend optional conferences and field trips relevant to my courses. So, except for my student loan, I haven't fallen into debt.'

For each year of his degree, Sam also received the full government maintenance grant, currently £2,906, a student loan for living costs (currently £3,497 for students also getting the full grant) and takes out a student loan to cover tuition fees (currently £3,225, increasing to £3,290 from October 2010).

'My grant and bursary completely cover my living expenses during term time, and my loan helps towards the costs of living during vacations. To top this up, I also work during the vacations, mostly on website design earning around £10 an hour. The last couple of years I've even managed to swing a week's work in Sri Lanka each Easter with fares paid, plus a fantastic £14-an-hour rate.'

During his year working for the Students' Union, Sam is earning £16,500. He pays £75 a week for accommodation and has a weekly food bill of around £45.

Student maintenance loans

The student loan is quite different from the fee loan. The student loan is cash in the bank: the fee loan is paid direct to your university and you never see the cash.

How much can I borrow?

Not enough – at least that is what most students think. The maintenance loan is reviewed annually and usually increased, but not this year. What you receive is dependent on where you are studying. (Note: the student maintenance loan, usually called the student loan, is quite different from the maintenance grant. The loan you have to pay back – the grant you don't.) The rates for a full maintenance loan for a full-time student in England in 2010–2011 are shown in Table 15. Rates for Wales and Northern Ireland vary slightly.

Table 15 Full maintenance loan rates (England 2010–2011)

		Full year max. available	Final year max. available
Students living away from their parents' home	In London	£6,928	£6,307
	Elsewhere	£4,950	£4,583
Students living in their parents' home		£3,838	£3,483
Studying overseas		£5,653	£5,214

Is the loan means-tested?

Yes. Not everybody can take out the full maintenance loan. It is means-tested according to your maintenance grant and family income. For low-income families, part of the grant is paid in lieu of part of the maintenance loan, so those receiving the full or a large proportion of the full grant may find they are not entitled to the full loan. If you are from a higher-income family (earning over the £50,778 income threshold), a quarter of the loan allocation is means-tested against your income or that of your family. It is hoped that any part of the means-tested loan you do not receive will be paid by your parents or spouse.

Table 16 shows the maintenance students can expect in England who are starting their course in 2010–2011.

Table 16 Maintenance available to students in England starting courses in 2010–2011

Family income	Assessed contribution	Maintenance grant	Maintenance loan	Total grant plus loan
Student living at home			Max. £3,838	
£25,000	£0	£2,906	£2,385	£5,291
£30,000	£0	£1,906	£2,885	£4,791
£40,000	£0	£711	£3,483	£4,194
£50,000	£0	£50	£3,813	£3,881
£50,778	£0	£0	£3,838	£3,838
£53,000	£444	£0	£3,394	£3,394
£56,153	£1,075*	£0	£2,763	£2,763
Student studying in London			Max. £6,928	
£25,000	£0	£2,906	£5,475	£8,381
£30,000	£0	£1,906	£5,975	£7,881
£40,000	£0	£771	£6,573	£7,344
£50,000	£0	£50	£6,903	£6,953
£50,778	£0	£0	£6,928	£6,928
£55,000	£844	£0	£6,084	£6,084
£60,478	£1,940*	£0	£4,988	£4,988
Student studying outside London			Max. £4,950	
£25,000	£0	£2,906	£3,497	£6,403
£30,000	£0	£1,906	£3,997	£5,903
£40,000	£0	£711	£4,595	£5,306
£50,000	£0	£50	£4,925	£4,975
£50,778	£0	£0	£4,950	£4,950
£55,000	£844	£0	£4,106	£4,106
£57,708	£1,386*	£0	£3,564	£3,564

*Approx. max. for family contribution for one student
Note: figures are not exact and should be taken as a guideline only

How the calculations are made

Where students receive a maintenance grant, the amount of loan for which they are eligible will be reduced by 50p for every £1 of grant. University bursaries are not included in this calculation. This means that if you come from a lower-income household, you will have a smaller loan to repay. All students will be able to receive 72% of the maximum student loan for maintenance.

Where the student is not receiving a grant, the other 28% will be assessed on family income over £50,778 at a rate of £1 for every £5 earned. As you can see, students from better-off families are highly dependent on parents making their contribution.

My academic year is longer than at most colleges: can I get extra money?

Yes. If your course is longer than 30 weeks you can claim for an extra loan, which will be means-tested, for each week you have to attend your course.

Weekly rates for 2010–2011 are:

► London: £106
► elsewhere: £83
► living at home: £54
► studying abroad: £115.

Where does the student loan come from?

The SLC, which is a special company set up by the government to provide loans for students.

Student loans: a few facts

When the student loan was first introduced in 1992, there was uproar. Many thought that higher education in this country should be completely free; others said that students should contribute to the cost of their education. At the time, the loan was around £580. People predicted student numbers would plummet. They were wrong. In fact, while the loan increased year on year, so did student numbers.

But 2006, the first year of the top-up fees, saw a drop in student numbers. Applicants for courses were down by 3% to 506,304, and the number of students actually starting courses was down by 3.6% to 390,809 (UCAS figures). Fast forward to 2009 and, according to UCAS, application figures increased by a massive 8.7% to 639,860. And it now looks as if 2010 may well be another bumper year, with applications by March up by 8.8% on the same time last year.

But the cost is still a deterrent for some. Our research among students in December 2009 showed that around 11% of students knew of somebody who didn't go to university for financial reasons, and 72% said they knew someone who had decided to study in their home town to save money; 22% said they knew someone who had dropped out of university for financial reasons.

Whatever your views about funding yourself through university, if you are a student just starting in higher education in the UK you will probably end up with a hefty loan and graduating with a sizeable debt. Most students do. In fact, 86% of *Guide to Student Money* student contacts expected to be in debt – the same figure as last year.

Sixth formers who started university in 2008 expected to pay on average £34,740 for a three-year degree course. This was up from £33,512 on the previous year, according to the *NatWest Student Money Matters Survey*. However, one medical student we spoke to at St Andrews reckons she will have debts of around £50,000 when she graduates.

What students say about debt

'When my bank offered an interest-free overdraft I thought the £1,500 was mine to spend. Now I have to think about paying it back. Very distressing!'

'It is unfair to judge the financial status of a student on the parents' income, since it's the student who will be paying off the debt.'

'It's the middle-class students that are suffering, with no grants and parents who can't afford to sub them.'

'In my first year I spent all my loan in two weeks, so I had to live on noodles for three months. Ugh!'

'I don't like living at home, but I have to because I'm skint!!'

'Student debt is bad enough, but the "invisible" debt is worse – overdrafts, credit cards, borrowing from family – all of which has to be paid back.'

'Depression is a problem that hits everyone who lives on a tight budget.'

Facts and Figures

▶ 57% of students said they were worried about the debt that they were accumulating while 40% said they were not.

▶ Average anticipated debt of students £15,000–£20,000

▶ £50,000 was top debt figure quoted.

▶ £15,600 was the average salary expected to be earned on graduating.

Source: *Guide to Student Money* survey

There are students who take a different view:

'Generally, studying is an indulgent luxury which improves prospects and so people should take as much responsibility as possible.'

'Most students don't mind the thought of paying back money once they are earning.'

Student advice on making your money go further

'Budget and stick to it!'

Jennifer, second-year Film student, Falmouth

'Don't spend it all in freshers week, it's hard to be the one without money to go out with later!'

Nicola, second-year Choreography student, Dartington

'Live at home, and chose a cheap uni. My twin brother saved literally thousands.'

Kimberley, third-year Broadcasting student, Falmouth

'Be classed as an independent student – live away from home for three years before uni and get loads of bursary and grant money!'

James, third-year Music Systems Engineering student, UWE

'Don't go into your student overdraft just because it's there!'

Kati, Psychology graduate, UWE

'Nights in are a better idea than nights out.'

Jacob, third-year English Literature student, Lancaster

'Look for accommodation early so you're not left paying for something very expensive.'

Rachael, second-year Biology student, St Andrews

Who can get a maintenance loan?

UK students who undertake full-time first degree or diploma of higher education courses at universities or HE colleges. While there is no age limit on students taking out a fee loan, maintenance loans are only available to students aged under 60.

I'm an overseas student: can I get a maintenance loan?

No. Even students from the EU who are classified as 'home' students for fees are not entitled to apply for a maintenance loan. For further details see Chapter 5, page 109.

Are there loans for part-time students?

No. But there is help (see Chapter 5, page 114).

I want to do a second degree: can I get a loan for maintenance and fees?

It depends on how long your first course was and the length of your second course. In general, support will be available for students for the length of a course plus one extra year. Say your new course is three years – add to that one year, subtract the length of your first course (say three years) and you would receive funding for one year. But if, for example, your previous course was three years and your new course is four years, add another year to that and you would receive funding for two years. Of course, it could work the other way: if your previous course was four years and your new course is only three, you would end up receiving no funding at all. However, if you are thinking of taking a second undergraduate degree at Oxford or Cambridge you could be in fee loan luck – see Chapter 5, page 109.

I want to change my course: what happens to my loan?

If you change to another course in the same college, your entitlement to a maintenance loan may well stay the same, but your fees could be different.

Equally, if you transfer to another college the fees may be different. The major problem arises if you change to a college or a course that does not attract student support or if there is a break in your studies before you join the new course. If you transfer from one course to another or withdraw from your current course, it is very important that you not only discuss this with your college but also talk to Student Finance England as soon as possible.

I am doing a further education course: can I get a loan?

If you are doing a course that leads to a first degree, HND, HNC, PGCE or National Vocational Qualification (NVQ) at Level 4 you can get a student loan. The information in this book is aimed mainly at HE students. Students in the 16–19 age group attending further education colleges may be eligible for financial help through their college.

What are Professional and Career Development Loans?

These loans are designed for people on vocational courses (full time, part time or distance learning) of up to two years where your fees aren't paid, and you can't get support from your LA. They cover course fees (only 80% given if you are in full-time employment, 100% if you have been out of work for three months or more) plus other costs such as materials, books, childcare and living expenses. You can apply for £300–£10,000. The scheme is funded by a number of high-street banks (Barclays, the Co-operative and the Royal Bank of

Scotland) and administered by the Learning and Skills Council, who will pay the interest on your loan during training and for up to one month afterwards. If the course you take lasts more than two years (or three years if it includes work experience), you may still be able to use a Professional and Career Development Loan to fund part of your course. Shop around the different providers and compare the terms offered before making a choice.

For a free booklet on Professional and Career Development Loans, phone 0800 585505. More information can also be found on www.lifelonglearning.co.uk and www.direct.gov.uk/en/EducationAndLearning/AdultLearning. See also Chapter 9 for other sources of finance to tap.

'Get a job – the student loan seems like a lot of money, but it doesn't cover even the essentials.' (See Chapter 6 for more on getting a job.)

Psychology student, Hull

Why are the student loan rates lower for the final year?

These loans are lower because they do not cover the summer vacation. You are expected to be working by then, or you can draw social security. However, if your final year is longer than 30 weeks you can apply for more loan for each week. If it lasts 40 weeks or more, you can get a loan at the full rate. This is often the case for students on 'accelerated' degree courses. Rates for 2010–2011 are shown in Table 17.

Table 17 Student loan rates for 2010–2011

	Full year	Final year
Home	£3,838	£3,483
Elsewhere	£4,950	£4,583
London	£6,928	£6,307

Further information

Who to contact/what to read

▶ Student Finance England helpline: 0845 607 7577 between 8a.m. and 8p.m. Monday to Friday and from 9a.m. to 5.30p.m. weekends for financial information, including information on your loans.

▶ Also, Student Finance England main number: 0845 300 5090, online www.direct. gov.uk/studentfinance. Full information about fees, maintenance grants and loans is given in the following free booklets, which you would be well advised to get and study:

- For students in England: *Student Finance England – A Guide to Financial Support for Higher Education 20010/11*, which is the source for the loan statistics in this chapter, is available from tel: 0800 731 9133 or 0845 300 5090, website: www.direct.gov.uk/studentfinance. Braille and audio editions are also available.

- For students in Scotland: *Student Support in Scotland: A Guide for Undergraduate Students 20010/11* is available from any Scottish university or the SAAS, Gyleview House, 3 Redheughs Rigg, South Gyle, Edinburgh EH12 9HH, tel: 0131 476 8212, email: saas.geu@scotland.gsi.gov.uk or website: www. saas.gov.uk.

- For students in Northern Ireland: *Financial Support for Students in Higher Education 20010/11* is available from Student Support Branch, Department for Employment and Learning (Northern Ireland), Rathgael House, Balloo Road, Bangor, Co. Down BT19 7PR or tel: 028 9025 7710 or (for booklet) 0800 731 9133 or visit the website: www.delni.gov.uk.

- For students in Wales: *A Guide to Financial Support for Higher Education* is available from the National Assembly for Wales, Higher Education Division 2, 3rd floor, Cathays Park, Cardiff CF10 3NQ, tel: 0845 602 8845 or websites: www.studentfinancewales.co.uk and www.learning.wales.gov.uk.

Thrift Tips

'Reduce your cuppa expenditure – buy a kettle and a cafetière.'
Third-year Geography student, Oxford

Or better still:
'... a flask.'
First-year Medicine student, Aberdeen

'Move to eco-friendly products – e.g. home-made vinegar/bicarb cleaning sprays.'
Fourth-year Classics student, St Andrews

'For the price of a sandwich you can buy a whole loaf, a packet of meat and even the mustard.'
PhD English Literature student, St Andrews

'Market your talents. If you play an instrument, teach – £15 p.h. If you play tennis, coach – £10 p.h.'
First-year Music student, City

'Busk.'
Third-year spatial design student, Falmouth

CHAPTER 3

Applying for funding and paying it back

In this chapter you will find information covering:

Applying for grants and loans

You should start thinking about applying for financial support as soon as you have applied for a place on a course. Do not wait until you have a confirmed place: just quote the course you are most likely to attend. Apply even if you don't think you will be entitled to a maintenance grant as you will also be assessed for how much loan you are entitled to and how much (if anything) your family is expected to contribute. New students will apply to Student Finance England and not to their LA as in the past.

Important steps to follow

1. The student finance service for 2010–2011 should be online from early December 2009 and you can apply at www.direct.gov.uk/studentfinance. You can also download an application form to print out from the website or phone 0845 300 5090 to get one sent to you. Students from the rest of the UK should see Chapter 4: Scotland page 94, Wales page 98, Northern Ireland page 100.

2. Fill in your application form and return it on the web or by post to Student Finance England. The address is on the website and the form. Give all the details you are asked for and say whether you intend to apply for a loan. Remember to include your National Insurance number if you want a loan. You might also be asked to send your UK passport or birth certificate as identification. Your parents/partner may also be asked to supply information.

3. Once Student Finance England has received your application, you will be assessed to see what finance you are entitled to. You will then be notified by letter of what your entitlements are – this should be within six weeks of your application being received. You will then be able to track the progress of your application and manage your own student finance account online. If you get in a muddle or need some advice, just log into their helpful webchat service or secure messaging.

4. Before you start your course, you will be sent a payment schedule showing when you can expect to receive money.

Timing is important.

▶ New students applying for student finance that depends on household income should get their application in by 25 June 2010.

▶ Students applying for student finance that does not depend on household income should get their application in by 23 April 2010.

▶ Late applications may result in late payments.

▶ If your circumstances change after this date you should let Student Finance know as soon as possible. You can do this by filling in a 'Change of Circumstances' form, which can be downloaded from the Student Finance website.

If you want to discover what help you are entitled to, check out the online calculator at www.direct.gov.uk/studentfinance. Deadlines for applications for funding for 2011–2012 have not yet been set but the dates quoted should give you a good idea of what those deadlines will be.

For the application process for students based in Wales, Scotland and Northern Ireland, turn to Chapter 4.

When and how will I get the money?

There have been some frightening stories in the media of students not getting their loan money for weeks after the first term started. The Student Loans Company (SLC) assures us that these problems will have been sorted. To be on the safe side, get your application in on time – early if possible. It was the increase in applicants and the influx of late applicants that threw a spanner in the works.

This is what should happen:

▶ *Your student loan and grant*: once you have registered your arrival at university and have started to attend the course, your university will notify Student Finance England and your student loan and grant (if applicable) will be paid into your bank account. However, it could take three working days after your college has confirmed that you have arrived for the money actually to reach your bank account, so you may need funds to tide you over. Payments will be in three tranches, made at the beginning of each term.

▶ *Your fees*: will be paid direct to your university.

▶ *Your university bursary*: likely to be paid into your bank account by your university. It will generally be paid out in two tranches, one in the second and one in the third term. You may need to inform your university that you think you are eligible for a bursary. Make sure you have filled in the right section on your application form to ensure financial information is passed to your university so they can assess you for a bursary.

'I was living on £5 a week since an error had been made in processing my application form and I didn't receive my bursary until the last week of term.'
Second-year Biochemistry student, Oxford

'Major problem in student loan coming in late in the term.'
Third-year Classical Civilisation student, Warwick

It's a Fact

Student Finance England, the online service for students applying to go on to higher education in 2010–2011, makes the process faster and more straightforward than ever before. You can now apply for student finance at the same time as making your UCAS application so you only have to fill in your details once. See for yourself: visit www.direct.gov.uk/studentfinance.

Panic! My loan and grant haven't arrived!

It happens – not that often, but it can be dramatic when it does. In an ideal world, your cheque should be waiting for you when you arrive at your university or college, but things can go wrong. Some typical reasons we discovered were:

- you applied late, so the amount of the loan has not been assessed
- the loans company has been inundated
- wrong information on your bank account
- you didn't give all the information required, e.g. National Insurance number.

Whatever the reason, it doesn't help the destitute student to eat, so …

What can I do?

- *Try the bank.* If you already have a bank account, they may help you out with a loan – most banks offer free overdrafts to students. Talk to the student adviser at the campus or local branch. This, of course, is no help to the first-year student who needs that cheque to open a bank account, so make sure you have an account before you start your course.

- *Try your college.* Ask them for temporary help. Most institutions have what's called a hardship fund set up to cover just this kind of eventuality.

- *Try the Access to Learning Fund.* This has been set up to help students. Full details are given on page 79.

- *Friends?* They may well take pity on you when it comes to socialising, buying you the odd drink, but it is rarely a good idea to borrow from friends.

- *Check your application.* Check where it has got to and what is holding it up online – www.direct.gov.uk/studentfinance.

How late can I apply for funding support?

Up to nine months after you have started your course. Applications can be made at any time during the academic year. The cut-off date for a maintenance loan application is one month before the end of your academic year.

Parents: what to expect

What are parents expected to contribute?

If the family income is £50,778 or over and you live in England then you could be assessed to contribute towards your son or daughter's maintenance. But that is still better than in the rest of the UK, where the norm is around £40,000.

How much you are expected to contribute is on a sliding scale: the maximum amount parents or spouses in England are expected to contribute for one student in the year 2010–2011 is approximately:

- students studying in London: £1,940
- student studying elsewhere: £1,386
- student living in parents' home: £1,075.

(See Table 16 in Chapter 2, page 59.)

advice note *i*

You will need to have some cash in hand when you arrive at university, since your loan or grant payment will not hit your bank account on the first day, and it could in fact be several days before you receive any money.

Note: Scotland has a different system of funding for students, and parents are expected to contribute substantially more than parents in the rest of the UK. The figures are also different for Wales and Northern Ireland; see Chapter 4 for more details.

Note to parents

No parent is expected to contribute more than the maximum means-tested portion of the loan for each student, however high their income – but many do. (See the paragraphs below for details of what you might have to pay.)

How do they calculate how much loan I can have?

The actual calculation of whether and how much your family is expected to contribute towards maintenance and how much grant you are entitled to is very complex. It is based on 'residual income': this means what's left after essential expenses have been deducted. The assessment will be on family income, so if both parents are earning both incomes will be assessed.

So what are essential expenses? It works like this: they take your parents' or parent plus partner's gross income before tax and National Insurance and then subtract allowances for things such as pension schemes, dependants and superannuation payments that qualify for tax relief and whether you will be receiving any maintenance grant. Having done this, they then assess what your household contribution should be. It is not until the family income is over £50,778 that parents are expected to contribute. See Table 16 on page 59.

Facts and Figures

Parents are contributing more than ever before.

▶ 52% of students receive financial support from their parents. (Our *Guide to Student Money* survey put the figure higher at 63%).

▶ 61% of contributing parents pay an average of £69.51 a week.

Source: *NatWest Student Living Index Survey*, August 2009

My parents are divorced: whose income will they assess?

Your LA will decide which parent they consider you are living with and assess their income, ignoring the income of the other parent.

I have a step-parent: will their income be included?

Yes: the income of a step-parent, if that's the parent you live with, or a cohabiting partner, whether of the same or opposite sex, will be taken into account. However, maintenance received from an absent parent will not be considered as part of the household income when assessing income.

What happens if my parents are not prepared to divulge their income?

You will not be assessed for a maintenance grant and will only be eligible for three-quarters (the non-means-tested portion) of the maintenance loan.

What if I have a sibling claiming for a maintenance grant and a loan?

If there are several children in higher education in the family, the grant and loan entitlements are calculated on the same scale as for one student; those parents whose residual income is below £50,778 would not have to contribute for either student and you would both be eligible for a full loan. If the family income is over £50,778 but below £57,708 (£60,478 in London), parents would have to contribute no more than for one student, and any additional loan received would be divided proportionately between the students. Any parental contribution should be divided in the same way. It must also be remembered that any other dependent children they have will come into the calculation. Parents with a higher residual income will have to contribute more if they have more than one child at university. The maximum parents can be asked to pay, regardless of how many children they have at university, is £6,210 if students are under the new top-up fee system.

Does the parental contribution ever change?

Generally, the threshold at which parents begin to contribute towards maintenance is raised each year as the loan is increased. But this year, the loan has *not* been increased, so parental contributions have stayed the same. Remember, as a parent you are only expected to contribute – nobody can force you.

What if my mum or dad is made redundant?

If your parents' income suddenly drops, you should contact Student Finance England immediately as you could be entitled to a maintenance grant and more maintenance loan. You should also tell your university, since many bursaries are linked to the amount of maintenance grant received.

If my parents can't afford to or won't pay the shortfall in my maintenance loan, is there anything I can do?

No. There is no way that parents can be made to pay their contribution towards your maintenance, and your LA or Student Finance England will not make up the difference. Equally, your parents can choose how they give their contribution: cash in hand or paying for something such as rent, utility bills or books.

Are there any circumstances in which my parents would not be expected to contribute towards my maintenance?

Yes – if you:

▶ are 25 or over

▶ are married

▶ are in care

▶ have been supporting yourself for three years.

Is the debt worth the struggle?

Judge for yourself!

Graduates earn on average 20–25% more over their lifetimes than people who don't continue their formal education beyond A levels. On average, this amounts to £160,000, according to the research in 2006, but how much the difference is depends on what you study.

- ▶ *Medicine*: £340,315 more
- ▶ *Humanities*: £52,549 more
- ▶ *Arts*: £34,494 more.

Source: Universities UK report, 2006.

Some important questions and answers

I want to go to a university in my home town but don't want to live with my parents. Can I get the full financial package?

Students living at home are eligible for the lower 'living at home' maintenance loan only. There is no regulation preventing you from living away from home, but funding is at the discretion of your LA.

Our research for the *Guide to Student Money* showed that 72% of students knew someone who had decided to study in their home town to save money.

I'm thinking of getting married: will it affect my maintenance grant and loan entitlements?

Yes. Students who get married before the academic year are considered as independent and their support is no longer assessed on their parents' income but on that of their partner, provided he or she is earning enough. This is calculated in a similar way as for parental income.

I'm not married but living with a partner: will this affect my support?

Yes – you will be considered independent in the same way as a married student would be and income will be based on your partner's income.

What is the maintenance loan meant to cover?

Lodgings, food, books, pocket money, travel, socialising – but not fees.

My academic year is longer than at most colleges: can I get extra money?

Yes. If your course is longer than 30 weeks you can claim for an extra loan, which will be means-tested, for each week you have to attend your course.

Rates for 2010–2011 are:

- London: £106 per week
- elsewhere: £83 per week
- living at home: £54 per week
- studying abroad: £115 per week.

If your course year is 45 weeks or longer, you will receive a loan based on 52 weeks.

Table 18 Which subjects were up and which are down among students applying for uni in 2009?

Subject up	Percentage change	Subject down	Percentage change
Imaginative Writing	+26.8%	Archaeology	–6.2%
Aerospace Engineering	+21.7%	Pre-Clinical Veterinary Medicine	–6.2%
Nursing	+19.9%	Human Resources	–7.9%
Animal Science	+18.8%	Finance	–8%
Agriculture	+16.3%	Production and Manufacturing Engineering	–8.6%
Journalism	+16%	Theology and Religious Studies	–9.5%
Dance	+13.2%	Planning (Urban, Rural, Regional)	–10.3%
Philosophy	+13%	American Studies	–10.5%
Forensic Archaeology	+12.2%	Complementary Medicine	–11.1%
Mechanical Engineering	+12.1%	Linguistics	–17.7%

Note: large combination subjects not included
Source: UCAS application figures, 2009

If I work part time, will it affect my student financial package?

No. Students can work during their course and the money earned will not be considered when their loan or grant is calculated.

What will happen if I drop out of my course?

You will have to pay off any loans taken out for fees and maintenance. Your LA might also ask you to repay some of the fees they have paid.

Table 19 Lowest drop-out/failed to get a degree rates

Courtauld Institute of Art	0%
Cambridge	1.0%
Glasgow School of Art	1.6%
Oxford	1.8%
St Andrews	2.1%
Central School of Speech and Drama	2.6%
University of Bristol	2.8%
Imperial College	3.0%
Universities of Durham and Exeter	3.1%
Leeds College of Music	3.2%

Source: HESA performance indicators for UK universities and colleges – full-time study for courses started 2005–2006 (predicted), published September 2008

Table 20 Highest drop-out/failed to get a degree rates

UHI Millennium Institute	28.2%
Bolton University	20.7%
Napier College	16.9%
University of Sunderland	16.8%
Roehampton University and Swansea Metropolitan University	16.6%
London South Bank University	16.5%
London Metropolitan University	16.2%
University of Glamorgan	16.0%
Glyndwr University	15.5%
University of Wolverhampton	15.3%

Source: HESA performance indicators for UK universities and colleges – full-time study for courses starting 2006–2007, published September 2009

Dropping Out

Avoid being a university drop-out. At the last count, around 7% of students dropped out of university or failed to get a degree. In some universities, the drop-out rate is as high as 16%; in a couple it's over 20%. The universities with fewest drop-outs are shown in Table 19 and highest drop-out rates in Table 20. Freshers who think they've taken the wrong course should beat a hasty path to their course director or careers service for advice as soon as possible. Nothing is set in stone. The critical date is 1 December: the SLC doesn't actually pay your fees before then.

Reasons students gave in the *Guide to Student Money* survey for their friends dropping out of their course included:

'Ran out of money.'
Aberdeen student

'Received no loan because of previous degree.'
Falmouth

'University would not give him breathing space even though he still had two years to graduation because he was an international student.'
Aberdeen

'Couldn't survive.'
Falmouth

'Stopped getting child support after children left school.'
Dartington

'He was an international student from America and his loan company went bust.'
UWE

'They blew their student loan in two days!'
UWE

'Couldn't afford to repeat a year without SAAS paying the tuition fees.'
St Andrews

'Loan wouldn't cover accommodation.'
St Andrews

When is the best time to take out a maintenance loan?

There are three options:

1. When you need it.
2. As late as possible – because it's index-linked to inflation (see page 83).
3. As soon as possible. Some financially astute students take out their student loan even if they don't need it and invest it in a good interest-paying account with a bank or building society (not so easy to find in these credit crunch times). But these accounts generally pay more than the inflation rate and more than the interest on a student loan. Make sure you know what you are doing. Check out interest rates first, and ensure you can get at your money quickly and easily if you are likely to need it – some high-interest rate accounts give limited access.

'Because I had sponsorship, had worked for a year before uni and had a Saturday job, I didn't need a student loan – but I took it out anyway, and put it in a good building society account, just in case I wanted to go on to do further study. As it is, my sponsor has offered me a job that's too good to turn down, so I won't need it, but it was nice to have that security cushion there. I haven't checked it out yet, but I think the loan has actually made me money; at least it hasn't cost me anything, which has to be good.'

Third-year student

Do I have to take out the whole maintenance loan amount?

No. You can take out however much you want, up to the maximum for which you are eligible that year. If you do not apply for the full amount at the start of the academic year, you can apply for the rest later.

Will the loan be paid all at once in a lump sum?

No. The loan will be paid termly, in two or three instalments depending on when you apply for it.

Is there any help with travelling expenses?

The first £303 of any travelling expenses is disregarded. Above that, you can claim a grant for certain expenses if you are attending another establishment as part of a medical or dental course or attending an institution abroad for eight weeks or more as part of your course. The grant is means-tested. (Scottish students should see page 97.)

Additional help

Access to Learning Fund

What is it?

The Access to Learning Fund is a special fund available through your college that helps students who may need extra financial support to stay in higher education.

Who gets Access help?

If you are in real financial difficulty, this is the source to tap. The fund is open to both full-time students and part-time students studying 50% of their time on a full-time course. It is there to help those facing particular financial hardship, those in need of emergency help for an unexpected financial crisis and those who are considering giving up their studies because of financial problems. Priority is given to students with children, mature students, those from low-income families, disabled students, students who have been in care, and students in their final year.

cash crisis

As your loan cheque will not be banked until you have arrived at your university or college, you will need to have some money of your own to get yourself there, and possibly to maintain yourself for several days until the cheque is cleared. Check out the cost of train fares.

If you are living in halls of residence, your college will probably be sympathetic if your cheque hasn't arrived and will wait until it does. But don't be too sure about this – check it out. Some colleges will add a penalty to the bills of students who don't pay up on time. And if you run out of money and can't pay your bill at all, you will not be allowed to re-register for the next academic year. If it's your final year, you will not get your degree until the bill is paid.

If you are living in rented accommodation, you can expect no leniency. Landlords expect to be paid on the dot, usually ask for rent in advance and may request an additional deposit. You will need funds to cover this.

'Ask for help as soon as you realise you have a financial problem, as it takes at least four weeks to assess an Access to Learning Fund application. But in the end I got £200 – a lifesaver when you can't pay your rent.'

Fourth-year Astrophysics student, UCL

'I was having trouble meeting my mortgage repayments: the university was very helpful with an emergency loan and very understanding. Talk to them. At the end of the day, they don't want you to drop out.'

Fourth-year Pure Mathematics student, St Andrews

'Don't choose the wrong degree first time around.'

Second-year BA Photography student, Falmouth, who receives around £400 p.a. from the Access to Learning Fund to top up her pub earnings.

How much can you get?

That depends on your college. It could be just a few hundred pounds to tide you over a sticky patch, it could be £3,000-plus. Your college will use its discretion. The amount given will depend on a number of factors – your circumstances, how many other students are applying and how much they have in the kitty. You can apply for help more than once in a year.

In Wales, similar payments are made through the Financial Contingency Funds (FCFs) scheme. Scotland provides help through Hardship Funds, while Northern Ireland provides help through Support Funds.

advice note

Postgraduates are not entitled to a student loan unless they are taking a PGCE course. So if as an undergraduate you do not need the loan or all of the loan now but are thinking of going on to do a postgraduate course, it might be worth your while taking out the student loan and investing it so the money is there to help you through your postgraduate studies later on. If you are not a financial whizz kid, take advice. The student loan is a really cheap way of borrowing money, but you don't want to build up debt unnecessarily.

Will I have to pay the money back?

Access payments are usually given as a grant, but they could be given as a short-term loan.

'I tried to get funds from Access but felt I was on trial.'

Mature Physics and Engineering student, Heriot-Watt

'The college hardship fund is a wonderful scheme to help you survive.'

Mature Midwifery student with four children, Canterbury Christ Church

How do I set about getting money from the Access to Learning Fund?

Apply to your college. Every institution will have a different procedure and different criteria for measuring your needs. You will probably have to fill in a form giving details of your financial situation. Most institutions will have somebody to help and advise you. They may even have a printed leaflet giving you details.

When should I apply for Access funding?

As soon as trouble starts to loom. The fund is limited to the amount that is allocated, so it is largely first come, first served. We have heard of institutions that have allocated most of their funds by the end of November of the academic year.

I'm a student from abroad: can I apply for Access money?

Sorry, but no. The Access to Learning Fund is restricted to domestic students only, so overseas students are not eligible.

Are there any other hardship funds?

Some institutions and also some students' unions have resources to help students in real financial difficulty. They all vary according to the institution, and they will pay out money for a variety of reasons. Funds are generally given when all official avenues are exhausted. Priority is often given to students who are suffering financially because of unforeseen circumstances such as a death in the family or illness. Sometimes small amounts are given to tide you over or to pay a pressing bill. Increasingly, hardship payments take the form of an interest-free loan, which can be especially useful if your grant or loan cheque doesn't arrive on time. They may also offer help to students from abroad.

Leeds University Union, for example, offers a range of financial assistance to students who find themselves in difficulty. There is a Fund-raising Group, which considers all applications. As most of the money comes from external charitable trusts, their hands are tied to some extent because they are governed by each individual trust's guidelines and criteria. But they do offer much-needed support.

Facts and Figures

Of the students graduating last year:

▶ 333,720 first-degree students obtained a degree

▶ 14% of students obtained a first-class degree

▶ 48% obtained a 2:1

▶ 57% of first-degree graduates were women

▶ 41% of students received a science degree, of whom 50% were women

▶ 204,560 students obtained a postgraduate qualification.

Source: HESA statistics for academic year 2008–2009

Are there any other allowances, grants and bursaries I could apply for?

Yes. Check Chapter 5: you might fall into a special category. Otherwise try Chapter 9, 'Other sources to tap'.

Gordon's story

Gordon is a Latin American Studies student at Glasgow.

'When I came to university I had an electric guitar, an amp, a bass guitar, a stereo and a camera,' he says. 'In times of financial need, these have all had temporary lodging in the pawnshop. Gradually, this became less and less temporary, so now I no longer have a bass guitar, a camera or a stereo.'

He adds: 'The loss of the latter is no great hardship, as I have already sold my CDs and DVDs one by one to the second-hand record shop.'

Thrift Tips

'Try the Access to Learning Fund: it isn't widely advertised. I got £200.'
Third-year Sociology student, Aberdeen

'Try to get your book list early and be first in line for second-hand books – then sell them back to your uni library later.'
Third-year Physics student, UCL

'Take a gap year and save.'
Third-year Geography and Management student, York

'Find food nearing its sell-by date and being sold off cheaply, then freeze it.'
First-year Social and Political Science student, Cambridge

Loans: paying them back

Will I be able to afford to pay back my loans?

It may take a long time, but a system has been worked out that allows you to pay back what you borrowed in line with what you earn.

When do I have to pay back my loans?

You repay nothing until the April after you have graduated, and then only when your income is over £15,000 p.a. will you begin to pay off the loans. The amount you pay is related to your salary, so whether you have borrowed £1,000 or £35,000, have had a maintenance or fee loan or both, your monthly repayments will be the same as long as you stay on the same salary. You will go on paying until the debt is paid off. However, if after 25 years you still haven't paid it all off, the government will write off anything left outstanding (except arrears). Rates are currently worked out at 9% of income over £15,000. The current scale is shown in Table 21.

Table 21 Loan repayment rates

Annual income up to	Monthly repayments (approx.)	Monthly salary (approx.)
£15,000	£0	£1250 and below
£16,000	£7	£1,333
£18,000	£22	£1,500
£21,000	£45	£1,700
£24,000	£67	£2,000
£27,000	£90	£2,250

How will I make the repayments?

Repayments will be collected through the Inland Revenue and will be deducted from your pay packet at source. Probably all you will know about it is an entry on your pay slip.

Will I have to pay back more than I borrow?

In real terms, probably not. The interest rates on loans are linked to inflation, so while the actual figure you pay will probably be higher, the value of the amount you pay back is broadly the same as the value of the amount you borrowed. And it is certainly lower than the interest paid on other loans.

You will be charged interest on your loan from when you receive your first payment, and this will be added to your debt. The interest rate in the year to August 2007 was 2.4%; the rate from September 2007 to August 2008 was 4.8%; but by December, with the banking crisis taking a grip on the country, it was down to 3% and by January to 2.5%. From September 2009 to 31 August 2010, the rate was 0%. For 2010–2011, the rate has not been set yet. But yes, rates do vary. For current rates see www.direct.gov.uk/studentfinance.

Will all students graduate with a huge debt?

Most students starting a course now will have to face up to the prospect of starting work with a debt to pay off, and this could be substantially more than the amount totted up under the Student Loans Scheme.

it's a Fact

▶ Dramatic graduate job cuts feared have not materialised.

▶ Vacancies for graduates are stabilising, with a modest decrease of 1.6% predicted.

▶ Transport sectors expect cuts.

▶ More graduate vacancies are predicted in oil companies and consulting.

▶ Graduate salaries frozen for the second year running.

▶ Postgraduate study is not the solution – employers urge struggling graduates to research jobs and prepare for interviews more thoroughly.

Source: AGR *Winter Review 2010*

Our research among undergraduates this year showed a massive 86% expected to be in debt either to the bank or to the SLC, or possibly both, by the end of their course – by anything from a few hundred pounds to over £15,000. The most-quoted figure over £15,000 was £20,000, but £40,000–£50,000 was not uncommon, especially among medical students.

It doesn't take much mathematical ability to work out what your debt is likely to be. Take how much you pay for fees – this year £3,290. Multiply that by the number of years of your course and add a further amount for each year for inflation – the hike up from last year was around 2.04%. Then take the amount of loan you receive (remember, not everyone can take the full loan), multiply that by the number of years of your course. Usually we'd suggest adding something for inflation, but as the loan was not increased this year we suggest you just bear it in mind.

Add on your interest-free loan from the bank if you intend to use it (60% of our student contacts said they did) – which could be anything up to £3,000, depending on the generosity of your bank (see page 260) – and you will have some idea of what your debt is likely to be.

Table 22 Estimated maximum debts for students whose household income is around £50,775

	Outside London		In London	
Fee loan	£3,290 × 3 + 2.04% =	£11,072	£3,290 × 3 + 2.04% =	£11,072
Maintenance loan	£4,950 × 3 =	£14,850	£6,928 × 3 =	£20,784
Free overdraft from bank		£3,000		£3,000
		Total: £28,922		Total: £34,856

Note: this table does not take account of interest on the loan or the slightly lower loan given in final year

We estimated the worst debt on a three-year course outside London at nearly £29,000 and in London at over £35,000. The example shown in Table 22 is for those unlucky students whose family income is around £50,775, and who would be entitled to take out the full loan. (Below £50,020 you would receive a portion of the grant and your loan would be cut. Above £50,778 your parents would be expected to chip in, so your loan would also be cut.)

The fact is, no two students' expenditure and income are ever the same, but it's good to be aware of the worst scenario.

Do the rules about paying your loan back ever change?

The rules are reviewed every year to make sure graduates can realistically pay back what they owe. The payback threshold has been £15,000 for the last few years.

Will I be able to pay it all back?

Although facing the possibility of graduating with a massive debt, most students have the prospect of starting a job with a fairly substantial salary. Starting salaries

It's a Fact

Medical students seem to be the hardest hit, which is hardly surprising since the course is at least five years long. Last year, nearly a third of our student contacts at St George's in London anticipated debt of over £30,000, and half of those thought it was more likely to be over £40,000. One 'poor' student from abroad expected to graduate to a debt of £150,000, which says something about the lengths to which students will go to get a good training.

for graduates with good second-class honours degrees in a blue-chip company in 2010 were expected to be around a median of £25,000 (no change from last year). Recruiters also predicted vacancy cuts would level off, according to the AGR *Winter Review 2010*.

▶ Check out Chapter 11 on budgeting – it might save you a few sleepless nights.

▶ Compare current bank overdraft rates for newly qualified graduates.

Loan repayment holiday for students cut

It couldn't last! Graduates in England will no longer be able to take a five-year loan 'repayment holiday' – it has been cut to two years. You will still have the opportunity to put your repayments on hold at any time of your choice, which could be a great help if you want to buy a house, go travelling or have got into debt, but the deferment can now only be for two years. However, if your partner also has a loan to pay off, together you can budget on four years.

If you are earning around £2,000 a month, the repayments won't seem quite so grisly. But will you find a job? Are you going to be a 2:1 success story?

Many graduates start work on salaries of less than £16,000. At the time of writing, the employment market for graduates in the UK is likely to be the worst it has been for many years. Table 23 gives an idea of the top-paying professions for graduates.

The graduate market is currently very volatile, so what it will be like in three or four years' time, when this year's first-year students graduate, is anyone's guess. But it's worth remembering that, if you can't find work, the SLC will wait for

Table 23 Where are the big graduate starting salaries to be earned?

Investment bank or fund managers	£38,250
Law firm	£35,000
Oil company	£33,500
Banking or financial services	£28,500
Consulting or business services firm	£27,750
IT/telecommunications companies	£27,000
Motor manufacturing	£26,000
Insurance company	£25,500
FMCG company	£25,500
Accountancy or professional services firm	£25,000
Energy, water or utilities company	£25,000

Source: AGR *Winter Review 2010*

repayment; the banks, however, may not be so sympathetic, although most do offer special overdraft facilities to graduates, which you should investigate.

I'm a graduate with £25,000 student loan debts to clear: is my new employer likely to pay this off?

When the loan scheme first came in, many employers thought they might need to offer the 'carrot' of paying off students' loans if they wanted to attract the best graduates. Whether the government was hoping that employers would step in and clear students' debts in this way was a question often discussed in the national press.

Don't forget, if you're anticipating a 'golden hello', the taxman will expect his cut.

cash crisis

In fact, at least one major company did draw up contingency plans for a 'golden hello' scheme, and a number of companies we contacted said they were watching the market and their competitors very closely.

Then the 1990s recession hit the UK hard, graduate openings were in short supply and graduates were competing for jobs rather than employers competing for graduates. Employers put all ideas of loan pay-off schemes for students on the back burner.

However, market trends and influences change very rapidly. Good-quality graduates were in short supply again and employers were quite genuinely concerned about the amount of debt graduates have.

So the 'golden hello' quietly materialised. 'Quietly' because few employers were keen to call it that. You might think, in these troubled credit-crunch times, when everyone is predicting a cutback on graduate opportunities, the golden hello would be a distant memory – but according to the AGR *Winter Review 2010*, this is not so. In 2010, around a quarter of AGR members are reported to be offering a golden hello to graduates, with figures ranging from £1,000 to £4,000, and a median payout of £2,500.

Can I get out of repaying student loans?

Yes you can, but only:

► if you never earn more than £15,000 a year
► if you become permanently disabled

> Women face unequal opportunities: you are likely to earn £1,000 a year less than your male counterparts, and this is apparent within three years of leaving university, according to a major survey on graduate experience published in January 2008 by the HESA. Whatever happened to equal opportunities?

- ▶ if you die!
- ▶ after 25 years the loan will be written off.

Is bankruptcy an option?

Not any longer. A few years ago, we reported that some 9,000 students and graduates were considering making themselves bankrupt to avoid debt. New laws making it easier to become bankrupt were being introduced, and in straightforward cases you could probably clear your debts within 12 months. But the government, it would seem, were hot on their heels and moved rapidly to close this obvious loophole in its system of student finance, and today the SLC tells us that making yourself bankrupt is not an option for clearing your student loan debt – well, at least your good reputation will be intact.

Is the Student Loans Scheme better than borrowing from the bank?

Most banks and some building societies will give students overdraft facilities on special terms, usually including an interest-free £1,000–£3,000 overdraft facility (see Table 24).

This is intended mainly to help you during that difficult period when your loan hasn't yet arrived or you've run out of cash at the end of the term. The overdraft is wiped out as soon as the loan cheque arrives. It is better only to use the bank's interest-free facility if your financial problems are temporary or you are certain you will be able to pay the overdraft back once you graduate. Most banks won't start charging interest on student overdrafts immediately after you graduate, giving you time to get a job. This can be several months, but check it out with your bank. Banks also offer students longer-term loans at competitive rates, which should be investigated.

But, in general, banks are not the best bet for long-term borrowing for students – the Student Loans Scheme is, since the interest rate is no more than inflation and paying it back is related to your salary and ability to pay. (See details on payback arrangements in Table 21 on page 83.)

It's worth remembering, however, that to get a loan you have to have a bank or building society account. As mentioned, if you already have an overdraft with your bank, as soon as the loan hits your account it will automatically be used

It's Official ...

... the great British entrepreneurial spirit is not dead and only slightly dampened by rising student debt. The number of students planning to set up their own business after qualifying remains consistent at 4%, or around 30,000 students. Even in the current economic downturn, as employers' graduate intake targets are reduced, many students are considering self-employment.

Prominent entrepreneur Lord Karan Bilimoria, the founder of Cobra Beer, started his business in the last major recession. He said recently

that opportunities still abound for determined graduate entrepreneurs. However, student debt is likely to slow down their plans: while 75% of students with ambitions to go it alone would either scale back or defer their plans until their debts were paid off, a brave (possibly unwise) quarter would carry on regardless.

If you see yourself as a potential entrepreneur, register for free mentoring and support at www. flyingstartonline.com. If you have the right ideas, they will help you on your way.

Source: Survey commissioned by the National Council for Graduate Entrepreneurship in conjunction with Barclays, 2006

Table 24 Interest-free loans offered by banks to students in 2009–2010

	Santander	Bank of Scotland	Barclays	Halifax	HSBC	Lloyds TSB	Nat West	RBS
1st year	£1,000	£3,000	£2,000	£3,000	£1,000	£1,500	£1,250	£2,750
2nd year	£1,250	£3,000	£2,000	£3,000	£1,250	£1,500	£1,400	£2,750
3rd year	£1,500	£3,000	£2,000	£3,000	£1,500	£1,500	£1,600	£2,750
4th year	£1,800	£3,000	£2,000	£3,000	£1,750	£2,000	£1,800	£2,750

to pay off the overdraft, so you might not find that you have any more cash in hand, though you'll certainly have more peace of mind.

The bank is the student's friend

For most students the best thing the bank offers is the interest-free overdraft. But remember:

▶ to get the interest-free overdraft facility you must tell your bank you are a student

▶ if your overdraft goes over the set interest-free limit, you will be charged interest

▶ you may be able to negotiate a larger interest-free overdraft, but don't rely on it

▶ use the bank's interest-free limit rather than build up debt on a credit card.

Which is best, a big or small overdraft facility? The bigger the overdraft facility, the greater the temptation to overspend and the more you will have to pay back. On the other hand, a smaller overdraft facility may mean you go over the limit sooner and you start paying bank charges. You decide!

See what else the banks offer in Chapter 11, Table 45 (page 262).

Health Check

I'm sick and myopic, and I've got toothache – can I get free treatment?
As a student you don't actually qualify for any help, but as someone on a low income you could qualify for free or reduced:

▶ dental charges

▶ glasses

▶ eye tests

▶ prescriptions.

Form HC1 is the starting point, available from high-street opticians, the Benefits Agency or the Post Office. That will probably send you off on a trail leading to form HC2 or HC3; if you haven't received either of these items you will need form HC5, and don't forget to ask the chemist for receipt form FP57 (EC57 in Scotland) to claim for free prescription charges. If you are confused – and who isn't? – then leaflet HC11 (*Are you Entitled to Help with Health Costs?*) will put you straight on the NHS in general and HC12 on costs – both are available

from your Benefits Agency or by phoning 0845 850 1166 (local rates).

Try to get things going before treatment begins, or at least before you need to pay up. Otherwise, make sure you keep all bills and receipts, as evidence of costs. If after filling in HC1 you are told you are not entitled to any help and you think you are, give the Department of Health or Benefits Agency another try. It could be that the computer is 'confused' as well – it has been known! It can be a long process, but it's often worth the effort.

For immediate medical advice, phone NHS Direct on 0845 4647.

It's serious – I could be off sick for weeks. What should I do?
If you become seriously ill and are likely to be off sick for months then you should obviously let your university department know, but also your local authority and the SLC, since your student loans might be affected if you are off for more than 60 days.

Further information

Who to contact/what to read

▶ Student Finance England helpline: 0845 607 7577 between 8a.m. and 8p.m. Monday to Friday and from 9a.m. to 5.30p.m. weekends for financial information, including information on your loans.

▶ Also, Student Finance England main number: 0845 300 5090, online www.direct. gov.uk/studentfinance. Full information about fees, maintenance grants and loans is given in the following free booklets, which you would be well advised to get and study:

   ▶ For students in England: *Student Finance England – A Guide to Financial Support for Higher Education 20010/11*, which is the source for the loan statistics in this chapter, is available from tel: 0800 731 9133 or 0845 300 5090, website: www. direct.gov.uk/studentfinance. Braille and audio editions are also available.

   ▶ For students in Scotland: *Student Support in Scotland: A Guide for Undergraduate Students 20010/11* is available from any Scottish university or the SAAS, Gyleview House, 3 Redheughs Rigg, South Gyle, Edinburgh EH12 9HH, tel: 0131 476 8212, email: saas.geu@scotland.gsi.gov.uk or website: www.saas.gov.uk.

   ▶ For students in Northern Ireland: *Financial Support for Students in Higher Education 20010/11* is available from Student Support Branch, Department for Employment and Learning (Northern Ireland), Rathgael House, Balloo Road, Bangor, Co. Down BT19 7PR or tel: 028 9025 7710 or (for booklet) 0800 731 9133 or visit the website: www.delni.gov.uk.

   ▶ For students in Wales: *A Guide to Financial Support for Higher Education* is available from the National Assembly for Wales, Higher Education Division 2, 3rd floor, Cathays Park, Cardiff CF10 3NQ, tel: 0845 602 8845 or websites: www.studentfinancewales.co.uk and www.learning.wales.gov.uk.

Thrift Tips

'*Spend time in the library in winter as it's warm and saves on heating bills.*'
Second-year Politics and History student, Aberystwyth

'*Take all the food you can at breakfast, which is free, and eat it for lunch.*'
First-year Medical student living in halls of residence, Dundee

'*If you think £1 is nothing, try saving one a day for a year. £365 is two months' rent.*'
Second-year Electronics student, Robert Gordon University

Can't Face all this Debt?

There's always the Open University (OU). More and more young people are choosing the OU study-at-home way. With more than 230,000 undergraduate and postgraduate students enrolled, the OU is the UK's largest university. It offers 570 courses, covering 70 subject areas and leading to 100 different qualifications. These range from certificates to foundation degrees to full undergraduate and postgraduate qualifications. The cost of an open degree is around £3,500, a Bachelor's (honours) degree around £4,500, and an MBA through the AMBA-, EQUIS- and AACSB-accredited Business School from £12,000–£14,500. Compare that with the costs of a three-year degree in a conventional university – estimated figures are now reaching £33,000.

Most students would probably argue that the OU route isn't much fun but it is actually Britain's favourite university, topping the league tables with a 94% student satisfaction rating in the National Student Survey. Seventy per-cent of OU students are in full- or part-time employment during their studies as well, which means they're earning as they're learning and not racking up huge debts.

If you're thinking about returning to studying but not sure if you've got the time, motivation, money or know-how, the OU offers free online materials at www.open.ac.uk/openlearn, iTunes U and YouTube EDU to give you a taster of the courses and help you assess your ability before committing to a course.

There is also the OU's recession portal that gives advice on updating skills, getting back into work, redundancy help and how to make the most of your CV, from the people who have studied and researched these economic trends for the majority of their lives – visit www.open.ac.uk/recession.

For information or to order a prospectus, visit their website www.open.ac.uk or phone 0845 300 6090.

CHAPTER 4

Devolutionary differences

Not all regions of the UK follow the same student funding system as outlined in the previous chapters. Scotland, for example, decided to introduce a no-fees funding approach for its own students soon after the Scottish Parliament was set up. Wales also decided to take an independent approach, but is now falling more into line with England. In this chapter, we look at the major differences to be found if studying in devolved regions of the UK rather than in England.

Scotland

Less debt is the big plus if you live and study in Scotland. In brief, the deal is as follows:

- if you live and study in Scotland you pay no fees for your university education, and because of EU regulations this also applies to non-UK EU students
- students from the rest of the UK who study in Scotland do pay fees but pay less than in the rest of the UK
- Scottish students attending universities in England, Wales and Northern Ireland pay fees of up to £3,290 p.a.
- as in the rest of the UK, those paying fees will be able to get a loan to cover them while they study
- all Scottish students studying in or outside Scotland can apply for a maintenance loan
- non-repayable bursaries (called grants in the rest of UK) will be given to students from low-income families. These will replace part of the loan so you will not incur so much debt
- the graduate endowment, previously paid by Scottish and EU students who study in Scotland, has been abolished, representing a saving to students of over £2,000
- better-off Scottish parents are assessed to contribute more than in the rest of the UK.

I'm a Scottish student studying in Scotland

Table 25 shows the loan amount for which you are eligible if you are a Scottish student studying in Scotland.

Table 25 Loans available for Scottish students studying in Scotland

	Minimum	Maximum
Living in parental home	£605	£4,107
Living elsewhere (amount depends on family income and bursary; loan rates for final-year students are slightly lower)	£915	£5,067
Non-repayable Young Students' Bursary (means-tested on family income of up to £34,195; bursary replaces part of loan)		£2,640
Additional loan for young students where family income is £22,789 or below		£785

Extra loan for longer courses

If your course is longer than 30 weeks and three days you can claim for an additional loan:

▶ living in parental home: £54 per week

▶ living elsewhere: £83 per week.

I'm a part-time student: will I get any help?

Yes, a £500 part-time HE fee grant (the amount is under review for 2010–2011) is given to new and existing part-time students who earn £22,000 or less and are studying 50% or more of a full-time degree course. For more details, see Table 32 on page 114.

Do you think your course is value for money?

Of the students attending Scottish universities who expressed a view in the *Guide to Student Money* survey, 89% said they thought their course was value for money while only 11% thought it was not. However, the reason often given was because it was free or because the fees were reasonable.

I'm a Scottish student studying outside Scotland

If you are studying in the UK but outside Scotland, you will have to pay the full fees demanded by the university for your course, up to £3,290 p.a. Table 26 shows the money available to help finance your studies.

You may be eligible for a bursary from your university: see Table 12 on page 53.

Extra loan for longer courses

If your course is longer than 30 weeks and three days you can claim for an additional loan:

▶ living in parental home: £54 per week

▶ living elsewhere: £83 per week

▶ London: £106 per week.

Table 26 Loans available for Scottish students studying outside Scotland

	Minimum	Maximum
Student fee loan		
Non-means-tested loan to cover fees		£3,290
Non-repayable means-tested bursary[1]		£2,150
Student maintenance loan[2]		
Living away from home in London	£915	£6,153
Studying elsewhere	£915	£5,067
Studying outside Scotland but living at home	£605	£4,107
Additional loan for students from low-income families[3]		£785

1. On family income up to £34,195; full bursary given where family income £18,825 or less
2. The maintenance loan is based on family income and bursary received; loan rates for final-year students are slightly lower
3. On family income up to £22,789

Note: loan money for Scottish students studying in Scotland is paid out monthly

What parents in Scotland are expected to pay

Table 27 will give some idea of what Scottish parents could be facing. But remember, students in families where the residual income is up to £34,195 should be receiving an income–assessed Young Students' Bursary.

Families with a residual income below £24,275 (or £20,645 for spouses/partners) are not expected to contribute.

A deduction of £195 will be made from the assessed contribution for every dependent child other than the student. No parent is expected to contribute more than £5,237 p.a. for one child studying in London, £4,152 p.a. if the

Table 27 Parental contribution in Scotland

Residual income	Assessed contribution
£24,275	£45
£25,000	£126
£30,000	£681
£35,000	£1,237
£40,000	£1,792
£45,000	£2,348
£50,000	£2,903
£55,000	£3,631
£60,000	£4,400

Note: income threshold is slightly lower for partners/spouses

student is living away from home and studying anywhere else or £3,502 p.a. if the student is living at home, however much they earn. These figures are based on the full loan minus minimum loan that a student can take out. If there is more than one child at university the maximum contribution a parent can be expected to make is £8,000 p.a., regardless of how many offspring they have at university. Although Scottish parents may look with envy at parents in the rest of the UK, who will be assessed to contribute considerably less than those in Scotland, English students will be accumulating a great deal more debt than their Scottish counterparts.

Travel for Scottish students

If you are living away from home, three return journeys per year to your place of study can be claimed for, plus additional term-time travel to and from your institution. (This does not include students whose parents live outside the UK.) The first £159 of any claim will be disregarded. Only the most economical fares will be allowed. (The cost of a student railcard or bus pass may also be reimbursed.)

How do I apply for financial support in Scotland?

Last year, over 80% of Scottish students applied online at www.saas.gov.uk/student_support, and ministers have agreed that this makes it the preferred method. If you prefer the paper method, however, go to Guides and Forms on the website and download what you need. Alternatively, phone 0845 111 1711 or 0845 111 0243, email saas.geu@scotland.gsi.gov.uk, or write to – or even visit – SAAS, Gyleview House, 3 Redheughs Rigg, Edinburgh EH12 9HH.

I'm a student from outside Scotland studying in Scotland

If you are from outside Scotland, you will pay a set fee of £1,820 p.a. This may seem like a lot less than the £3,290 students are paying in other parts of the UK, but the reasoning is that Scottish degree courses last for four years whereas degrees in the rest of the UK generally last for three. However, if you multiply £1,820 by four you'll see you're paying a lot less than the £9,870 some students will have to find. But Scottish universities are under no obligation to pay bursaries to students from lower-income families and

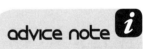

advice note

In a sticky financial situation? Don't suffer in silence, all universities in Scotland have access to hardship funds, which may be able to help out deserving students.

they are unlikely to do so. The rest of your funding will follow the English pattern, so see Chapter 2 for details on fee loans (page 50), maintenance grants (page 54) and maintenance loans (page 58). For fees for Medicine, see page 116.

Financial advice given to the *Guide to Student Money* by students …

… at Aberdeen University

'Get a job before university and save up money to help cover your costs. SAAS do not appear to cater for middle-class families and don't provide anywhere near enough of a "living costs loan", unlike in England!'
Benjamin, third-year Computing Science student

'Don't confuse wants with needs.'
Alyssa, postgraduate Soil Science student

'Keep track of spending in the first month, because that's when it tends to be the highest.'
Bregje, third-year Geography and International relations student

---

… at St Andrews University

'Don't stay in the most expensive halls in first year. I blew savings etc. and now have the burden of that debt.'
Christopher, second-year Medicine student

'Don't buy chips and cheese after a night out – you'll save a bucket!'
Gemma, first-year Mathematics student

'Keep a log of what you're spending.'
Kerry, History student

Wales

New students will face higher fees in Wales. Although Wales has taken an independent line on fees for the last couple of years, the principality is falling more in line with England.

So what's the deal? Swings and roundabouts!

- The Welsh Assembly has decided to do away with the fee grant they introduced for Welsh students studying in Wales, so new students starting their course in 2010 will now pay the same fees of £3,290 as students studying in England. It's tough. If only you had started your course a year earlier you would be paying half that.
- However, the maximum grant paid to lower-income families has been raised to £5,000 – nearly double that in England.
- The above will apply to all students, wherever they study.

The Assembly grant in detail

All Welsh students from lower-income families, wherever they study, will be able to apply for a Higher Education Assembly Grant of up to £5,000 to help with maintenance. This is means-tested and, while it operates in a similar way to the grant in England, it has a much lower family income cut-off threshold. Amounts available are as follows:

- for incomes of £0–£18,370: £5,000 grant
- for incomes of £18,371–£50,020: partial grant depending on family income
- for incomes over £50,020: no grant.

You can also apply for a maintenance loan, up to the amounts shown in Table 28.

Table 28 Loans available for Welsh students

Place of residence	Loan available
Away from home and studying in London	Up to £6,780
Away from home and studying elsewhere	Up to £4,840
Living in parental home	Up to £3,750
Studying abroad	Up to £5,770

For every £1 of grant received, the amount of maintenance loan will be reduced by 60p up to £2,844. This means that up to £2,844 of repayable loan will be replaced by a non-repayable grant. You may also be eligible for a bursary from your university: see page 55.

I'm a part-time student in Wales: will I get any help?

Yes. See pages 103 and 114.

I'm a student from outside Wales studying in Wales

Students who come from outside Wales and study at Welsh universities will not benefit from the higher maintenance grants offered in Wales because their financial package will be the package offered by their home region. However, they may benefit under the Welsh Bursary Scheme. Students who receive the maximum Assembly Learning Grant in Wales, regardless of where they come from in the UK, will be eligible for a minimum bursary of £329 a year (this figure is for continuing students and may well be revised for new students); this is instead of the university bursaries given in England. Welsh universities, like English universities, may choose to give higher bursaries (see Table 32, page 114). If you are hoping for a university bursary, don't forget to tick 'Consent to share financial information with your university' on your application form when applying for financial support.

All students: if you get in a sticky financial situation then your university may be able to help you out through the Access to Learning Fund. Help is generally given as a grant but could be a loan. See Chapter 3, page 79.

I'm Welsh: how do I apply for student funding?

You can apply for support online by logging on to www.studentfinancewales. co.uk, or you can make a paper application by contacting your local authority for a form or downloading a form from 'Forms and Guides' on the Student Finance Wales website. As with the English application procedure (see page 68), once you have registered you will be given a customer reference number and password so you can track your account online.

Northern Ireland

I'm a student from Northern Ireland: what funding can I get?

Northern Ireland generally follows the same funding system as in England (see Chapter 2), but each year there are more differences. For example, the basic grant (£3,475) is higher in Northern Ireland than in England, but the family income cut-off point for receiving a grant is lower – at £41,065 – whether you study in Northern Ireland or anywhere in the rest of the UK. Maintenance grants and loans in Northern Ireland are different too (see Table 32, page 114).

These figures are still lower than in England but an increase on last year.

Table 29 Maintenance grants and loans for students from Northern Ireland (assuming student is living away from home and not studying in London)

Family income	Grant	Maintenance loan	Total
£19,203	£3,475	£2,953	£6,428
£20,000	£3,300	£2,999	£6,299
£25,000	£2,201	£3,289	£5,490
£29,019	£1,318	£3,522	£4,840
£30,000	£1,215	£3,625	£4,840
£35,000	£689	£4,151	£4,840
£41,065	£50	£4,790	£4,840

▶ The maintenance grant is £569 higher than in England at £3,475 (though less than the £5,000 in Wales). It is non-repayable and, of course, means-tested. But as you will see from Table 29, the amount of loan that students from lower-income families are able to take out is also reduced.

▶ Cut-off point for grant is when family income is over £41,065.

▶ Any university or college in Northern Ireland charging the full fees (£3,290) must give students receiving the full maintenance grant a bursary of £329 p.a. Many give more.

▶ If you are planning to study at a publicly funded college in the Republic of Ireland, see below.

▶ Extra help if in a sticky situation: support funds are available through your university in Northern Ireland. These operate in a similar way to the Access to Learning Fund in the UK. See Chapter 3, page 79 for details.

Studying in the Republic of Ireland

The financial arrangements are very different from studying in the UK.

▶ There are no fees for you to pay.

▶ Registration fee of €1,500 (the 2009–2010 figure) is currently paid by the Department of Employment and Learning.

▶ Maintenance loan and means-tested higher education bursary of up to £2,000 are available from your local Student Finance NI office.

I'm a part-time student in Northern Ireland: will I get any help?

Yes. See page 114.

How do I apply for student funding?

You can apply online from November/December 2009 at www.studentfinanceni. co.uk or request an application form from your local Student Finance NI office. You do not have to wait until you have a confirmed place on a course to apply. Return the application form, making sure you provide all the information requested. Deadlines for applications for new students who choose not to supply financial information, 23 April 2010; other new students, 26 June 2010.

Where is the 'best' place to live and to study in the UK?

Check our comparative funding guide in Table 30.

- ▶ If studying in England, Wales (new students) or Northern Ireland, you will be expected to pay up to £3,290 p.a. towards your fees.
- ▶ If you are from Scotland and studying in Scotland, you pay no fees.

Extra help from your university

- ▶ Scotland: provides help through Hardship Funds.
- ▶ Wales: similar payments are made through the FCFs scheme.
- ▶ Northern Ireland provides help through Support Funds.
- ▶ England provides help through the Access To Learning Fund.

Information about fees, maintenance grants and loans

- ▶ For students in Scotland: *Student Support in Scotland: A Guide for Undergraduate Students 2010/11* is available from any Scottish university or the SAAS, Gyleview House, 3 Redheughs Rigg, South Gyle, Edinburgh EH12 9HH, tel: 0131 476 8212, email: saas.geu@scotland.gsi.gov.uk or website: www.saas.gov.uk.
- ▶ For students in Wales: *A Guide to Financial Support for Higher Education* is available from the National Assembly for Wales, Higher Education Division 2,

Table 30 Comparative funding for UK students studying in England, Scotland, Northern Ireland or Wales

Student support	English students everywhere except in Scotland	Welsh students everywhere except in Scotland	Northern Irish (NI) students everywhere except Scotland	Scottish students in Scotland	Rest of UK in Scotland	Scottish students in England/ Wales/NI
Fees	Up to £3,290 p.a.	Up to £3,290 p.a.	Up to £3,290 p.a.	None	£1,820 p.a. (£2,895 for Medicine)	Up to £3,290 p.a.
Fee loan	Up to £3,290 p.a.	Up to £3,290 p.a.	Up to £3,290 p.a.	None	£1,820 p.a. (£2,895 for Medicine)	Up to £3,290 p.a.
Maintenance grant	Up to £2,906 p.a.	Up to £5,000 p.a.	Up to £3,475 p.a.	Up to £2,640 p.a.	Up to £2,906 p.a. from England; up to £3,406 from NI; up to £5,000 from Wales	Up to £2,150 p.a.
Full grant: earning up to …	£25,000	£18,370	£19,203	£22,789	England £25,000; NI £19,203; Wales £18,370	£22,789
Earnings threshold for grant	£50,020	£50,020	£41,065	£34,195	England/Wales £50,020; NI £41,065	£34,195
Max. maintenance loan: London	£6,928 p.a.	£6,648 p.a.	£6,780 p.a.	N/A	N/A	£6,152 p.a.

(Continued)

Student support	English students everywhere except in Scotland	Welsh students everywhere except in Scotland	Northern Irish (NI) students everywhere except Scotland	Scottish students in Scotland	Rest of UK in Scotland	Scottish students in England/Wales/NI
Max. maintenance loan: elsewhere	£4,950 p.a.	£4,745 p.a.	£4,840 p.a.	£915– £5,067 p.a.	England £4,950; NI £4,840; Wales £4,745	£5,067 p.a.
Living in parental home	£3,838	£3,673	£3,750	£605– £4,107 p.a.	England £3,838; NI £3,750; Wales £3,673	£4,107 p.a.
Extra maintenance loan	No	No	No	£785	No	£785 p.a.
University bursary if receiving grant	Min. £329 p.a. (av. on full grant £1,000)	Min. £329 p.a. (av. on full grant £1,000)	Min. £329 p.a. (av. on full grant £1,000)	No	No	Min. £329 p.a. (av. as English students)
Family contribution for one child	Max. £1,939 approx. Up to 28% of loan means-tested	Max. £1,861 p.a. approx. Up to 28% loan means-tested	Max. £1,898 p.a. approx. Up to 28% means-tested	Max. £4,152 p.a. (£3,502 p.a. if student living at home)	Max. £1,386 p.a. up to 28% of loan not given England (£1,329 Wales/ £1,356 NI)	Max. £5,237 p.a. London, £4,152 p.a. elsewhere, living at home £3,502

3rd floor, Cathays Park, Cardiff CF10 3NQ, tel: 0845 602 8845 or websites: www.studentfinancewales.co.uk and www.learning.wales.gov.uk.

▶ For students in Northern Ireland: *Financial Support for Students in Higher Education 2010/11* is available from Student Support Branch, Department for Employment and Learning (Northern Ireland), Rathgael House, Balloo Road, Bangor, Co. Down BT19 7PR or tel: 028 9025 7710 or (for booklet) 0800 731 9133 or visit the website: www.delni.gov.uk.

▶ For students in England: *Student Finance England – A Guide to Financial Support for Higher Education 2010/11*, which is the source for the loan statistics in this chapter, is available from tel: 0800 731 9133 or 0845 300 5090, website: www.direct.gov. uk/studentfinance. Braille and audio editions are also available.

CHAPTER 5

Am I a special case?

This chapter looks at the funding and extra help that is available for students in special categories. In some cases this is in addition to the funding outlined in the previous three chapters; in others there is a completely different system; for yet others, sadly, there is no funding at all.

Courses with a difference

I'm a sandwich student doing an industrial placement: will I have to pay fees during my industrial placement?

Yes. Whether it is a thick or thin sandwich placement, all students will have to pay fees. Those who spend an entire year of a course on an industrial/sandwich placement at home or abroad will pay reduced fees. However, students will find that universities can set their own figure, to a maximum of £1,629.50 – nearly 50% of the current fee.

But why, you might ask, do you have to pay fees when you are not enjoying the advantages of university? This is said to be a contribution towards the cost to the institution of administrative and pastoral arrangements relating to the placement. If the placement is for less than a full year, full fees will be charged, up to £3,290 p.a. You may apply for a fee loan (see page 50) and also for a maintenance loan (see page 58). If you are on a full year's industrial training you will only be eligible for the reduced rate of loan, which is approximately half the full rate of loan, as follows:

- ► London: £3,263 approx.
- ► elsewhere in UK: £2,324 approx.
- ► parental home: £1,744 approx.
- ► overseas: £2,780 approx.

I'm going to take a foundation course: will I get funding?

Some courses include a preliminary or foundation year. These are designed to prepare students for study in their chosen subject if their qualifications or experience are not sufficient to start a degree-level course of study. The same support is available to students on a foundation year as for undergraduates if – and this is crucial – the following conditions are met:

- ► the foundation year is an integral part of the course
- ► the course as a whole is eligible for student support
- ► you enrol for the whole course and not just the foundation year.

For full details of funding, see page 46 for England, page 94 for Scotland, page 98 for Wales and page 100 for Northern Ireland.

I'm taking a second undergraduate degree at Oxbridge: is there any help?

If you are thinking about studying for a second undergraduate degree at either Oxford or Cambridge in one of the disciplines listed below, you could be eligible for a College Fee Loan (CFL). You will need to hold a UK honours degree from a publicly funded institution to be eligible. A CFL information leaflet and application form is available from your college.

Eligible courses are as follows:

▶ Medicine (undergraduate and four-year graduate-accelerated)

▶ Dentistry

▶ Veterinary Science

▶ Architecture

▶ Social Work

▶ a course for which graduates are eligible for a healthcare bursary (see below).

I'm going to do a distance learning course: is there any help?

Yes: if you are on a 'designated' full-time distance learning course, you can apply for a fee grant of up to £1,230 a year and a course grant of up to £265 a year (funding depends on family income). If you are disabled, you may also qualify for allowances for disabled students (see page 122).

Facts and Figures

The number of students accepted for foundation courses in 2009 was up by 17.3% to 25,031 (UCAS figures).

Note: some universities charge lower fees for foundation courses.

Students from abroad

Table 31 shows the top 10 countries sending students to the UK.

But what will it cost you, and who will pay? That depends on where you come from.

EU students

EU students will be treated on a similar basis to their UK counterparts regarding fees. This means they will pay no fees if studying in Scotland, but are likely to be charged the full £3,290 p.a. if studying anywhere else in the UK.

Table 31 Top ten countries sending students to study in the UK

Country	2008	2009	Change
China	6,120	6,509	6.4%
France	2,703	3,194	8.2%
Ireland	2,609	2,823	8.9%
Cyprus	2,305	2,612	13.2%
Hong Kong	2,615	2,575	−1.5%
Germany	2,276	2,415	6.1%
Malaysia	2,016	2,390	18.6%
India	1,674	1,843	10.1%
Nigeria	1,681	1,592	−5.3%
Greece	1,652	1,527	−7.6%

Source: UCAS acceptance figures 2009

All EU students will be able to take out a loan to cover their fees and pay it off gradually once they graduate. EU students are not entitled to apply for a maintenance loan, are unlikely to receive a maintenance bursary and will not receive a maintenance grant.

'I am French, so studying in England is really expensive as there is not much help available. I will have to borrow money from my bank in France because I'm worrying about money. But at least I should have a job when I graduate, and the experiences I'm having are priceless!'

First-year Natural Sciences student, Durham

'Please give EU students loans and sponsorship – we need help too!'

Physics student, Oxford

Non-EU students

Even though most UK students pay fees, the full cost of a course is subsidised by the government. Students from countries outside the EU will be charged the full cost of the course and can legally be charged higher tuition fees than UK students – so for a first degree you can think in terms of the following figures (the median figures for 2009–2010, from Universities UK):

▶   classroom-taught course: £9,300 p.a.

▶   science/lab-based course: £11,500 p.a.

▶   clinical course: £22,100 p.a.

You will not be eligible for a fee loan, a maintenance loan, grant or any help with funding. Some universities do give bursaries to overseas students and some charities have special funds for overseas students – see Chapter 9, page 206. Fee rates for postgraduates can be higher (see page 220). However, most universities and colleges do have a designated overseas adviser whom you could ask for help. Non-EU students wanting to gain work experience in this country after they graduate will now find they can stay longer – up to two years.

Facts and Figures

More overseas students than ever (56,791) started degree courses in our universities in 2009, up 10.1% on the previous year.

Source: UCAS figures

Where to find help

For details on living in the UK, try the following contacts:

▶ the educational enquiry service at the British Council Information Centre, Bridgewater House, 58 Whitworth Street, Manchester M1 6BB, tel: +44 (0)161 957 7755, email: general.enquiries@britishcouncil.org or website: www.educationuk.org

▶ the UK Council for International Student Affairs (UKCISA) advice line, tel: +44 (0)20 7107 9922, open 1p.m.–4p.m. Monday–Friday, or website: www.ukcisa.org.uk. UKCISA's Council for International Education handles around 10,000 enquiries from students each year

▶ you can also try the British Council, High Commission or Embassy in your own country.

Refugees and asylum-seekers: what help is there?

Very little!

If you have the right qualifications and can afford it, you are free to apply to any UK university. But any funding, and how much you must pay, will depend on your immigration status and how long you have been in the UK. Most refugees and asylum-seekers do not qualify for funding and are considered 'overseas' students, which means they may well be charged the overseas fee rate (see page 110, 'Non EU overseas students'). However, some universities will charge UK home student rates while your application is pending. Also, see the 'Facts and Figures' box for students from former British colonies (page 113).

Facts and Figures

The proportion of graduates recruited from overseas to fill vacancies is predicted to fall from 22.8% to 18.4% this year by AGR employers. In a difficult UK jobs market, this is thought to be a sign that UK candidates are matching up to the competition from abroad.

Source: AGR *Winter Review 2010*

If you're living and studying in Scotland, your situation may be slightly different. If you have already lived in the UK for three years, funding concessions are occasionally available, but don't expect it. However, if you are granted full refugee status, you will be eligible for the same funding as UK students – see Chapter 2. If you have already started your degree studies and your immigration status changes, it is important to tell your university as soon as possible. You must apply for any support within four months.

So where can refugees and asylum-seekers not entitled to funding find help?

Some universities offer bursaries to students from overseas – see *University Scholarships, Awards & Bursaries*, published by Trotman. Also check individual university websites and prospectuses.

There are many trusts and charities in this country that have funds to help students from overseas – see Chapter 9. The Education Graduation Advice Site (EGAS – see below) could be a good starting point. Scholarship search databases can be found on www.educationuk.org and www.hotcourses.com.

For more information, check out the following websites:

- www.britishcouncil.org.uk
- www.egas-online.org.uk
- www.ukcisa.org.uk
- www.refugeecouncil.org.uk
- www.educationaction.org
- www.hotcourses.com
- www.educationuk.org
- www.direct.gov.uk
- www.refugeeaccess.info.

'You think you've got it hard. As an overseas student I get no government support and I'm working my ass off to support myself.'
Connie, Physics student Imperial College London; she earns £84 a week during term time and £175 a week during vacations as a sales assistant

Further information for international students

EU students

For details on tuition fees for European Union students, plus other information contact:

▶ Student Finance Online website: www.direct.gov.uk/studentfinance

▶ Student Services European Team, PO Box 89, Darlington DL1 9AZ, tel: +44 (0)141 243 3570 (Monday–Friday 9a.m.–5.30p.m.) or email: EUTeam@slc.co.uk

▶ UK Erasmus, 28 Park Place, Cardiff CF10 3QE, tel: +44 (0)29 2092 4311, email: Erasmus@britishcouncil.org or website: www.britishcouncil.org/erasmus

▶ Leonardo da Vinci programme: check with your university or college

▶ Investing in the Future – Financial Support for EU Students from Student Finance England Publications Department, tel: +44 (0)800 731 9133.

> **Facts and Figures**
>
> Students from the former colonies of Britain and some non-EU European countries will pay the same fees as students in England – generally £3,290 p.a.

All students from abroad studying in the UK

The British Council website Education UK provides detailed information about life in the UK for international students. It should answer many of your general questions on subjects like accommodation, living costs, study options, cultural issues and much more. Go to www.educationuk.org and choose the option 'Living in the UK'. The main site itself is worth looking at as well.

See also:

▶ UKCISA website: www.ukcisa.org.uk

▶ VisitBritain, the official website for tourism in Britain: www.visitbritain.com

▶ UCAS 'Instructions for Completion of the Application Form by International Students' – this is free from UCAS with your application form

▶ British Council Information Centre: a useful contact for funding enquiries or more information about courses, Bridgewater House, 58 Whitworth Street, Manchester M1 6BB, tel: +44 (0)161 957 7755, email: general.enquiries@britishcouncil.org or website: www.educationuk.org

▶ A Guide to Studying and Living in Britain is a book full of practical advice published by How To Books, website: www.howtobooks.co.uk, also available from Grantham Book Services, tel: 01476 541 080.

Part-time students

Do part-time students get any help?

Yes, up to £1,495 p.a. in England and Northern Ireland, or over £2,000 in Wales – see Table 32.

Table 32 Grants and fee grants for part-time students

Course	England and NI fee grant	England and NI course grant (max.)	Wales fee grant	Wales course grant (max.)	Scotland fee grant*
50–59% of the full-time course	£805	£260	£635	£1,075	Up to £500
60–74% of the full-time course	£970	£260	£765	£1,075	Up to £500
75%+ of the full time course	£1,210	£260	£955	£1,075	Up to £500

*2009–2010 figure – under review for 2010–2011

Part-time students doing 50% or more of a full-time course can apply for an income-assessed grant towards fees and a course grant of up to £1,435 in England and £2,030 in Wales to help with travel and books, depending on intensity of course and income. Both are means-tested.

There are around 500,000 part-time students in HE in England, and the government expects around 85,000 to benefit from this financial package.

At the moment, part-time students have to pay all their fees upfront. Universities' think-tank the Million+ group is fighting to give part-time students a fairer deal by abolishing upfront fees and providing a proper support package backed by the NUS.

Attending a private higher education institution

Students attending a private HE institution that was designated for funding by the Department for Innovation, Universities and Skills (now part of the Department of Business, Innovation and Skills) should be able to take out a loan to cover fees of up to £3,290. It may not be enough to completely cover your fees as these can be higher than in other types of university. You may also be able to take out a maintenance loan and could be eligible for a maintenance grant. The course could cover any topic – theology and complementary medicine, for example. See also the information on dance and drama, page 119.

Healthcare courses

What's the package for those taking a nursing and midwifery Diploma of HE (DipHE) course?

- You will not have to pay fees.
- You will receive a non-repayable, non-means-tested bursary provided you have been accepted for an NHS-funded place.
- If you receive a bursary, you will not be able to apply for a student loan.

Bursary rates for nursing and midwifery

Bursary amounts depend on where you live. Based on 45 weeks' attendance on courses in:

- England and Wales, from April 2009–2010, the rate is:
    - studying in London: £7,827
    - elsewhere: £6,701
    - living in parental home: £6,701
- Scotland, from August 2009, the rate is £6,578 plus £60 initial expenses allowance in first year
- Northern Ireland, the rate is £6,055.

In the future, all nurses and midwifery staff in NHS hospitals will have to have a degree. Diploma courses will be phased out between September 2011 and early 2013 and new entrants to the nursing profession from September 2013 will take a degree. Some universities may only offer the new degree courses from September 2011, so you should contact your university of choice before applying to see which courses are being offered.

I'm taking an allied health professional course: what support is there for me?

The UK health authorities pay the fees of full- and part-time pre-registration students on courses in: audiology, chiropody, dental hygiene, dental therapy, dietetics, occupational therapy, orthoptics, physiotherapy, prosthetics, radiography and speech and language therapy. A maintenance bursary is available, but means-tested according to family income. (This funding package also applies to some students taking a nursing or midwifery degree.) It is, however, a bursary and not a loan, so what you get does not have to be paid back. You will also be able to apply for the lower-rate student loan to make up the balance of your living costs, and you may be eligible for help from the Access to Learning Fund (see Chapter 3, page 79). Rates are shown in Table 33.

Table 33 Allied health professionals bursary and loan rates

	Bursary rates			Reduced loan rates for 2010–2011	
	England/Wales	Scotland	NI	England/Wales/NI	Scotland
London	£3,392	£3,020	£2,900	£3,263	£2,800
Living away from home	£2,810	£2,455	£2,355	£2,324	£2,265
Living in parents' home	£2,346	£1,865	£1,920	£1,744	£1,740

Extra allowances may be available for extra weeks of study, and also for older students, single parents, those who have dependants or students who incur clinical placement costs. Table 34 will give you an idea of the contribution parents/spouses are expected to make.

Table 34 Expected parental/spousal contribution to allied health professional courses

Residual income	Contribution
Under £24,279	None
£25,000	£120
£30,000	£647
£40,000	£1,699
£50,000	£2,752
£60,000	£3,805
£70,000	£4,857

Medical and dental students: is there any extra help?

Medical and dental students who are on standard five- or six-year courses will be treated as any other student in that area for the first four years of their course and will have to pay the fees required.

Those from outside Scotland who are studying in Scotland will be charged fees of £2,895 p.a., lower than in England; Scottish students studying in Scotland will not be charged fees.

In your fifth and any subsequent years funding will be provided by the NHS, which means your tuition fees will be paid and you will be eligible to apply for a means-tested NHS bursary and a reduced maintenance loan from the SLC (see details under 'I'm taking an allied health professional course' above).

If you live in England and want to study in Scotland, Wales or Northern Ireland, the NHS Student Grants Unit will assess and pay your bursary. If you live in Scotland, Wales or Northern Ireland and want to study in England, you should consult the relevant national authorities. Students taking the four-year accelerated course in medicine for graduates should see Chapter 10, page 244.

'I've known a couple of medics who joined the army for a year, interrupting their five-year course to earn money to help with the costs of doing their degree.'
Second-year Medical student, St George's

A medical student's story

'When you get to your first year of clinics (fourth year) you are still expected to survive on not much more than undergraduates (i.e. the student loan),' explains a fourth-year medic from UCL. 'However, your days and weeks are longer, there are weekend and night shifts, and it's a 48-week year – so not much time for other work. All through uni I had relied on a holiday job to keep me afloat. Now it was not so easy. I was maxed out on an already over-extended overdraft and the bank was threatening to charge me, while my landlord wanted the rent.

'All I needed was £100 to pull me back from the brink. I applied to my university, but the dean of students could not be contacted and the finance office said I would have to wait seven days even for an appointment to be considered for "emergency" funds. So what did I do? Borrowed from a friend.'

NHS bursaries

- In England, contact the NHS Student Grants Unit, 22 Plymouth Road, Blackpool FY3 7JS, helpline: 0845 358 6655 or website: www.nhsstudentgrants.co.uk.

- In Wales, contact the NHS Student Awards Unit, 2nd floor, Golate House, 101 St Mary's Street, Cardiff CF10 1DX, telephone bursary enquiries: 029 2019 6167 or website: www.nliah.wales.nhs.uk.

- In Scotland, contact the SAAS, Gyleview House, 3 Redheughs Rigg, South Gyle, Edinburgh EH12 9HH, tel: 0131 476 8227 or 0845 111 1711, email: saas.geu@scotland.gsi.gov.uk or website: www.saas.gov.uk.

- In Northern Ireland, contact the Bursaries Administration Unit, Central Services Agency, 2 Franklin Street, Belfast BT2 8DQ or tel: 028 9055 3661, or contact the appropriate ELB, websites: www.delni.gov.uk or www.dhsspsni.gov.uk.

Specialist courses

This section covers information on teaching, social work, and dance and drama courses.

What's the deal for trainee teachers?

If you already have a degree and are considering a postgraduate initial teacher training (ITT) course, turn to Chapter 10, page 240, for details of the incentive package that is being offered. You could be in for a nice surprise.

There are no special incentives for undergraduates any more. Undergraduate trainee teachers receive the same funding as other students – sorry!

Trainee teachers in Wales

In addition to the normal funding for undergraduates, there's a special deal in Wales called the Secondary Undergraduate Placement Grant, which is available on an annual basis to support you during school-based teacher training. Under this scheme, £1,200 will be paid to undergraduate students who are on a secondary ITT course specialising in one of the priority subjects at that level (which are design and technology, information and communication technology, maths, modern languages, music, religious education, science and Welsh).

This information applies to the academic year 2009–2010 and is subject to change in future years. The grant is paid in two instalments by ITT providers; enquiries about your eligibility should be directed to the ITT provider with which you wish to study.

Small hardship grants are also available for those who get into unforeseen difficulties that might prevent them completing their course. Postgraduates should also see Chapter 10 page 241 for more funding information.

I'm taking a degree in social work: can I get a bursary?

The Social Work Bursary is available to students ordinarily resident in England studying on an approved undergraduate course (full or part time). The bursary is not income-assessed, which means that earnings, savings and other sources of income are not taken into consideration. It includes a basic grant, a fixed contribution towards practice learning opportunity-related expenses and tuition fees. Financial awards are dependent on individual circumstances.

▶   Undergraduates: the amount you will get is shown in Table 35.

▶   Graduates: see page 232.

The basic grant includes £575 towards placement travel.

Table 35 Rates of Social Work Bursary available

	London-based HE institution	HE institution elsewhere
Full-time students subject to top-up fees	Up to £4,975	Up to £4,575
Part-time students	Up to £2,487.50	Up to £2,287.50
Full-time students not subject to fees	Up to £3,475	Up to £3,075

Note: figures are for 2009–2010, based on a 52-week period

Full details on eligibility criteria and funding availability can be found at www.ppa.org.uk/swb or you can email swb@ppa.nhs.uk. Alternatively, call the bursaries customer service team on 0845 610 1122.

I want to study dance and drama: will I get funding?

If you are offered a state-funded place on an HE course you should be eligible for the same funding as students on degree courses. The Royal Academy of Dramatic Art (RADA), the Guildhall School of Music and Drama, the Central School of Speech and Drama, Bristol Old Vic Theatre School, Rose Bruford College and many other institutions fall into that category (see Chapter 2).

A majority of accredited dance and drama courses at private HE institutions offer some form of funding to help with fees and living expenses. While HE courses in dance or drama no longer offer Dance and Drama Awards (having introduced the 'state-funded places' scheme), the awards are still offered by some 20 performing arts schools. Competition for all these awards is very fierce, however, and not all students who achieve a place will receive an award.

If you get a Dance and Drama Award, it will cover the majority of your tuition fees. However, you will also need to make a personal contribution. For the academic year 2009–2010, this personal contribution is £1,275. The Dance and Drama Award is given regardless of your household income. But whether you get additional help depends on your circumstances.

▶ Students from England, Wales and Scotland may also be able to get help with living costs. How much extra will depend on your household income.

▶ Students from Northern Ireland should contact the student financial section at the Western ELB for help with fees and maintenance – email student.awards@welbni.org.

▶ Students from EU countries should apply to their home country for help with living costs.

If you are offered a place as a private student by your college and it is not state-funded, you will have to pay the full cost of the private tuition fee. For those who do not receive an award, a three-year course (including living costs) could set you back £50,000. However, you should still contact your local authority (LA) for details of how to apply for help as a private student on a designated course because some funding might be available. Not all accredited courses attract government funding, so if funding is essential check the status of a course before you start applying. The booklet *A Guide to Vocational Training in Dance and Drama* is full of useful information, including full details of funding – to obtain a copy, call 0845 602 2260 or see www.direct.gov.uk/en/EducationAndLearning/14to19/MoneytoLearn/DanceandDrama/index.htm.

Additional help for special groups

I'm a mature/independent/married student: is there any special funding or advice for me?

An independent student is someone who no longer lives with their parents, has been working for at least three years or is over 25. As an independent student, you are entitled to the general funding package for students (see Chapter 2, or Chapter 4 if you're based in Scotland, Wales or Northern Ireland). Independent English students can earn up to £25,000 before losing any of their funding entitlement. For students from Northern Ireland, the figure is £19,203 and Wales, £18,370. If you are married or living with someone in a stable relationship, your partner's income may well be means-tested should you apply for a maintenance loan or grant. There is no age limit on taking out a fee loan; the cut-off point for taking a maintenance loan is now 60 years.

If I become a student will I still receive benefits such as Income Support?

Instead of the maintenance grant, students who receive Income Support or Housing Benefit are eligible for a non-repayable Special Support Grant. This works in a similar way to the maintenance grant (see Chapter 2, page 54) – it is given to low-income families. If you receive the special support grant you will not be eligible for the maintenance grant.

Facts and Figures

The number of mature students (aged 25 and over) starting an undergraduate degree in UK universities in 2009 was 55,900, up 8.7% on the previous year.

Source: UCAS figures

I have children to support: are there any other allowances, grants and bursaries I could apply for?

▶ A non-repayable special support grant of up to £2,906 a year (£3,475 in Northern Ireland) is available for new full-time students who are eligible for benefits such as Income Support or Housing Benefit while they are studying. The main beneficiaries are likely to be lone parents, other student parents and students with disabilities. The grant is based on household income and does not have to be paid back if you're eligible for the maintenance grant. This will not affect any university bursary you are offered.

▶ The Parents' Learning Allowance: up to £1,508 p.a. (£1,538 in Northern Ireland) helps with course-related costs for students with dependent children. This is income-assessed.

▶ Childcare Grant: up to £148.75 a week for one child and £255 for two or more. The amount given is based on 85% of actual childcare costs. It is paid in three instalments by the SLC; it does not have to be repaid.

▶ Child Tax Credit: available to students with dependent children and paid by the Inland Revenue. Students receiving the maximum amount will be entitled to free school meals for their children. The amount you get will depend on circumstances. Call 0845 300 3900 for more details or visit www.inlandrevenue.gov.uk/taxcredits and check out how much you could get.

▶ Adult Dependants' Grant: up to £2,642 p.a. (£2,695 in Northern Ireland) for full-time students with adult dependants. This is paid in three instalments.

▶ Access to Learning Fund: see page 79. Universities generally look very favourably on mature students when allocating access funds.

Scotland

Please note: help for parents in Scotland and the amounts available are different from those listed here (see www.student-support-saas.gov.uk/student_support/supplimentary_grants.htm).

I'm disabled and I want to go into higher education: can I get extra help?

There are a number of ways you can get extra help, depending on your disability. If you follow up every lead offered here it's going to take time, but the results could be worthwhile.

What's the starting point for somebody who has a disability?

First choose your course, then choose the university or college where you would like to study. Next, check out the college facilities and their ability to cope with your specific disability, by:

- ▶ writing for details of facilities
- ▶ visiting suitable institutions
- ▶ having a 'special needs' interview with the institution.

Then fill in your UCAS application.

When should I start getting organised?

It's a good idea to start getting organised in the summer term of your first A level year as you may have to revise your choice of institution several times.

What financial help can I expect from my local authority?

Like most students on full-time HE courses in this country, you would as a disabled student be eligible for the full financial support package described in the previous chapters.

I am severely disabled: can I get a student loan?

Yes. As an undergraduate you would be eligible for a student loan. In fact, the regulations laid down when the SLC was set up allow for the loans administrator to delay the start of repayment for people with disabilities, and any disability-related financial entitlements you receive will be disregarded when calculating your repayment amounts. Phone the SLC helpline free on 0845 607 7577.

Can I apply to the Access to Learning Fund?

Yes. Each institution decides its own criteria for payments – there are no set rules. You might find being disabled gives you more entitlement (see details on page 79).

Disabled Students' Allowances

Disabled Students' Allowances (DSAs) are available for full- and part-time students and these offer support to those with a disability or specific learning difficulty such as dyslexia.

There are four types of DSA.

1. Up to £20,520 per year for non-medical personal help – e.g. readers, lip-speakers or note-takers (up to £15,390 if studying part time).
2. Up to £5,161 for the whole course for specialist course equipment – e.g. computer, word processor, Braille printer, radio microphone or induction loop system (whether studying full or part time).
3. A general DSA – up to £1,724 p.a. (up to £1,293 for part-time study) for minor items such as tapes, Braille paper or extra use of phone.
4. Extra travel costs incurred as a result of your disability.

Distance learning

Full-time undergraduates who cannot attend their course because of their disability will be eligible for full-time student support in addition to DSAs (see page 109).

Can I get help with travel?

The loan for students includes a set amount for transport costs (£303) – as a disabled student you can claim for travel expenses incurred over this amount if your disability means, for example, that you are unable to use public transport and must travel by taxi (see point 4 in the DSAs list above).

What about social security benefits?

Most full-time students are not entitled to benefits such as Income Support and Housing Benefit. However, such benefits can be available to students in vulnerable groups such as people with disabilities, but the situation is complicated. The people to put you in the picture are your Job Centre or Job Centre Plus, or Skill: the National Bureau for Students with Disabilities (see below); alternatively, phone the Benefits Inquiry line on 0800 882 200 or for minicom users 0800 243 355 (opening hours: 8.30a.m.–6.30p.m. Monday–Friday; 9a.m.–1p.m. Saturday).

Can I get a Disability Living Allowance?

Yes. This allowance is available to you as a student. It provides funds on a weekly basis for those who need help with mobility – e.g. the cost of operating a wheelchair or the hire or purchase of a car. It also covers those who need care and assistance with any physical difficulties such as washing or eating, or continual supervision. The allowance will not affect your DSAs in any way. See the answer to the previous question for people to contact.

Further information for specialist groups

Mature students

▶ *Returning to Learning: A Practical Handbook for Adult Learners Returning to Education* is published by How To Books and available from www.howtobooks.co.uk.

Disabled students

▶ Contact the students' welfare officer at your university or college, or contact the students' union or local Citizens' Advice Bureau.

▶ Skill: National Bureau for Students with Disabilities, runs a special information and advice service, open Tuesday 11.30a.m.–1.30p.m. and Thursday 1.30p.m.–3.30p.m., tel: 0800 328 5050, and also publishes a number of useful leaflets (free to students) and books for disabled people, available from its website: www.skill.org. uk, or fax: 020 7450 0650, textphone: 0800 068 2422 or email: info@skill.org.uk.

▶ Benefits Agency or Job Centre/Job Centre Plus: contact details should be in your local telephone directory.

▶ Royal National Institute of Blind People (RNIB), RNIB Education and Employment Network, 105 Judd Street, London WC1H 9NE, tel: 020 7388 1266 or helpline: 0303 123 9999, open Monday–Tuesday/Thursday–Friday 9a.m.–5p.m., Wednesday 9a.m.–4p.m. (messages can be left on the answerphone outside these hours), email: helpline@rnib.org.uk or website: www.rnib.org.uk.

▶ Royal National Institute for Deaf People (RNID), 19–23 Featherstone Street, London EC1Y 8SL, tel: 0808 808 0123, textphone: 0808 808 9000, fax: 020 7296 8199, email: informationline@rnid.org.uk or website: www.rnid.org.uk.

▶ *Bridging the Gap: A Guide to the Disabled Students' Allowances* is available from tel: 0800 731 9133, textphone: 0800 328 8988 or fax: 0845 603 3360. Also available from www.direct.gov.uk/studentfinance.

Studying abroad

I have to spend part of my course studying abroad: will I get extra help?

Yes, but it will be a loan. If you study abroad for at least 50% of an academic quarter (which normally means a term), you are eligible for an overseas rate of loan, which for 2010–2011 is as follows:

▶ England: max. £5,895 (Wales and Northern Ireland may vary slightly)

▶ Scotland: highest-cost countries £1,215–£7,162; high-cost countries £1,095–£6,097; all other countries £915–£5,067.

Don't forget, unless you are on an Erasmus exchange (see below), you will still have to pay reduced fees to your own university if you spend a year away in another country. These are set by your university up to a maximum of £1,645 (50% of the normal fee). You will be able to take out a loan to cover these.

Scottish students who normally study in Scotland will pay no fees.

My course abroad is longer than my course in the UK: can I get more money?

Yes. The rate given is worked out on a year of only 30 weeks and three days. If you need to stay longer, you can increase your loan. The rate for 2010–2011 is up to £115 per week (up to £150 per week in Scotland).

'Students who have a compulsory study period abroad can get into serious financial difficulties. Nobody warns you of the cost of this before you choose a course such as European Studies and Modern Languages.'

Third-year French and Russian student

It's going to cost me a lot more to fly to Tokyo than to take a train to Leeds: can I get any help with travel?

Yes, but not for the full fare. Your loan already includes some travel element (£303 in England, Wales and Northern Ireland); anything over this will be taken into consideration when calculating how much grant and loan you are entitled to receive. It is probably best to let Student Finance England calculate what you are entitled to.

Remember when putting in for costs to give all the facts – the journey from your home to the airport costs something, too. (Arrangements differ in Scotland, where the disregarded amount is £159.)

Is there any other help for students who want to study abroad?

Two organisations have been set up to assist students wanting to study in the EU:

1.   Erasmus (sometimes known as Socrates–Erasmus), the European Community Action Scheme for the Mobility of University Students, is designed to encourage greater co-operation between universities and other HE institutions in Europe.

Under this scheme, students taking courses including foreign languages in other European countries may be given a grant towards extra expenses while studying abroad for a period of three to 12 months. These could include travel expenses, language courses or living and accommodation costs. If you're part of this scheme, you should also be exempt from paying the reduced fees that sandwich students taking a year out have to pay. For more details phone 029 2092 4311, email erasmus@britishcouncil.org or visit www.britishcouncil.org/erasmus.

2. The Leonardo da Vinci scheme provides opportunities for university students and recent graduates to undertake periods of vocational training of up to 12 months with organisations in other EU member states; placements are largely technology-based. While individual employers will provide any salary, the Leonardo scheme can make a contribution towards language tuition and expenses. For more details, phone 0845 199 2929.

Who to contact

Funding from these organisations is arranged mainly through your university or college. They should have full information and should therefore be your first point of call. Otherwise, contact the organisation direct.

What happens if I get sick while studying abroad?

Don't wait until you get sick: take out health insurance cover before you go (see information about travel insurance on page 179.) Your LA will probably reimburse the costs of health insurance, providing they consider it 'economical'. Check out the situation with them first. If you are going abroad as part of your course, seek advice from your university; they will know the score. You may have to pay a social security charge (see page 128, 'Focus on three popular places for studying abroad').

Remember, above all, to hold on to your receipts. Without these you are unlikely to be reimbursed by your LA.

Can I study for my whole degree abroad?

You can, but it's not going to be cheap because you won't be entitled to a student loan, unless you are studying at the University of London Institute in Paris. As it is part of the University of London, the institute's three-year French course can be studied in Paris, but you would be treated as any UK student and be eligible for UK funding. This means you could be eligible for a maintenance grant and the maintenance loan at the overseas rate (which this year is up to £5,895) and could be offered a university bursary. The down side is you would have to pay UK fees of £3,290 p.a. (2010–2011 figure). If you go to an EU country and study at a non-UK institution, as a resident of the UK you will be treated like the students in that country and will normally pay no tuition fees. In most European countries, HE institutions do not charge tuition fees; if they are charged, they are generally set at a nominal rate.

But a number of universities do have registration fees, and there are additional health and personal insurance costs, students' union fees and other expenses to consider. Many countries have special arrangements for their students, such as concessionary rates for meals, transport and accommodation and as an EU student you would benefit from these. The most expensive part of your stay will be maintenance costs, and because you are not taking any part of your course in the UK you will not be eligible for the student loan or maintenance grant.

Will my EU university give me a bursary or scholarship?

It's unlikely. As EU students find when they come to the UK, you will be treated like a home student as far as fees, entry and other costs and concessions are concerned but you are not covered by the funding package for the country in which you study, while bursaries and scholarships for first degrees are not easily found.

What will it cost me to live abroad?

Living costs vary depending on where you are studying. As in the UK, capital cities are more expensive places to live than country towns.

When it comes to the price of food in the EU, the UK is among the more expensive places. If you are thinking of studying further afield than Europe, the cost factor is appreciably higher as it is unlikely that you will get your fees for a full degree course covered, and travel will be a major expense.

Will studying abroad be very different?

Every country has its own particular approach to study and its own characteristics. In Europe, for instance, individual universities tend to cater for a greater number of students. Lectures, classes and seminars are more crowded and there is a greater dependence on printed course material. There is less contact between tutor and student and the system generally is more impersonal.

Another major difference is the exams. Often there is a greater reliance on oral examinations. In Italy, for example, the majority of the exams are oral.

While this tends to give students additional self-confidence and make them more articulate, it is something new to UK students that they will need to get accustomed to.

European students are more inclined to attend their local university, and many live at home. As a result, universities do not provide the wide range of social and recreational facilities you would expect to find at a UK university. Students use the local city or town's facilities, which can be expensive. The universities of Europe are often situated in fine old towns and in regions you will want to explore, which again will be a drain on your (limited) resources.

'My third year was spent abroad, but I still had to pay half tuition fees – for what? It's outrageous!'

Fourth-year Languages student, Durham

'The fourth year of my degree is in France. Even though I don't need a student loan at the moment, I have taken it out and put it in a high-interest account because I know I will want to travel once I get to Europe.'

First-year Chemistry student, Imperial College, London

Focus on three popular places for studying abroad

Please note, all figures in the examples below are approximate.

France

You need to prove you have sufficient resources to maintain yourself while studying in France. The threshold is about €5,160, with a minimum level of €430 a month, but this will barely be enough to cover your living expenses. In reality, you will need more like €600 a month. What are these expenses likely to be? Figures for 2007–2008 are as follows:

Your monthly costs might break down as follows:

▶ accommodation: €150 per month in the university, €300 per month for a studio in the city
▶ food: €230 per month
▶ transport: €31 per month
▶ Student fees: average €92 per month (annual cost of a course: €150–€900 in a public institution, €3,000–€7,000 in a private university)
▶ telephone: €30 per month.

For the first month it is estimated that you will need around €1,500. This will cover:

- rent: €150– €300
- deposit for accommodation (two months): up to €600
- annual insurance for accommodation: €50
- social security: €180
- health insurance: €70–€285 depending on risk taken
- registration fee: €150.

There are very few scholarships available, but postgraduates could try the Entente Cordiale Scholarships – contact the French Embassy in London. A helpful website is www.cnous.fr.

FACTS and FIGURES

Countries that attract the most students from abroad:

- USA: 22%
- UK: 12%
- Germany: 10%
- France: 9%
- Australia: 6%
- Canada: 5%.

Source: OECD *Education at a Glance* 2007

Germany

A degree in Germany takes between four and six years, so you must anticipate a long stay. Each year is divided into two semesters.

The first hurdle is registration: this gives you that all-important student card, which will entitle you to special rates on local transport, reduced rates for cultural events and use of the refectory. Tuition in universities is generally free, but a number of states have introduced fees of up to €500 per semester. Foreign students need to prove they have sufficient funds for their stay – around €770 per month (€7,716 p.a.) is about what German students have, but you can get by with less, certainly in the former East Germany.

Rents vary – in the larger cities such as Frankfurt and Hamburg the average is €310 a month, in smaller places such as Dresden, Jena or Chemnitz the average is around €186 a month. Balance that against the fact that it is easier to find a job in a bigger city.

Although EU students are allowed to work in Germany this is not a good way to fund your studies because unemployment is high at the moment. Expenses will include:

- enrolment and administration fee: €100 per semester
- semester ticket for travel (some universities): €50.

Your average monthly expenses could total €703:

- ▶ rent (including additional charges): €250
- ▶ food: €160
- ▶ clothing: €60
- ▶ travel (car/public transport): €86
- ▶ health insurance: €60
- ▶ telephone/internet/TV licence: €50
- ▶ work/study materials: €37.

Books, depending on your course, could be €200–€250 a semester.

German institutions do not generally award scholarships and grants, and if given they are generally based on academic ability. The most extensive scholarship programme is organised by the German Academic Exchange Service (DAAD), but this is only for postgraduates. Try the websites www.study-in-germany.de/english/grants and also www.daad.de/deutschland/foerderung/stipendiendatenbank.

The USA

It may not be as costly as you think!

Tuition fees can vary enormously between individual colleges and depend on a range of factors, such as whether they are state-run or private: costs average around $18,548 for out-of-state students at public four-year institutions and $26,273 at private four-year institutions. Two-year colleges' tuition rates are around $6,000. Then there are additional costs such as books and equipment, which could add another $1,000–$1,500 p.a. On top of that you have living costs, which again vary drastically between regions of the country but could add another $4,000–$14,000 to your bill for each nine-month academic year. You will also need money for travel from the UK and back, and for health insurance and personal expenses.

Can I get funding to study in the US?

The above figures are averages rather than the amount most students pay. There is over $140 billion in financial aid available for study in the US; approximately two-thirds of full-time undergraduates receive some type of grant aid, and that includes international students. So don't rule out studying in the US on the grounds of finance, even if you come from a low-income family.

Yes, fees are much higher over there, but many of the hundreds of universities and colleges in the States have large endowments. There is a tradition in the US of alumni supporting their old colleges, so most offer bursaries and scholarships.

Some awards are for academic performance, sport or music, but many are given for financial need.

Well-known Ivy League institutions such as Princeton, Yale and Harvard and other prestigious universities such as Stanford and Berkeley all offer help to students from low-income families. For example, the Harvard Financial Aid Initiative provides full funding without loans to students with a family income below $60,000 – see www.admissions.college.harvard.edu/apply/international/ international_aid.html for more details. Scholarships from professional, charitable or governmental organisations external to the university are also available.

In addition, international students can work on campus for up to 20 hours a week during term time and 40 hours a week during holidays. However, this cannot be listed as a source of income for visa applications.

But of course, first you have to get a university place – and this process can be expensive with entrance fees. Fortunately, every institution has its own website and that is the place to start.

For more informatuion about study in the USA, contact the US–UK Fulbright Commission – Education USA advice centre, and see www.fulbright.co.uk. Fulbright offers seminars for students, parents and advisers and holds a USA College Day university fair each autumn.

Top US University Targets UK Students

Think Harvard, one of the America's leading universities, is beyond your financial reach? Think again. Harvard has a policy of giving students from low-income families generous financial assistance. In fact, students whose parents earn less than $60,000 (£31,500) a year could find they can study free. Harvard is keen to attract some of Britain's finest.

Harvard is not alone: over 4,000 UK undergraduates and around 2,500 UK postgraduates were said to be making their way to the USA last year.

Further information for students from the UK studying abroad

► UNESCO publication *Study Abroad*: try www.amazon.co.uk.

► *Getting into US & Canadian Universities* by Margaret Kroto, published by Trotman, website: www.trotman.co.uk.

► *You Want to Study Where?! Alternative Degree Destinations* by Philip Dring, Barbara Lynn and Jim O'Brien, published by Trotman, website: www.trotman.co.uk.

► *Summer Jobs Worldwide* by Susan Griffith, published by Vacation Work, includes over 50,000 jobs worldwide and is updated annually; website: www.trotman.co.uk.

► UK Socrates–Erasmus, tel: 029 2092 4311 or website: www.britishcouncil.org/erasmus.

CHAPTER 6

Paying your way

This chapter looks at the main reasons why students work, what they can do and what they can expect to earn.

Why do students work?

There are many reasons why students work, either before or during their course. In this chapter, we investigate some of those reasons and give advice on what sort of work you can expect to find, how to go about getting it, who to contact and what to read. But the main reason why students work is to …

Make money to fund your degree

If you have read the first five chapters of this book, you will realise that what you are likely to get to finance you through university just won't be enough.

A large number of students work, most from sheer financial necessity, and their aim is to earn as much as possible.

▶ Just over a third of the UK student population (38%) were thought to have part-time jobs when the 2009–2010 academic year started.

▶ On average, UK students were found to earn £91.92 a week through part-time work, making more than £3,100 during the academic year – collectively, that's £2.7 billion.

▶ Over 100,000 more undergraduates took up part-time work during term time in 2009 than in 2008.

▶ 43% of students were working to pay their way through university, saying it would be too expensive without additional income.

▶ Average rate of pay was £6.53 per hour.

▶ Over the academic year 2009–2010, university students are expected to spend £362 million on living and accommodation costs.

Source: *NatWest Student Living Index Survey 2009*

Should you/can you work during term time?

Most universities and colleges allow students to work during term time; in fact, many universities have set up job shops, so you could say they are actively encouraging it. But most suggest a limit on the number of hours you work during term – generally 15 hours a week, although some say 10–12 hours and others up to 16. The university students' union is a great source of work, providing job opportunities in its shops and bars.

The number of students who actually work during term time varies between universities. Many institutions just don't know. However, Table 36 offers an idea of the percentage of students working at some UK unis.

Table 36 Proportion of students who work

University	Proportion of working students
Dundee	25%
Aberdeen, Bath, Glasgow, Sheffield, Surrey	30%
Brighton, Edinburgh, Staffordshire	35%
Coventry, Lincoln, Oxford Brookes, Slade	50%
Aston, Gloucestershire, Middlesex, Portsmouth, Northampton, Sheffield Hallam	60%
Sussex	70%
Hertfordshire	80%
Huddersfield	90%

Going against the trend are Oxford and Cambridge, where many (but not all) colleges actively forbid or strongly discourage students from working during term time, except perhaps if they work in the student bar. Since the Oxbridge term is just eight weeks long and, as one lecturer pointed out, 'very intensive weeks at that', perhaps the colleges have a point. (For full and more up-to-date figures and information on individual universities, see the *Guide to UK Universities 2010*, published by Trotman.)

The tutor's view
'When it comes to work, academic staff attitudes vary from the positive to the negative. Obviously, they would like it if students didn't have to work, but are realistic, especially with the introduction of fees. If you want to encourage students from diverse financial backgrounds, then you have got to be prepared to let them work.'

Co-ordinator of Student WorkPlace, University of Manchester job shop

The students' view
'The necessity of finding part-time work means the quality of your college work suffers.'

PGCE student, Bangor

'Get a job with a good employer – for money, experience, skills and references.'

Final-year Sociology student, Kent

'Part-time work teaches you discipline and keeps you from being in the bar every night.'

Third-year Sociology student, De Montfort

How important is it to get a job? Will it make a difference to my finances?

It certainly will, as Table 37 shows. If you want evidence that students are being hit by the increasing cost of living, look at the previous year's figures for average weekly expenditure (the figures in brackets) – they tell a sorry story.

Table 37 Student's average weekly budget

Town/ city	Av. weekly rent	Av. total weekly expenditure*	Av. weekly earnings	Av. hours worked per week	Extra cash needed per week
Birmingham	£74	£171 (£193)	£77.24	11.47	£167.76
Brighton	£87	£220 (£198)	£128.29	15.11	£178.71
Bristol	£76	£190 (£183)	£93.13	14.30	£172.87
Cambridge	£82	£205 (£154)	£98.10	14.89	£188.90
Cardiff	£68	£202 (£200)	£86.18	15.05	£183.82
Dundee	£71	£203 (£155)	£72.67	12.44	£201.33
Edinburgh	£81	£205 (£166)	£92.79	15.50	£193.21
Glasgow	£72	£187 (£188)	£106.88	17.15	£152.12
Leeds	£72	£210 (£171)	£94.46	16.09	£186.54
Leicester	£66	£191 (£221)	£92.98	14.88	£164.02
Liverpool	£69	£205 (£192)	£119.29	17.02	£154.71
Manchester	£74	£174 (£168)	£85.51	13.61	£162.49
Newcastle	£68	£204 (£191)	£84.09	12.95	£187.91
Nottingham	£75	£208 (£191)	£72.21	11.04	£210.79
Oxford	£85	£238 (£198)	£109.13	14.88	£213.87
Plymouth	£74	£193 (£148)	£84.86	14.39	£182.14
Portsmouth	£76	£215 (£189)	£89.93	16.15	£201.07
Reading	£74	£197 (£n/a)	£101.72	15.45	£169.28
UEA	£74	£195 (n/a)	£68.91	13.22	£200.09
York	£68	£197 (£146)	£64.14	11.37	£200.86
All	£74	£201 (£192)	£91.92	14.47	£183.08

*Previous year's figures are given in brackets
Source: NatWest Student Living Index Survey 2009

Glasgow looks like the most cost-effective place to study, followed closely by Liverpool – providing, that is, you find a job and don't mind putting in the hours, which at an average of 17 a week are the highest among the universities we looked at, and well above the average. However, Brighton students seem to be earning the most – on average, around £8.50 an hour for a 15-hour week – which is essential since their cost of living is one of the highest.

But the real questions are:

▶ Will the student finance package you receive (grant, bursary, loan, parental help) be enough to make up the extra cash needed? See previous chapters

▶ Will you find a job when there is so much unemployment?

University job shops

Among the most important innovations in recent years are university job shops – they can be found at most institutions in the UK. They all seem to operate on their own individual system but have one aim in common – to find work for students during term time and the holidays. Pay is never less than the minimum wage, which is currently £4.83 for 18–21-year-olds (£4.92 from October 2010) and £5.80 for those 22 or over (£5.93 from October 2010).

Information collected by the *NatWest Student Living Index Survey* in 2009 showed that students earned on average £6.53 per hour.

Focus on three job shops

Job shops come under a variety of names. There is Joblink at Aberdeen, the Student Employment Service at Edinburgh, WorkStation at UCL, CUBE at Coventry and PULSE at Liverpool. All seem to have different ways of working. Details of three different job shops are given below.

Cardiff

Cardiff University's Jobshop was one of the first student employment services established in the country. It offers both a student employment agency and a Job Centre-style service, and keeps students who are registered up-to-date with new vacancies every day via email. Around 4,500 students register with the Jobshop every year and it provides a flexible service that enables them to balance paid work with their study commitments. All kinds of work are offered, from bar work and waiting to clerical, administrative, flyering and library shelving. The Jobshop provides casual staff for not only the university and students' union but also the growing number of local companies who are now taking advantage of the service.

Jayne Howorth, who works for the Unistaff Jobshop, says of the credit crunch: 'It has inevitably affected us in the last 12 months. We are still getting plenty of casual work in from the university, but there has been a noticeable downturn in work from external companies since January 2009. The message we are getting is that a lot of casual staff budgets are being cut. In addition (as you would expect in the current climate), we have lots of students looking for work so there is generally less to go around this year.'

Southampton

The University of Southampton's Career Destinations service has a free online vacancy service called e-jobs. There are over 100 vacancies coming in weekly, with more than 500 available at any one time to the 8,000 or so students who use the service in their job search.

As well as graduate vacancies, there are a wide range of part-time, freelance and summer placement opportunities listed on the site. The vacancy service is open to all undergraduate and postgraduate students – just log on to www. soton.ac.uk/careers and register for e-jobs via the blue 'e-jobs' button on the homepage.

This year sees the introduction of a new vacancy management system, which will allow students and graduates to set preferences and receive vacancy email alerts accordingly. It will also allow employers to log in and advertise their vacancies.

The service oversees the execution of a number of internship programmes as well, which run from four weeks to three months or longer both at the University and with external organisations. Calls for applications regularly run on the Career Destinations homepage and via weekly emails to students.

The service's employer events calendar is another important tool for meeting potential recruiters and encourages students to come out and make a name for themselves with employers face-to-face.

Typical areas of work include communications, engineering, finance, retail, promotional and marketing activities, IT and administrative positions.

Lou Hempton, who works in the Employer Engagement team at Career Destinations, says: 'We check all vacancies that come in. We have a vacancy code of practice and don't carry commission-only or pyramid-selling vacancies.' How are unsuitable vacancies kept off the site? Lou and her colleagues scrutinise each and every employer to ensure organisations whose aims do not coincide with the University's employability goals don't make it past the starting gate. As a result, commission-only jobs at the local casino were trashed pretty smartly.

Career Destinations says students can rest assured that the bulk of the country's recruiters have picked up with hiring again, and many are substantially increasing their number of vacancies. The service advises getting applications out early as competition is tight and the recession is over as far as graduate recruiters are concerned.

Manchester

The University of Manchester Careers Service has a specialist work experience unit that handles all types of student work, including part-time jobs, industrial placements and vacation work positions. Students can search vacancies online or register to receive appropriate vacancies by email.

Around 150 jobs are advertised each month. Manchester students can also find information on a wide range of national and international work experience schemes. The Student WorkPlace job shop also provides advice on creative job hunting in the credit crunch and writing applications for part-time work. Recent jobs advertised include web developer, foreign language teacher, brand ambassador, performing arts tutor, event management, illustrator, media analyst, children's fun science presenter, and photographer.

Talking about the current job market, Student WorkPlace Student Recruitment Manager Scot Foley says: 'When the recession started, there was an exaggerated drop in part-time vacancies. However, they bounced back in spring and summer 2009, and there are still many jobs being advertised. Speaking to some businesses, I found that they were still recruiting but didn't want to advertise because they already had plenty of applicants.'

His advice to students is: 'Ask around in shops, bars and restaurants. If you are job hunting at the beginning of a new academic year, start early! August or early September will help you stay ahead of the rush for student jobs. Be prepared to put in the leg work and search further than the main student areas, where you will have lots of competition. Work hard on polishing your CV, and develop your skills through voluntary work or unpaid projects if you have no

Thrift Tips

'Potatoes and more potatoes – mixed with cheese, with ham, with butter – at least you're full.'
Third-year Egyptian Archaeology student, UCL

'Forget the gym – walk. You'll be fit and save a fortune.'
First-year Korean Studies student, Sheffield

'Cover your plates with cling film and save on the washing up.'
Third-year Forensic Science student, Wolverhampton

'Cut toothpaste tubes open to get the bit at the end.'
Second-year Broadcasting student, Falmouth

work experience or can't find paid work. But most important, target your CV and show more than ever what skills you have which are relevant to the job: e.g. for a bar job – communication and working under pressure.'

Does your university have a job shop?

Check it out as soon as you arrive. Jobs go very quickly. Most students want or need to take jobs during the long summer vacations. Your university job shop or that of a university closer to home may be able to help you here.

Try Slivers of Time

Can't commit to regular hours of working, but need to earn money? Then Slivers-of-Time working could be just for you.

▶ Slivers-of-Time working is for anyone with spare hours to 'sell' to local employers. Ideal for students, this new way of working takes the idea of casual work a sophisticated step further and will give you immediate cash, a range of skills and a verified CV of successful short bookings.

▶ Work-seekers are called 'sellers' because they sell their time and skills and interested companies will buy. Once you have registered on the Slivers of Time website, you supply online details of when you want to work – and then sit back and wait for a text message about

work available. You can change your mind at any time. Perhaps you have a couple of hours to spare or a regular free evening. If you are a good, reliable worker, you will get a higher rating and more jobs.

▶ The scheme was successfully piloted in East London in 2006. Since then, a number of new areas have come online. The most recent include Kirklees, Westminster, South Liverpool, Hull, Cambridgeshire, Sheffield, Leeds, Harrow, Exeter and Bristol, and there are more in the pipeline. If your area doesn't come up on the Slivers of Time website, check with the local authority to see if they have an upcoming scheme.

▶ To find out more and get registered log onto www.sliversoftime.com.

Jono's story

Term-time working can be fun, as Jono, a third-year Innovative Manufacturing and Technology student at Loughborough University, discovered when he joined the Officer Training Corps (OTC).

'It was 3a.m., dark, cold and the middle of winter; I was sleeping in a ditch. A hand grabbed my shoulder and shook me violently – it was my turn to go on sentry duty, there was three inches of snow on the ground and we were under fire ...'

Jono explains: 'If you want to earn money and have some fun, join the OTC (it's a kind of cop-out Territorial Army for students). There are field weekends once every five weeks, when you are paid over £80 to crawl around in the cold and wet from Friday evening to Sunday with a gun in your hand shooting at the enemy (blanks of course).

'All too often you'll be sleeping out in the open. If you're lucky, you can sling a hammock between two trees and kip down, but that's luxury. Snow isn't as bad as rain. One weekend it tipped it down for 48 hours non-stop, and it doesn't matter how waterproof your gear is: after 10 hours of throwing yourself on the ground and getting into trees, you are soaked to the bone. That's when you start wondering what on earth you are doing there. But believe me, it is cracking fun.

it's a fact

Pay for students in the OTC is currently £35 to £57 per day depending on time served, qualifications and rank.

You feel you've achieved something. It's the camaraderie, the challenge, often the sheer absurdity of it all. There are some fantastic expeditions, like parachute jumping in Cyprus. There was just one drawback – I was on work experience at the time and missed it!'

What work are students doing and how did they find it?

Students seeking evening or weekend work during term time will probably find it easier in a large city than in a small town. London students should fare better than most – which is just as well, since they are among the most financially stretched.

You are most likely to find work in bars, restaurants or general catering, dispatch-riding (you'll need your own wheels and a fearless mentality!), pizza delivery, office or domestic cleaning, child-minding, market research, modelling, offices (temporary work), hotels, and of course, shops and supermarkets.

Table 38 shows a few examples of what students have been doing.

Table 38 Some student jobs and rates of pay

Type of work	How job was found	Pay per hour	University
Horticulture manual work	Family	£6.30	Lancaster
Museum steward	Web	£8.00	St Andrews
Charity mugger	Friend	£7.00	UWE
Uni ambassador	Uni	£7.45	UCL
Bike mechanic	Asked	£5.35	Huddersfield
Front of house for arts venue	Friend	£6.47	Aberdeen
Zoo supervisor	Word of mouth	£5.02	Durham
Website designer	Offer to students	£10.00	Oxford
Nightclub	Job centre	£5.50	Essex
National Trust admin	Temp agency	£6.50	Lancaster
Petrol station manager	Local newspaper	£5.65	Falmouth
Football club turnstile operator	Advert in programme	£7.50	Southampton
Lifeguard/sports coach	Asked (email)	£6.46	UWE
Basketball coach	Interview	£10.00	Wolverhampton
Holiday cottage cleaner	Friend	£8.00	Falmouth
Language teacher	Contacts	£12.00	Sussex
Party planner	–	£5.00 approx.	Hull
Singer – gigs	Word of mouth	£60.00	City
Piano teacher	–	£6.80 approx.	Robert Gordon
Uni admissions dep't	Freshers fair	£7.00	St Andrews
Gym instructor	Gym member	£5.57	Wolverhampton
Ironing	Imagination	£5.00 approx.	De Montfort
Secret shopper	Job shop	£5.50–£11	Hertfordshire

Further information

Who to contact

► University job shop.

► Employment agencies.

► Job Centres.

► Local employers on spec.

What to read

► Local newspaper job ads.

► *Summer Jobs Worldwide* by Susan Griffith, published by Vacation Work/Trotman, includes over 50,000 jobs worldwide and is updated annually; website: www. trotman.co.uk.

Work experience and internships

What counts as work experience?

'All experience is good and can count as work experience,' according to Liz Rhodes of the National Council for Work Experience (NCWE). 'A placement in an industry where you are being considered for a career is of course excellent and a great way for you to find out if it's right for you, but even a job in the local restaurant, shop or office can help build key transferable skills – from dealing with people to prioritising and keeping a cool head in a crisis,' she says. Make the most of the opportunities and experiences that come up. You'll be surprised just how much you have learned and the challenges you've faced, and it could do wonders for your CV. Visit www.workexperience.org.uk for more advice on getting work experience, from different types of programmes to how to go about setting up the placement.

What is really meant by work experience?

For students, it means the opportunities offered by different organisations to gain specific experience of working in an area that will help them with their degree studies or entrance into a career. Of course, it helps that students are paid to do this work, so finding a placement during the vacations is a double whammy.

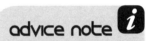

advice note

Don't leave it too late! If you want to work over the Christmas holidays, start planning early, even before you go to uni – competition is high.

What is an internship?

Work experience by a different name. The word 'internship' came from the USA and was spread throughout Europe by multinational companies, where it is now widely used. In the States some internships are unpaid, so it is always worth checking. Sometimes the phrase 'vacation placement' is used.

Who provides work experience?

Many organisations that are unable to offer sponsorship or industrial placement do offer vacation work experience – banks, insurance companies, accountancy and law firms, for example.

Big companies such as BP, Shell, Credit Suisse, Barclays, Microsoft, National Grid, and Exxon Mobil take on a number of students for vacation work each year (or at least they did – in these troubled financial times, places may not be

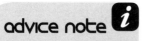

advice note

Check out the National Work Placement Exhibitions held generally in October – see www.work-placement.co.uk.

so easy to find). Many of these companies offer placements abroad; some of these placements are better than others. The NCWE holds an annual competition to find the company offering the best work placements. There are a number of categories covering different sizes of organisation, charities and lengths of placement. Winners for 2010 included TUI Travel PLC (overall winner), Enterprise Rent-A-Car, Centrica ProspectSoft Ltd, Audiences North East, the BBC, *Which?*, International Sourcing Limited, Lockheed Martin UK and Pinsent Masons LLP.

How do you find a vacation placement?

Companies advertise in your university careers advice centre, and you can try www.workexperience.org or www.prospects.ac.uk. Expect a fairly intensive interview, as many companies think vacation work might lead to a more lasting relationship, e.g. full-time employment after you graduate, and are looking at you with this in mind.

You may also find openings in areas where sponsorship is out of the question and industrial placements are difficult to find, such as personnel, marketing or publishing. If you are considering the media, advertising or journalism, you may well find securing paid work impossible. However, if you are prepared to work unpaid, just for the experience, then you might have better luck. Try some of the local radio stations, the many TV channels and TV production companies, local papers (especially the freebies) and the wide range of different magazines that are published. It will take a lot of energy to secure success, as you will need to write to individual editors giving details of how you could add value to their publication or programme.

Facts and Figures

Former work placement students are the third most effective means of selecting graduates, according to major employers.

Source: *IRS Employment Review* 2008

Ideally, select ones you know something about. Work experience placements are not all one-sided: the employer gets something out of it, too – the chance to look at a possible new employee while providing you with real and interesting experiences and the opportunity to work on 'live' projects as part of a closely integrated and supportive team. But actually getting a work placement is incredibly competitive.

'Vacation placements and workshops are an excellent opportunity for you to learn first-hand what a particular career would involve,' says Caroline Beaton, Graduate Recruitment and Development Manager at law firm Clifford Chance. 'Choosing the right career and the right employer are important and often difficult decisions. There will be a whole range of options to consider and you will want to be as well informed as possible. Spending a couple of weeks with a prospective employer gives you a very good idea of what the work would involve and what kind of atmosphere you would be working in. In addition to vacation placements, there are also opportunities to attend workshops which can offer a more compact way of gaining an insight into a career as a lawyer.'

Clifford Chance offers a four-week vacation placement during the summer break, which currently pays £270 a week. There are also places available on the firm's winter and spring workshops, which are open to finalists and first-year students respectively. As well as gaining an insight into law at Clifford Chance, students also benefit from unlimited use of outstanding facilities, including the staff restaurant, swimming pool and state-of-the-art gym.

How will I find a placement?

Big employers

Large companies such as Procter & Gamble offer what they call summer internships to students on a worldwide scale. They see it as a fair means of assessing students' ability and hope eventually to recruit most of their graduates through this scheme. AkzoNobel (which now incorporates ICI) is another major company that offers summer internships and industrial placements, which provide students with an excellent opportunity to gain hands-on work experience. They also see their internships as a chance to assess students' talents and potential for their Graduate Development Programme. They say they look for drive and motivation in students who are team players with good interpersonal skills. Is that you? Your university careers office should have details of these and other programmes with major companies. Otherwise, contact employers directly or look online.

advice note ℹ️

Go Wales

For students who live or are studying in Wales, Go Wales offers project-based placements currently attracting wages of £230 per week plus some excellent experience to add to your CV. Also on offer are work tasters – unpaid, temporary placements which allow students and graduates to to gain a little 'taste' of a career or job before taking the plunge. Call 0845 225 6050 or visit www.gowales.co.uk for more information.

Based in the West Midlands?

Try Graduate Advantage. They offers students and graduates short- and long-term paid work placements in all sectors of business and industry; see www. graduateadvantage.co.uk.

Small employers

Small companies can be contacted direct, or you could try Step. This UK-wide scheme is designed to encourage small- and medium-sized employers to take on undergraduates for an eight-week summer placement to carry out a specific project of benefit to both the employer and the student.

Students have the opportunity to use their existing skills and the chance to develop new ones while experiencing life in the workplace. Opportunities are open to second- and penultimate-year undergraduates of any degree discipline.

You'd earn £210 per week. This is in the form of a 'training allowance' and so is exempt from tax and National Insurance contributions. In 2009, over 600 projects were undertaken across the UK. Money, of course, is important, but so too is getting the right job at the end of your degree course. The competition out there is very strong, even for top graduates, so you need to make your CV stand out. Taking part in a Step work placement in an area relevant to your future career aspirations is certainly one way to achieve this.

Around half a million students look for work placements for the summer vacations. Competition is fierce. To avoid disappointment, start looking as soon as you have your university place. Work experience is becoming an important deciding factor on a student's CV, and an important aid to financial survival. Check out your uni job shop or the website www.prospects.ac.uk.

Step now also offers placements for recent graduates (Graduate Step), and for students looking for a year-long sandwich placement (Step into Industry). For details, visit the Step website, www.step.org.uk, where you'll find more information, a database of current opportunities and an online application form for the summer programme, or contact your university's careers advisory service.

Student feedback from the 2009 Step programme has been excellent:

► 100% of student participants felt they would use the skills they had learnt in the future
► 94% found the work challenging
► 65% actually received a job offer through the placement
► 94% would recommend Step to a friend.

Charlotte's story

The 2009 Step winner was Charlotte Fayle, a 21-year old Biology student from Leeds University, who was crowned the 'UK's Most Enterprising

Student 2009' for developing an energy reduction service that could secure a significant increase in turnover for her host business.

Charlotte wowed the panel of judges with her achievements working at RCE Services UK Ltd, an electrical contractors based in Leeds. She created a viable energy reduction consultancy service for low-energy lighting solutions that could generate a potential £300,000 a year for the business.

'The opportunity to gain a new understanding of business and develop my communication skills has been invaluable', explains Charlotte. Robert Cardis, RCE's Managing Director, adds: 'The Step placement far exceeded our expectations and we're delighted that Charlotte has been recognised for the fantastic contribution she made to the business. She is destined for great things and we wish her all the best in whatever career she pursues.'

Internships vs Work Experience

Will the new deal proposed by the government to save new graduates from the dole by offering them internships with major companies dry up the internship market for undergraduates? Only time will tell. NCWE Director Heather Collier has this to say: 'Inevitably some companies are cutting back, but it's a question of striking a balance between cost savings in the short term and investing long-term in the talent who would be in place and ready to aid company competitiveness when the upturn comes.

'We're not sure whether the government initiative is going ahead at the moment. Advice for students is that fewer graduate opportunities means more competition for every undergraduate opportunity for work experience. Joining a university society would give them something to articulate at interview and make them stand out from the hundreds of hopefuls, as would, of course, any previous work experience. There are lots of good skills learned behind a bar or even waitressing – students shouldn't discount the value of anything they have done or learned outside of their studies.

'Salaries during work experience depend very much on the industry and location of the opportunity. They are very competitive in London, but in the North, typically £14,000–£16,000 pro rata.'

Ethnic minorities

The Windsor Fellowship Undergraduate Programme

The Windsor Fellowship is a unique charitable organisation that designs and delivers high-impact personal development and leadership programmes. It works in partnership with leading UK employers and educational institutions to ensure that talent from diverse communities is realised. The Leadership Programme for Black and Asian Undergraduates includes residential seminars, outdoor challenges, voluntary work, mentoring and a minimum six-week paid internship with a sponsor, providing a real-life insight into employment with leading organisations. Sponsors vary year by year but have regularly included Deutsche Bank, GlaxoSmithKline, John Lewis Partnership, Morgan Stanley, Friends of the Earth and several government departments and universities. Application forms and further information about this and other programmes can be downloaded from www.windsor-fellowship.org.

'The foundation has been laid. I believe I have more edge than my counterparts and this is a fantastic position to be in at the beginning of one's career. Thank you!'

Zanele Hlatshwayo

'The Windsor Fellowship experience has benefited me by making me more confident, giving me direction and skills needed for the working world as well as introducing me to like-minded people who have become my closest friends.'

Aarti Patel

The University of Oxford

The University of Oxford Careers Service offers a great deal of support for those looking for work experience. Its website has an extensive, searchable database with many types of work experience opportunities advertised on it at any one time. Opportunities include summer internships, part-time work, careers-related courses, longer placements, volunteer work and overseas work. This is backed up by a well-resourced information room with further details about the organisations concerned, and a wide range of other resources to assist those looking for suitable opportunities. A team of professional careers staff helps with students' work experience queries – ideal for those wanting tips to track down the more elusive work experience opportunities.

The service also runs a work experience fair in November, which is useful for those looking for work experience. In addition, the Careers Service offers advice, guidance and information specific to work experience via its website. Oxford students and graduates who completed their courses up to four years ago can access all these services by registering online, free, at www.careers.ox.ac.uk.

Most other university careers services offer similar help. Check with your own university careers service to see what is available. See also the section on 'University job shops' on page 137.

Who to contact

Who to contact for work experience:

- ▶ local employers
- ▶ major employers
- ▶ course directors
- ▶ college noticeboards
- ▶ your university careers advisers
- ▶ university job shops
- ▶ Step
- ▶ local employment agencies.

Will my work experience pay off?

It certainly has in the past. And things don't look as gloomy as you might think for the future. This year's *High Flyers Survey*, published in January, reports that employers expect to recruit 11.8% more graduates in 2010 than last year. Over a quarter of the 2010 entry-level jobs have been filled by deferred job offers and students who had done previous work experience with the employer.

With the supply of graduates continuing to grow, it is difficult to predict the effect the economic climate will have on the 'credit crunch' generation in the short or long term. Let's hope that by the time this year's new cohort of undergraduates hits the job market the good times will be here to stay. Even in this downturn there has been a demand for top graduates with good experience, so the thing to do is to make sure you are in the running.

Don't just sit back and think, 'I have a degree – everybody will want me,' because the sad fact is they won't. The notion that students can walk into top jobs simply because they have a degree, even in good times, is a fallacy. Not everybody is a blue-chip high-flyer. So if you want one of those top jobs you have got to be proactive and start lining up the kind of skills and experiences that employers are looking for now – which is why getting the right work experience is so important.

What are employers looking for?

Whatever the state of the employment market and whatever area of work interests you, getting your foot in the door is incredibly competitive. All employers are seeking the best candidates, and with increasing numbers of graduates coming out of our universities the pool is getting larger and larger. It is not unusual to have 4,000 applicants chasing 100 places. Despite the number of graduates around, many companies surveyed said they were not able to find graduates with the skills they required to fill all their vacancies. Obviously, companies can interview only a small proportion of prospective applicants.

So how do they seek out the best? What are their criteria? And what do you need to have on your CV, in addition to a good degree and possibly work experience, to make you stand out from the crowd and turn an application into an interview? We asked some major employers.

'We find that candidates who have some work experience, or who have taken the opportunity to broaden their horizons by working in the community or even travelling, have normally had a greater chance to develop and practise the sort of skills we are looking for.'

Graduate Resourcing, Royal Bank of Scotland

'Initiative and follow-through; leadership; thinking and problem-solving; communication; ability to work with others; creativity and innovation; and priority-setting. We look for evidence of these skills, which together we'll be able to develop further to run the organisation of the future.'

Human Resources Manager, Recruitment, Procter & Gamble UK

'We are looking for the next generation of senior managers, the people who will drive our business forward in the future, so the kinds of qualities we are seeking – conceptual and analytical thinking, strong interpersonal skills, ability to influence and motivate others – can't all be demonstrated through a good academic record, important though it is. We want to know about other areas of achievement as well.'

Graduate Recruitment, AkzoNobel (former ICI)

Job check

Always keep your future career in mind when you head for holiday and even term-time jobs – that's the advice of the NCWE. Skills learnt from time spent working can make a great contribution to your CV and help convince a future employer that you are better than the competition. Whatever and wherever the job – supermarket, pub, the students' union – make the most of the opportunity to enhance your employability. To help you, here is the NCWE checklist.

- Set some personal objectives for the period of employment before starting a job: what do you want to get out of it, beyond the pay packet?

- Don't be afraid to ask questions and take notes when being briefed by your boss at the outset. Better to ask now and be clear than make mistakes later.

- Keep a note of challenges you overcome each day and any problem-solving required. This demonstrates initiative and prioritising skills.

- Grab any chance to take on more responsibility: undertaking new tasks is a sure way of developing new talents.

- Do the best job you possibly can for self-satisfaction and the possibility of being asked back for the next vacation – maybe even for a permanent position in the future.

Graduate Recruitment Facts

Here are the findings of research carried out into 100 firms:

- graduate vacancies expected to rise by 11.8%

- while nearly half of employers expect to recruit more graduates, a quarter warn they will be making further cuts to entry-level positions. These include three main areas – consumer goods companies, engineering and industrial employers and the public sector

- the situation is more buoyant in the City with vacancies in investment banking jumping more than a third

- other areas seeing an increase in graduate vacancies are accountancy and professional services, high-street banking and retailing

- employers are receiving significantly more applications for their graduate programmes this year. More than 40% of applications so far have come from graduates who failed to find work last year

- the largest recruiters of graduates in 2010 will be PricewaterhouseCoopers, Deloitte, the Army, Teach First, KPMG and the RAF

- students remain very pessimistic about their career prospects and few believe there will be more opportunities than last year. Only 8% of finalists were confident they would find a job.

Finally:

- graduate starting salaries remain static at an average of £25,000 – that's if you can find a job.

Source: *High Flyers Survey*, published January 2010
AGR *Winter Review 2010* reported a slight decrease in graduate employment for 2010 and a median graduate starting salary of £25,000. More AGR findings can be seen on page 155.

Facts and Figures

Looking further ahead, what is likely to make you happy in ten years' time? Based on research carried out with 25,000 university applicants:

- having a job that is interesting (82%)
- spending time with family (68%)
- owning a home (46%)
- spending time with friends (46%)
- being in a long-term relationship (45%)
- having a job that contributes to society (40%)
- having a job that pays well (39%).

Source: *Future Leaders Survey*, conducted by Forum for the Future and UCAS and sponsored by Friends Provident

- Ask for feedback from your boss and the people you work with – there may be room for improvement – and note successes and achievements: these are what you need to put on your CV.

- Make suggestions – just because you're a holiday worker or work experience student doesn't mean you don't have good ideas, and your colleagues will always appreciate seeing things from a new perspective.

- Keep a diary of your thoughts throughout the placement. This will help you to add your achievements to your CV and will show you how far you've come.

- Ask for a reference from your boss; it will stand you in good stead for moving on to a permanent job.

- Work hard, but take the time to get to know your colleagues and enjoy the work atmosphere. After all, you may be spending every day there for a while!

Stop press!

- www.thestudentroom.co.uk, possibly the world's largest online student community giving study help, personal and professional advice and access to student guides. For the latest in job advice, see also e45.co.uk.

- www.prospects.ac.uk/chat is a communications channel enabling students to put their careers questions to big-name recruiters.

- Prospects also has a 24-hour chat room, where job-seeking students and graduates who wake up in a cold sweat in the middle of the night need not be in anguish alone. See www.prospects.ac.uk/links/gradtalk.

Further information

What to read

- *VT Lifeskills' Jobfile*: available from your careers service or public library.

Surf the net

There are a number of websites that can help you find work experience. Here are just a few of the best.

- Prospects, www.prospects.ac.uk, the graduate careers website, which has a work bank section.
- The NCWE, www.work-experience.org, which aims to support and develop quality work experience and encourage employers to offer more opportunities.
- Best part-time jobs: www.hotrecruit.com, or through UCAS: http://yougo.co.uk.
- Jobs for students: www.justjobs4students.co.uk, www.student-part-time-jobs.com and www.activate.co.uk.
- And for something different: www.sliversoftime.com.

advice note *i*

What's an employer looking for?
- motivation and enthusiasm
- team working
- oral communication
- flexibility and adaptability
- initiative/being proactive.

Industrial placements

Will I get one?

The idea of the four-year sandwich course that includes an industrial placement was never envisaged as a financial life-saver, but many students find that a year in industry with a good salary helps them to clear their debts while they gain invaluable experience. But with more HE institutions developing more sandwich courses, finding good industrial placements is becoming increasingly difficult. This is felt mostly where courses are fairly new and the institutions haven't yet built up a good rapport with industrial concerns.

When applying to universities, it is important to check out the extent and quality of the industrial placements offered to students, and whether in the current economic climate they are still readily available. There are essentially two sorts of sandwich courses: those where you take a year out – usually the third year – to work in industry, and courses in which you alternate six months at university with six months at work.

In the beginning, industrial placements were mainly for courses in engineering, but

advice note *i*

'Dress for success' is the advice to job-seeking students from Prospects. Whether attending an interview, recruitment fair or assessment day, creating a favourable impression is important. Getting the right look shows you understand the employer's business.

153

increasingly courses in business studies, retail, computer sciences and languages include an industrial placement year. Aberystwyth has taken this a step further with its YES scheme.

What is the YES scheme?

Aberystwyth University has pioneered an initiative to give any student in the university who is not already on a sandwich course the opportunity to take an industrial year out. The scheme is called YES (Year in Employment Scheme), and currently over 40 students at Aberystwyth are saying YES to the opportunity.

They come from a range of disciplines: arts, economics and social sciences, information studies, international politics and the sciences. You can choose a placement that is relevant to your degree subject, such as accounting, marketing, scientific research, events management or environmental conservation work, or use the time to experience work in an area that is totally new to you, such as human resources, retail management or production management.

You can even work abroad: YES students have recently worked in Europe, Australia, New Zealand, Africa and the USA. Students also work with major employers in the private, public and voluntary sectors such as IBM, KPMG, the Environment Agency, Perkins Engines and the Centre for Ecology and Hydrology. Salaries vary from around £8,000 up to £18,000, although some voluntary placements may only pay expenses. With everybody now having to pay fees, earning money for a year during study is a definite bonus.

Aberystwyth is adamant – with some justification – that the skills learned during the year out have enhanced both degree performance and employment prospects. The latest figures from the university show that students who have undertaken work experience gain employment after graduation more quickly than students who have not participated in any form of work experience. Joanne Hiatt, YES Project Officer, believes 'YES provides an opportunity for students to develop their employability skills while earning money and having some fun!'

Salary Check

- ► Graduate vacancies have stabilised after a massive fall in 2008. Expected decrease for 2010 is just 1.6%.

- ► Starting salaries are frozen for the second year running: median expected starting rate to remain at £25,000.

- ► Top starting salaries of £38,250 were paid in investment banking and fund management in 2009.

- ► Top starting salaries in legal firms were down to £35,000 in 2009.

Source: AGR *Winter Review 2010*

Michael's story

Michael, a third-year Business and Management student at Aberystwyth, is currently taking a year out through the YES scheme. This is what he is doing.

'While many of my university mates are applying for graduate job vacancies, and many wondering what they will be doing after leaving Aberystwyth, I'm going the extra mile and boosting my CV with experience that many of my mates may lack. Taking a year in employment with Howard Worth Chartered Accountants is helping me gain some essential and useful experience of work life.

'There are other benefits too. I'm saving money in an attempt to cut the debt I will graduate with. I am also living back home which is another saving.

'As well as putting in the hours in the office, which involves preparing accounts for a range of small businesses and limited companies, I'm in the company six-a-side football team where getting beat every week seems to be the norm.

'Being away from university does have its down sides – missing out on those nights out – but I think in the longer term the experience picked up

advice note

Graduate recruitment in the UK is still in the doldrums and competition for jobs is even greater ... Here are some suggestions from AGR recruiters to enhance your employment chances:

▶ research the company before applying

▶ apply early

▶ be prepared to relocate mentally by broadening your job criteria

▶ be positive – graduates who are indecisive are not hired

▶ get experience to enhance your soft skills, e.g. volunteering or a gap year

▶ get into work somehow – temporary paid employment is better than no employment.

Taking extra qualifications after graduation was not given the thumbs-up.

Source: AGR *Winter Review 2010*

since starting my placement will be far more valuable in a difficult job market.

'To anyone considering a placement year, my advice is take the opportunity if you can because you will benefit from the kind of experience you can't gain from reading a textbook or attending lectures, and there is always the chance that your employer may take you on after graduation.'

When is the best time to do a year in industry?

If you take your year in industry at 20 you are going to earn substantially more than you would at 18, so it could help pay off your debts – you will also know more about your subject so the experience can be more valuable. But if you take a year out before you start at university, the money you save will help to ease your finances once you start managing on student funding, and the experience will help with your studies.

Another point to consider: most universities charge fees during a year out in industry, and although these are much reduced – around 50% of the current fee – if your industrial placement is taken as a gap year either before or after university you won't have to pay this.

Could an industrial placement lead to sponsorship/employment?

Sometimes a year in industry is an integral part of a sponsorship scheme (see Chapter 8 for full details). If it is not, a successful period of work experience can result in your employer offering to sponsor you for the rest or the whole of your degree. With some three-quarters of employers who recruit new graduates providing work experience, there is no doubt that the student who has spent a successful placement with an employer is in a good position regarding future employment. An industrial placement provides the opportunity for you to get to know your employer and your employer to get to know you. It will help you to develop work-related skills that employers value.

The Year in Industry: Work, Earn, Win, Get Ahead

If you are looking for paid work experience in industry, which could really help your future career and possibly lead to university sponsorship, the Year in Industry (YINI) are the people to contact. YINI is a nationwide programme run by the education charity EDT. Working with internationally-renowned companies, YINI offers work placements that are challenging, rewarding and deliver real business experience to help you stand out from the crowd.

All YINI placements give you the skills and knowledge employers are looking for, the experience will help you make the most of university – and you get to earn while you learn.

A work placement with YINI will:

▶ give your CV the competitive edge

▶ let you try out your degree or career choice

▶ give you 'real work' experience

▶ pay while you learn

▶ help you make the most of university

▶ help set you up for life with contacts, experience and opportunities.

In some instances, placement companies have gone on to sponsor YINI participants through university, and even offer them jobs at the end of their degree.

Who will I work for?
YINI only works with companies who are committed to giving you real business and industry experience. Its partners range from leading FTSE 100 companies to small innovative start-ups.

What kind of job will I do?
YINI has placements for students interested in all areas of engineering, science, IT, e-commerce, business, marketing, finance and logistics.

You will become a trusted member of the team, be given your own responsibilities and be expected to deliver results. The satisfaction you get will be huge. Applications for placements should be made as soon as possible. The earlier students apply, the more opportunities are available. Placements follow the academic year and students earn competitive salaries during their placement. An administration fee of £25 is payable after application and acceptance onto the scheme.

For further information, contact the YINI National Office, University of Southampton, Hampshire SO17 1BJ, tel: 023 8059 7061, fax: 023 8059 7570, email: info@yini.org.uk or website: www.yini.org.uk.

What the students say
'I met great people and worked in a fast-moving and friendly team, and it gave me a much clearer idea of the kind of career I want after graduating. As a result of my experience I am a much more confident person than when I left school a year ago.'
William Jackson, Natural Sciences student, Cambridge, worked for 1 Ltd

'The projects I worked on were very challenging, but the feeling of satisfaction after they were complete made it all worth while.'
Emma Stephenson, Aeronautical Engineering student, Glasgow, worked for Shell

'By doing a YINI placement, I was given roles and responsibilities that would never usually be offered to a person of my age and experience. I know that I will carry the skills that I've learned back to my degree course, allowing me to gain a lot more out of the university experience. I know how to apply my knowledge from the classroom to the workplace and I am now more aware of managing my money.'
Nicol Perryman, Mathematics student, Newcastle, worked for Permoid Industries

Further information

Thinking about taking a sandwich course?

The internet is the place to look. There are a number of electronic resources that can help in the search for sandwich courses or other work placements.

- ▶ The UCAS website www.ucas.com/students/coursesearch – this will only bring up sandwich course information if the institution has included it.
- ▶ ASET, formerly the Association for Sandwich Education and Training, is the national body for work-based learning practitioners. It's an educational charity that promotes best practice for work placements, as well as providing support and advice for all professionals who work in the field. Contact: ASET, The Work-Based and Placement Learning Association, Broomgrove, 59 Clarkehouse Road, Sheffield S10 2LE, tel: 0114 221 2902, fax: 0114 221 2903, email: aset@asetonline.org or website: www.asetonline.org.
- ▶ The NCWE has useful information on a range of work experience opportunities – see its website www.workexperience.org. If you want advice on work experience, they are the people to ask.

Around 112,000 students went on sandwich placements each year, according to ASET.

Who to ask about placements

If you are not a sponsored student, contact your university careers service. It will have a list of possible employers who might offer placements. Contact employers directly – don't forget the smaller companies, which might have just one placement but don't advertise in case they get deluged.

What to read

► *Engineering Opportunities for Students and Graduates*, published by Professional Engineering Publishing Ltd, is available free from the Institution of Mechanical Engineers (IMechE), c/o Marketing & Communications Department, 1 Birdcage Walk, London SW1H 9JJ or email: marketing @imeche.org. uk. Don't forget to include your address.

► *Everything You Wanted to Know about Sponsorship, Placements and Graduate Opportunities*, regularly updated and published by Amoeba Publications – see the website: www.everythingyouwantedtoknow. com.

it's a fact

Credit crunch reassurance – research shows that graduates are more likely to be employed than those with the next highest qualification and are more likely to return to employment following periods of unemployment or economic inactivity.

Source: Universities UK

CHAPTER 7

Taking a gap year

This chapter looks at all the opportunities open to those who opt to take a gap year before or during university.

- ▶ Why take a gap year? (page 162)

- ▶ A gap year to raise money (page 162)

- ▶ A voluntary work gap year (page 165)

- ▶ A gap year for travel abroad (page 174)

- ▶ The student travel scene (page 177).

Why take a gap year?

Taking a gap year after A levels is becoming increasingly popular: each year around 230,000 students are thought to take a year out. After 13 solid years on the academic treadmill, many young people just feel that they need a chance to recharge their batteries. But last year, it is likely that there were many more on the gap year trail and you can put this down to the shortage of jobs. With more applicants trying for university, some 160,000 were unable to find places, and many of those opted for a gap year and are applying again this year. This means there is likely to be an even bigger scramble for places this year, and the gap year trail will be even more crowded. If you are likely to be one of them, this section may help.

If you have a uni place but want to go 'gapping', most universities will accept deferred entry; some institutions actively encourage it. But don't assume that deferred entry is an automatic right. You must always ask, and if the course is popular, you may be refused.

Many young people use their gap year to gain a skill or experience in a specific organisation as well as to make money. Often this results in them having a ready-made job to walk into during vacations, once they have started their degree course. Others just want fun and new experiences, or the chance to do something to help others. Here we look at three very different kinds of gap year: one to raise money, one to do voluntary work and one to travel.

it's a fact

A total of 520,000 UK residents take a gap year each year (not all of them students) and it's estimated that by 2010 that number will increase to two million, with the total expenditure reaching £11 billion (source: Mintel). Gaptravelguides.co.uk claims that a staggering 70% of students aim to take a gap year and 75% of people are seriously considering taking a career break as a means of broadening their horizons and experiencing new cultures. As yet, it is not known what effect the current economic downturn will have on these figures.

A gap year to raise money

If your aim is to save money, your best bet is to work as close to home as possible, where bed and board are likely to be at a very advantageous rate – if not free – and to avoid travel costs. In the past there were always plenty of jobs going in shops, restaurants and pubs, and you might still be lucky. Go for chains, such as Next, Tesco or a pub chain. You will then have street cred and may be able to find a part-time term-time job in your university town.

Since you have a whole year to work and a clutch of A levels to offer, you might be able to find a job with better pay and which stretches your ability more. But be realistic: you are not going to earn bags of gold. A gap-year student could expect to earn at least the minimum wage, which is £4.83 per hour for 18–21-year-olds (£4.92 from October 2010) and £5.80 per hour for those aged 22 or above (£5.93 from October 2010). Of the students who responded to the *Student Money* survey, fewer than half managed to save anything towards their university course, spending most of their earnings on travel. A gap year isn't only about earning money, though: many students see it as a chance to gain useful experience towards their career, to develop skills or to help others.

What students did in their gap years

- Lydia worked for the Royal Bank of Scotland and gained wide experience, made some useful contacts and earned £5,000 before starting a degree in Economics at UWE. But she blew most of her earnings travelling to Hong Kong, Australia New Zealand and South Africa. Check out her exploits on http://blogs.statravel.co.uk/anj-lydz.
- Rachel didn't feel ready for university or leaving home, so she worked in her local library and her old school's library, earning £7,000. She managed to save £3,500 so had no serious money worries when she started her course in Pharmacology at Aberdeen.
- Joanne worked for a supermarket driving a fork-lift truck, but managed to get heavily into debt before she even started an Equine Science course at Aberystwyth.
- Ruth travelled in Nicaragua for six months, but still managed to save £600 for uni working in a pub. She is taking Latin American studies at Essex.
- Lucky Ryan split his time between working in a ski resort and surfing in Australia before his Engineering course at Cambridge.
- Christopher worked in a sausage shop, where he learned how to mix up a 'mean banger'. It paid for driving lessons, got him his wheels and gave him a £2,000 bank balance when he started a course in Business Administration at the UWE.
- Kerry started her year working in Disneyland near Paris. She then worked at Eurocamp in Italy and Camp America in Northern California. She didn't save a bean, but had a great time. She went on to study Maths at Liverpool.
- Giles worked as an associate director on a film project before studying Politics at Hull.
- Jordan went to China to study martial arts at a school near Si Ping City but saved remarkably little. He is now studying Chinese Language and History at Sheffield.
- Conni took a job as a classroom assistant in the dance and drama department of a school and sometimes helped out with PE – useful experience for her degree course in Dance and Sport at Wolverhampton University.

- Edward spent his year singing in gigs and is still wowing the revellers in clubs around London while financing his music degree at City University.

- Kate had a fun-packed year, spending five months volunteering in Nepal, five months working and two months travelling around Canada before taking up Theological Studies at St Andrews.

- Laura taught English in Qatar before starting her own English Studies at St Andrews.

- Rebecca travelled to Japan and Australia, where she taught. She is now at Lampeter.

- Peggy lived and worked in a school in New Zealand, returning to start her studies at St Andrews after a year.

- Rachel devoted her year to others, working as a carer for the elderly for five months and then for a charity as a volunteer. She is now at St George's studying Medicine.

- Before going up to Oxford, Tim worked for the Department for the Environment, Food and Rural Affairs and then for a charity in South Africa.

- Lily worked as a trainee behaviour support worker in schools, which was good experience for her course in Applied Criminology at Huddersfield.

- Globe-trotting Laurel undertook volunteer conservation and community work in Kenya and then worked as an office assistant in an American summer camp. She is now studying Zoology at Durham.

- Anna's gap year was a glorious mix of holidaying in Australia and Canada, skiing in Switzerland and working as a nursery nurse. She is now studying Developmental Biology at UCL.

- Sapphire worked hard for 11 months at Merck Neuroscience Research Centre before taking a month off in Kenya. She is now studying Medicine at UCL.

- Mark took a Diploma in Art Design Foundation Studies but still managed to save £1,000 towards his course in Interior Architecture at Nottingham Trent University.

- Julia 'A' went to Calcutta with the Baptist Missionary Society, where she worked with street children and lived with the Mother Teresa nuns. She is now studying Law at Reading.

- Julia 'B' took a job in a factory to get enough money to join a volunteer conservation project in Australia. On her return, she worked at a scientific research centre to gain experience and save money – around £3,000 – for her degree in Natural Sciences at Durham.

- Rory was on duty at the Odeon cinema for six months, then blew everything he'd saved on a fabulous six-month trip to Australia. He is now studying English at Durham.

Students talk in more detail about their gap years on page 170.

Further information

Who to contact:

- Year Out Group – see below.
- Banks, insurance companies, accountancy firms – many offer work experience; always worth a try.
- Shops, supermarkets, chain stores – try to find an organisation with a number of local outlets and one that offers a training scheme.
- Teaching – you don't actually need any training to take up a temporary position as assistant teacher or matron in a preparatory school. As an assistant matron, you could find yourself darning socks and getting the kids up in the morning. As an assistant teacher, you'd probably be involved in organising sport and out-of-school activities, coaching and supervising prep and classes when staff are away. Current rates of pay are in line with the minimum wage with a small amount deducted if food, accommodation, etc. are included. Term ends in July, so you would then have two months' travelling time. For gap year vacancies, try Gabbitas Educational Consultants, Carrington House, 126–130 Regent Street, London W1B 5EE, tel: 020 7734 0161 or websites: www.gabbitas.co.uk or www.teachersrecruitment.com.

A voluntary work gap year

How would you like to undertake projects in Africa, Mexico or Peru while having the experience of a lifetime? Go on an Art History Abroad course to Venice, Florence or Bologna? Work and travel in the USA? Help the needy – homeless people, young offenders, children with special needs? Take a Trekforce or Greenforce expedition with the chance to help international conservation projects in such far-flung places as Belize and Guyana? Do you see yourself working to save endangered rainforests, wildlife or coral reefs, or perhaps developing some theatre techniques? All or any of these are possible.

Year Out Group

Once you've made the gap year decision, the Year Out Group is a good starting point if you are seeking adventure or a great experience. The Year Out Group is an association of 38 leading year-out organisations that was launched in 2000 to promote the concept and benefits of well-structured year-out programmes, to promote models of good practice and to help young people and their advisers select suitable and worthwhile projects. All the organisations have agreed to adhere to a code of practice and appropriate operating guidelines. Projects last from a few weeks to a year and are available in the UK or overseas. For many of them you will have to finance yourself (this is considered part of the challenge) – but others do pay quite well.

It is wise to start your planning early and to do it in as much detail as possible. In a full gap year there is time to work to earn money as well as to work on a project that is worthwhile, exciting and which could change your life forever. Each year, Year Out Group produces a booklet called *Planning your year out?*, which provides information on planning a well-structured gap year. The booklet is sent to all schools, colleges and careers offices each autumn and can also be downloaded from the group's website www.yearoutgroup.org.

To learn more about the members of Year Out Group and the opportunities they offer, read on. You can also contact them directly or via the Year Out Group website.

So what's on offer?

▶ Africa, Asia & Americas Venture – combines teaching and coaching sports, plus community projects, with adventure in Africa, India, Nepal, Thailand or Mexico; tel: 01380 729 009, email: av@aventure.co.uk or website: www.aventure.co.uk.

▶ African Conservation Experience – opportunities to work on game and nature reserves in southern Africa; tel: 0845 5200 888, email: info@ConservationAfrica.net or website: www.ConservationAfrica.net.

▶ Art History Abroad – courses including a Grand Tour; tel: 01379 871 800, email: info@arthistoryabroad.com or website: www.arthistoryabroad.com.

▶ Azafady – dedicated to supporting the people and ecosystems of Madagascar; tel: 020 8960 6629, email: info@azafady.org or website: www.madagascar.co.uk.

▶ Blue Ventures – projects and expeditions that enhance global marine conservation and research; tel: 020 3176 0548, email: madagascar@blueventures.org or website: www.blueventures.org.

▶ British Universities North America Club (BUNAC) work and travel programmes – USA, Canada, Australia, New Zealand and volunteer programmes in Africa, Asia and Latin America; tel: 020 7251 3472, email: enquiries@bunac.org.uk or website: www.bunac.org/yog (see also BUNAC, page 175).

▶ Camp America – join the staff at a summer camp; tel: 020 7581 7373, email: enquiries@campamerica.co.uk or website: www.campamerica.co.uk.

▶ CESA – language courses abroad; tel: 01209 211 800, email: info@cesalanguages.com or website: www.cesalanguages.com.

▶ Changing Worlds – offers volunteer and paid placements worldwide; tel: 01883 340 960, email: ask@changingworlds.co.uk or website: www.changingworlds.co.uk.

▶ Cross-Cultural Solutions – volunteer work with carefully-selected partner programmes in Africa, Asia, Eastern Europe and South America; tel: 0845 458 2781/2782, email: infouk@crossculturalsolutions.org or website: www.crossculturalsolutions.org.

- ▶ Flying Fish – full range of courses to help you upgrade your water and winter sport qualifications; tel: 0871 250 2500, email: mail@flyingfishonline.com or website: www.flyingfishonline.com.
- ▶ Frontier – conservation and volunteer projects worldwide; tel: 020 7613 2422, info@frontier.ac.uk or website: www.frontier.ac.uk.
- ▶ Gap Year Diver – diving training from beginner to divemaster plus learning, cultural, conservation and adventure activities in Egypt, Costa Rica, Venezuela, Fiji and the Bahamas; tel: 0845 257 3292, email: info@gapyeardiver.com or website: www.gapyeardiver.com.
- ▶ Global Vision International – conservation and humanitarian projects in over 30 countries; tel: 01727 250 250, email: info@gvi.co.uk or website: www.gvi.co.uk.
- ▶ Greenforce – join a conservation project and help scientific understanding; tel: 020 7384 3343, email: info@greenforce.org or website: www.greenforce.org.
- ▶ i to i – work worldwide in media, health, building, teaching, conservation, community work; tel: 0870 442 3042, email: info@i-to-i.com or website: www.i-to-i.com.
- ▶ International Academy – winter sport instructor courses in Canada and New Zealand; tel: 029 2066 0200, email: info@theinternationalacademy.com or website: www.international-academy.com.
- ▶ Lattitude Global Volunteering – assist in schools, hospitals or on conservation projects and outdoor projects in 34 countries; tel: 0118 959 4914; email: volunteer@lattitude.org.uk or website: www.lattitude.org.uk.
- ▶ The Leap – volunteer and paid work placements in Africa, Asia, South America and Australia; tel: 01672 519 922, email: info@theleap.co.uk or website: www.theleap.co.uk.
- ▶ Madventurer – volunteer projects as part of a team or as an individual in Africa and elsewhere; tel: 0845 121 1996, email: team@madventurer.com or website: www.madventurer.com.
- ▶ Nonstop Adventure – winter sport instructor courses in Canada, water sport experiences elsewhere; tel: 0845 365 1525, email: info@nonstopadventure.com or website: www.nonstopadventure.com.
- ▶ Outreach International – volunteer projects with local communities in Mexico, Costa Rica, Sri Lanka, Cambodia and Ecuador; tel: 01458 274 957, email: info@outreachinternational.co.uk or website: www.outreachinternational.co.uk.
- ▶ Oyster Worldwide – paid and voluntary work in Canada, Tanzania, Nepal, Chile, Brazil and Romania; tel: 01892 770 771 or website: www.oysterworldwide.com.
- ▶ Peak Leaders – winter sport instructor courses and more in Canada and elsewhere; tel: 01337 860 079, email: info@peakleaders.com or website: www.peakleaders.com.
- ▶ Personal Overseas Development – volunteer projects in Nepal, Peru, Tanzania and Thailand; tel: 01242 250 901, email: info@thepodsite.co.uk or website: www.thepodsite.co.uk.

- Projects Abroad – projects in Africa, Latin America, Asia and Eastern Europe; tel: 01903 708 300, email: info@projects-abroad.co.uk or website: www.projects-abroad.co.uk.

- Project Trust – worthwhile volunteer placements in 26 different countries; tel: 01879 230 444, email: info@projecttrust.org.uk or website: www.projecttrust.org.uk.

- Quest Overseas – projects and expeditions in South America and Africa; tel: 01273 777 206, email: info@questoverseas.com or website: www.questoverseas.com.

- Raleigh – challenging community and environmental projects overseas; tel: 020 7183 1270, email: info@raleigh.org.uk or website: www.raleighinternational.org.

- Real Gap Experience – a variety of programmes in over 30 countries; tel: 01892 516 164, email: info@realgap.co.uk or website: www.realgap.co.uk.

- Travellers Worldwide – voluntary teaching, work experience and conservation projects on many continents; tel: 01903 502 595, email: info@travellersworldwide.com or website: www.travellersworldwide.com.

- Trekforce Worldwide – project-based expeditions and volunteer placements in Central and South America, tel: 020 7384 3343, email: info@trekforce.org.uk or website: www.trekforce.org.uk.

- VentureCo – expeditions offering language training, conservation and community projects in challenging environments; tel: 01926 411 122, email: mail@venturecoworldwide.com or website: www.ventureco-worldwide.com.

- Village-to-Village – a project-driven charity providing volunteer placements in northern Tanzania involving teaching, sustainable agriculture, HIV/Aids awareness training and other local initiatives; tel: 01937 918 083, email: enquiries@village-tovillage.org.uk or website: www.village-to-village.org.uk.

- Worldwide Experience – conservation and community projects in southern Africa and elsewhere; tel: 01483 860 560, email: info@worldwideexperience.com or website: www.worldwideexperience.com.

- Year in Industry – places potential graduates in leading industrial companies in the UK; tel: 023 8059 7061, email: enquiries@yini.org.uk or website: www.yini.org.uk.

- Year Out Drama – develop your theatre skills while working with professionals; tel: 01789 266 245, email: yearoutdrama@stratford.ac.uk or website: www.yearoutdrama.com.

- Year Out Group – the association that has brought together all the leading year-out organisations mentioned here, and provides valuable advice on planning your gap year; tel: 01380 816 696, email: info@yearoutgroup.org or website: www.yearoutgroup.org.

Voluntary work abroad in developing countries is not as easy to find as it once was, especially if you have no recognised skill, and many organisations seek people over 21. Some projects will pay maintenance costs, and sometimes give pocket money, but it is not unusual for volunteers to be asked to pay their own fares.

Conservation work is much easier to find, both in the UK and abroad. Most of it is completely voluntary and unpaid. You might even be asked to contribute to your food and accommodation costs. You could become involved in projects for the National Trust or the Royal Society for the Protection of Birds, on the restoration of cathedrals, working with disabled people and underprivileged children, painting and decorating ... it's amazing what some students turn their hands to.

While the financial returns from both voluntary and conservation work are likely to be zero, in terms of your CV it could be of considerable value. Employers are impressed by the altruistic and enterprising qualities needed for voluntary work.

You could also try ...

Long-term volunteering

The National Trust

If you are looking to fill a gap year, change career or gain work experience, and you have six months or more to spare, then you could join the National Trust's full-time volunteering programme. As a full-time volunteer, you could get involved in many different activities at Trust properties throughout England, Wales and Northern Ireland. You could work alongside a warden or gardener, assist house staff with aspects of running and preserving historic buildings and help with learning and events co-ordination. Training is provided and accommodation may be available. There's no pay, but out-of-pocket expenses are covered. For further information, contact the central volunteering team on 01793 817 632, visit the National Trust website at www.nationaltrust.org.uk/volunteering or email volunteers@nationaltrust.org.uk.

You can also volunteer for National Trust Working Holidays. Fruit picking and costume conservation are just two of the more unusual opportunities on offer. The Trust runs more than 400 conservation working holidays a year throughout England, Wales and Northern Ireland for as little as £85 for a week's full board and lodging (or from £50 for a weekend). They take place at beautiful Trust locations and are open to volunteers aged 18 and over (Youth Discovery Working Holidays are open to volunteers aged 16–18). For a current brochure, write to Working Holidays, Sapphire House, Roundtree Way, Norwich NR7 8SQ, phone the brochure line on 0844 800 3099, email working.holidays@nationaltrust.org.uk or see their website: www.nationaltrust.org.uk/workingholidays.

Archaeological digs

It won't earn you a fortune – more likely nothing (subsistence pay is rarely given)   but it can be fascinating work. See the special section included in every issue of *British Archaeology*, published six times a year by the Council for British Archaeology (CBA), St Mary's House, 66 Bootham, York YO30 9BZ, tel: 01904 671 417. The supplement gives full details of current UK digs. For subscription rates (including student reductions) and forms see the CBA website at www. britarch.ac.uk/shop/index.html. But the magazine should be available in public libraries and selected retail outlets. For full details of membership and digs in your area, see the CBA website, www.britarch.ac.uk/briefing/field.asp.

Alternatively, contact the county archaeologist for your district: their details are available from www.torc.org.uk/orgsearch.asp under 'local government archaeologists'. For archaeological digs abroad, phone Archaeology Abroad on 020 8537 0849. You may find local voluntary sector field projects you could join. The website www.torc.org.uk has a searchable directory where you could find details of local groups.

BTCV

BTCV runs around 252 conservation holidays worldwide throughout the year; prices start at about £60 for a weekend in the UK. Projects include pond maintenance, tree planting, step building, hedge laying, scrub clearance, dry-stone walling and community development. For more details, contact BTCV, Sedum House, Mallard Way, Doncaster DN4 8DB, tel: 01302 388 883, email: information@btcv.org.uk or browse and book online at www.btcv.org/shop.

In the case studies below, three students talk about their gap year and the skills they gained.

Laura's year

For her gap year, Laura decided to join her parents in Qatar, where they had just moved. Her original plan was to do work experience with the Al Jazeera news organisation. When that fell through, she got work with an English language school just five minutes' walk from home. In Qatar everyone is keen to learn English.

Teaching was a new experience for Laura: '"Don't worry, we'll give you a full course of instruction," they said.' But after one day of learning the ropes,

Laura was trying to control a class of boisterous six-year-olds. 'I'd been thrown in at the deep end, and I was not happy. They were very sweet, very chatty, and very determined – if they didn't want to do something, you couldn't make them.'

She found teaching adult classes suited her better. Everyone in Qatar has a smattering of English – gained from TV, films, pop music, the web – so even with no Arabic herself she could make progress, and she learned a lot about their culture. All teachers have to speak English, so she also found herself travelling out into the country to teach teachers – now that *was* a challenge.

She was well paid – £15 an hour, very different from the £5.83 she currently earns as a waitress in Scotland. During her gap year, Laura saved £5,000 towards her first year at St Andrews where she is studying English.

Skills gained:

- ▶ the joy of teaching
- ▶ self-confidence
- ▶ ability to adapt to different cultures.

Edward's year

Edward's gap year began to take off four weeks after the end of A levels when a friend contacted him to say he had a record contract with Universal as a singer-songwriter and needed a backing group. Would he like to join? No need to ponder the idea – this was far better than stacking shelves in the supermarket.

Edward had known his friend Ben Earle since he was six, when they were both choristers at St George's Choir School, Windsor and sang daily in Windsor Castle. But this was a very different kind of music. Edward was to play keyboard and provide backing vocals. What an opportunity! It was mostly recording sessions with the occasional gig. He earned £100 a week to be on stand-by to perform, plus expenses of around £20 a day. He met many stars, such as K. T. Tunstall and Amy Winehouse.

'At the same time, I was working to get my own break as a solo singer-songwriter. What I needed was performance exposure, and I found it through open mic nights at local pubs and a couple of times on local radio,' he says. He also built on his classical music experience and was asked to sing as a tenor with Keble College, Oxford. To eke out his earnings, he worked as a barman in his local. So when his friend and Universal parted company, Edward had plenty to fall back on.

Now in his second year at City University studying music, he has moved on from open mic nights and has done a number of solo gigs at different venues in London, including the Troubadour in Old Brompton Road, where the likes of Jimi Hendrix and Joni Mitchell once played, and Ginglik in Shepherd's Bush. His earnings are around £60 an hour – but only when he gets a paying job.

Skills gained:

- ▶ confidence
- ▶ belief in his own ability
- ▶ working an audience
- ▶ handling difficult situations.

Emily's year

From the moment she finished her A levels, Emily worked like crazy as a part-time restaurant supervisor to fund her gap year. She already had a deferred place at Falmouth in English and Media Studies, so she didn't have to hang around to sort that out.

At the end of November, her adventures began. She left to work with Ski Esprit in the French Alps. One week's training and she was dispatched to her ski season base at Plan Peisey in Les Arcs to work as a chalet assistant – cooking, cleaning and managing the chalet for 20 guests.

She had free accommodation, food, a lift pass and ski hire plus £56 a week. 'We had one day off and enough free time to go on the slopes five days a week,' she says. 'The night-life was great and there was a really friendly, fun atmosphere.'

As soon as the season ended in May she was off again, this time travelling and camping around France and Spain with her then boyfriend. 'We tried to live as cheaply as possible. I only spent £1,000 and had been away nine months.'

Over the year Emily earned around £4,000, but managed to save less than £1,000 towards university.

Skills gained:

▶ belief in her own ability
▶ happy dealing with situations outside her comfort zone
▶ chance to reinvent herself as an individual
▶ budgeting.

Ten Tips for a Gap Year

1. Decide what you want to do with your year – work, travel or both – then make a plan and stick to it.
2. Either secure your university place or, if you have one, ask for deferment before going travelling.
3. Work locally and live at home, you'll save more.
4. Make sure you travel with a reputable organisation – the Year Out Group (see page 165) is a good start.
5. Work out the cost before you go – with some voluntary projects it's you who pays. Factor in socialising, food, clothes and topping up your iPod when budgeting.
6. Check health regulations and take out health insurance. Get necessary vaccinations. Do you need a work permit and visas?
7. Make sure you have a return ticket or enough money to get home.
8. Arrange accommodation before you go.
9. Limit luggage to the amount you can carry yourself.
10. Don't run up credit card/bank debts: you'll do plenty of that once at uni.

Further information

What to read

- ▶ *The Gap-Year Guidebook*, published by John Catt Educational Ltd; website: www. johncattbookshop.com.
- ▶ *A Year Off ... A Year On?*, published by Lifetime Careers; website: www.lifetime-publishing.co.uk.
- ▶ *The Big Trip* by George Dunford, published by Lonely Planet; website: www. lonelyplanet.com.
- ▶ *Your Gap Year* by Susan Griffith, published by Vacation Work; website: www. trotman.co.uk.

A gap year for travel abroad

What employer is going to give you time off to travel the world? None. You will never, ever get a chance like this again. So if you have a yen to travel, make the most of your time, and budget wisely. Many on their gap year, especially those who take one after their studies, do it to travel. Some work before they go and see it as a great holiday. Others work their way around from country to country.

When you start to investigate the student travel scene, you'll discover that there's plenty of help available. The paths to the Far East, the kibbutz and Camp America are well worn. There is a plethora of publications and organisations, cheap travel firms, ticket concessions – even government advice – handed out to get you safely there and back. If that makes it all sound rather overplayed, pioneers can be accommodated.

Backpacking and inter-railing are always journeys into the unknown. Things rarely turn out exactly as you had envisaged. That's the excitement. I read somewhere that one gap year in three ends in disaster – make sure that one isn't yours. As for working your passage, most students do a wide range of jobs in a variety of countries before they get back home again. Skiing instructor, courier, au pair, grape-picker, summer camp assistant ... the *Guide to Student Money* found them all.

Further information

Who to contact

The Year Out Group (see page 165) has more than 30 organisations eagerly looking for willing students to help fulfil their travel dreams. Or you can try the following.

- AIESEC runs an international exchange programme – the Work Abroad Programme – which provides an opportunity for undergraduates and recent graduates to work for companies and other organisations throughout the world. Placements can last from two to 18 months. Typical placements are for marketing and business studies (Management Placement), IT and engineering (Technical Placement), teaching (Education Placement) and voluntary work or work for non-governmental organisations (Development Placement). AIESEC operates in 108 countries and is represented in 23 universities across the UK. Check out its website, www.aiesec.co.uk, or contact AIESEC UK, 29–31 Cowper Street, London EC2A 4AT, tel: 020 7549 1800.

- Au pair/nanny: try adverts in *The Lady* magazine and *The Times*; also see *The Au Pair and Nanny's Guide to Working Abroad* by Susan Griffith and Sharon Legg, published by Vacation Work.

- BUNAC – to meet the cash crisis facing many students, BUNAC organises various paid work and volunteer programmes for students and young people interested in working in the USA, Canada, Ghana, New Zealand, South Africa, Australia, Costa Rica, Cambodia, India, China and Peru (see information on the Year Out Group on page 165). Those working on the Summer Camp USA and Kitchen and Maintenance Programme (KAMP) will find that their air fares are paid in addition to all food and accommodation. Every year, BUNAC awards three scholarships of up to £1,000 each to help applicants cover the costs of taking part in a BUNAC working abroad programme to the USA or Canada. To enter the Green Cheese Scholarships, all you need to do is submit a humorous piece of original creative writing based on a travel-related topic. You're free to write about anything at all – whether it's a trip to the other side of the world or a journey you made closer to home. Entries should be no more than 1,500 words. Contact your university/college or BUNAC, 16 Bowling Green Lane, London EC1R 0QH, tel: 020 7251 3472, fax: 020 7251 0215, email: enquiries@bunac.org.uk or website: www.bunac.org.uk.

advice note

While hunting out an amazing adventure, bear in mind that one day you will need to impress a future employer, and what you decide to do now could give you the skills needed to secure a career. That trek through the jungle when a wild beast slunk off with the rations might provide the ideal answer to the question, 'Have you ever been faced with a challenge when your swift actions saved the day?' Even losing your tickets need not be a complete disaster and dismissed as incompetence, but turned into a useful instance of resourcefulness. Get the picture – always keep your CV in mind.

You can also try the internet: enter 'student gap year' in your favourite search engine and you'll have an amazing choice – Ultimate Gap Year, Global Gap Xperiences, Mad Adventures and the Gap Year Directory – which will offer you ideas of what to do, where to go and a range of special travel offers and much more besides.

What to read

All these titles are published by Vacation Work/Crimson Publishing, visit the website www.crimsonpublishing.co.uk.

- *Live and Work in ... France, Spain, Portugal, Italy, Germany, Belgium, the Netherlands and Luxembourg*: a series of books giving details of temporary and permanent work in various countries.
- *Summer Jobs Worldwide*: covers paid and unpaid job opportunities worldwide.
- *Teaching English Abroad*: guide to short- and long-term opportunities for both the trained and untrained in Eastern Europe, Greece, Turkey, Japan ... the choice is vast and varied.
- *Work Your Way Around the World*: offers authoritative advice on how to find work as you travel, with hundreds of first-hand accounts. Find out how to become a barmaid, kiwi-fruit packer, ski guide or jackaroo.
- *Your Gap Year*: a comprehensive guide to planning and embarking on a gap year.
- *Hands-on Holidays*: provides extensive information on short term working holidays ranging from conservation and humanitarian work to helping at festivals or on organic farms.

If you can't afford the books suggested in this chapter, look in your local library; nearly all the books mentioned here should be found in the reference section, and if they are not your library might well order them for you. A group of you might think it worthwhile buying some of the publications mentioned.

Thrift Tips

'It is much more economical to pay rent with bills included. It may look more expensive initially, but works out cheaper in the long run.'
Third-year Performing Arts student, Derby

'Work in a fast-food takeaway and eat your favourite junk food for free.'
Fourth-year English student, Cheltenham

'Choose flatmates the same size – it extends your wardrobe.'
First-year Animal Management student, Bradford

> *'Students have the time and the opportunity to travel and experience the "ideal" of freedom. You won't get that chance again.'*
>
> Loughborough University student, back from Africa

The student travel scene

It's all very well to whet your appetite for travel, but how are you going to manage to get to that exotic destination? This section looks briefly at the student travel scene.

As a student, can I get cheap travel abroad?

Yes: there are a number of travel organisations that operate special schemes for students. In fact, you will find they are vying for the privilege of sending you off on your travels, often dropping the price in the process. If you decide to take the cheapest, make sure it is a reputable organisation and a member of the Association of British Travel Agents (ABTA). It's better to be safe than stranded.

How do I go about getting cheap travel?

If you are already a student, your college's student travel office is the best place to start. There, you'll find experts who will understand your particular needs and financial restraints and are ready to give you advice. If you are taking a gap year, or your college has no travel office, try STA Travel, which is one of the biggest names in the student travel business. You can check them out on www.statravel.co.uk or call 0871 230 0040. If you prefer face-to-face contact, they have some 43 branches in or close to universities throughout the UK.

There are on-campus STA Travel offices at the University of Bath, Birmingham University, the University of London Union, Leeds University Union and the University of Warwick. High-street branches near universities include those in: Aberdeen, Belfast, Birmingham, Bournemouth, Brighton, Bristol, Cambridge, Canterbury, Cardiff, Dundee, Durham, Edinburgh, Exeter, Glasgow, Kingston, Leeds, Leicester, Liverpool, London, Manchester, Newcastle, Norwich, Nottingham, Oxford, Portsmouth, Preston, Reading, Sheffield, Southampton and in various locations around London.

STA Travel offers a great choice of adventure trips, conservation and volunteer projects, accommodation and language courses. As STA's Ian Swain says: 'Whether you want to coach rugby in Fiji, take an African safari, InterRail around Europe or simply need a cheap flight home, STA Travel can help you get there.'

Also big on the student travel scene is the International Student Travel Confederation (ISTC) with 500 offices in 120 countries (including 33 in the UK) and some 10 million students and youth travellers on the move. Their website, www.istc.org, is a must for any would-be adventurer. Make sure you have an International Student Identity Card (ISIC): it gives you an entrée to an amazing range of around-the-world opportunities. See details below.

What should I join or get before setting off?

▶ ISIC: £9. The card offers you thousands of discounts in the UK and around the world – from high-street stores to hotels and hostels, weekend breaks (although not unless you take their SY airfare), flights, buses, trains, restaurants, guidebooks, entertainment, attractions, museums, galleries, CDs to travel gear, gym memberships, software and eating out. You can also get low-cost international calls and texts in over 100 countries, free voicemail and an international travel emergency helpline via the ISIConnect phone and SIM card. ISIC is available to all full-time students. See www.isic.org for details of where you can get your card, or pop in to STA Travel.

▶ International Youth Travel Card (IYTC): £9. If you are not a full-time student but are aged 26 or under, the IYTC is for you. It offers fantastic discounts and ISIConnect services, available through ISIC (see above) or STA Travel.

advice note *i*

The web is a great source for cheap travel and excellent deals for students, but make sure you are dealing with a reputable firm. Never pay full fare on bus, coach, train or plane. Take advantage of rail and coachcards, shops selling bargain tickets, classified ads, chartered flights, stand-by fares, advance bookings and deals offered by student travel companies. Some of the budget airlines are giving the most fantastic deals.

▶ Youth Hostel Association (YHA): £9.95. YHA (England and Wales) Ltd offers access to UK and international youth hostels. Changes made to membership rules a couple of years ago mean that you don't even have to be a member to use their youth hostels. Non-members just pay a £3 a night supplement, or £1.50 per night for under-18s. However, you do need a membership card to use all Hostelling International (HI) member hostels in other countries. An annual card is now down to £10. A two-year card costs £16.50 and a three-year card £20.95 (if you are under 26). There are more than 4,000 HI Hostels across 80 countries and they all have assured standards for hygiene and safety. An annual card for those over 26 costs £15.50, but couples can buy a joint annual card for £22.95. To join the YHA, write to YHA, Trevelyan House, Dimple Road, Matlock, Derbyshire DE4 3YH, tel: 01629 592 700 or visit www.yha.org.uk.

- 16–25 Railcard: £26. This entitles all young people aged 16–25 to a third off most rail fares in the UK. Did you know that it also covers the London all-zone One-Day Travel Card? See the leaflet for travel restrictions and useful discounts. (Mature students of 26 and over in full-time education are also included.)

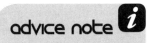

advice note ℹ

Cards to carry checklist

- 16–25 Railcard: £26
- 16 to 26 Coachcard: £10
- ISIC: £9
- IYTC under-26 card: £9
- YHA card: £9.95.

- 16 to 26 Coachcard: £10. This entitles all students aged 17 and over to a third off National Express and Scottish Citylink fares, and also some continental and Irish services – check with your local coach station or Victoria Coach Station, London, or phone the National Express Call Centre on 0870 580 8080.

What is InterRail?

InterRail gives you the flexibility to see Europe the way you want to – you can go where you like, when you like. Your InterRail pass gives you unlimited travel on the extensive network that covers over 30 European countries. Choose a one-country pass from £32 or a global pass from £152. It is available to European citizens and anyone who has been resident here for six months. Passes are available from STA Travel – pop into a branch, call 0871 230 0040 or visit www.statravel.co.uk.

Further information

Who else could I consult?

The national tourist office or board – many countries have one in this country and most are based in London. London telephone directories can usually be found in the reference section of your local library.

What to read

The *Rough Guide* books and *Lonely Planet* series cover almost every country and provide a useful insight into an area. Cost varies according to the country covered – try your local library.

As a student, do I need insurance?

Yes! Don't leave home without it. Travel insurance is often the last thing you think about, but it's the first thing you'll need if something goes wrong. Some

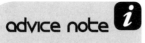

advice note

Find out about any rail passes offered by individual European countries. STA Travel should be able to help you out – 0871 230 0040 or www.statravel. co.uk.

work camps and voluntary agencies arrange insurance for those taking part in projects. Check this out, and check what it covers. There are certain reciprocal arrangements for medical treatment in some EU countries: you will need to apply for a European Health Insurance Card (www.ehic.org), but remember this may not cover all medical expenses, and your property won't be covered if it's stolen.

STA Travel offers three levels and three geographical areas of cover to suit every trip, whether your bag is bungee jumping, whitewater rafting or snowboarding, or even just soaking up the sun, from at little as 32p a day. (This assumes you are under 35 years of age and taking out European Budget cover for a period of 24 months.) Contact STA Travel on 0871 230 0040 or www.statravel.co.uk, or visit one of their branches.

Some banks offer travel insurance and you may get a good discount as part of the student package – see Chapter 11, page 262–264. Endsleigh's travel products are also designed to reflect the lifestyles of their customers, especially students, and they suit all types of holiday and travel experience. The firm offers a choice of cover options including basic, essential and comprehensive benefits in the UK, Europe or worldwide. Contact Endsleigh Insurance on 0800 028 3571 or www.endsleigh.co.uk.

Thrift Tips from Oxbridge

'Enter competitions you see. Sell things you don't need. Use teabags twice.'
Economics student

'eBay.co.uk is fantastic for selling anything.'
Veterinary Medicine student

'Get involved in student marketing and police ID parades – it means a little cash to make life easier.'
Chemistry student

'Mystery shopping! www.gapbuster.com: quick, good money.'
English and Drama student

Just a few examples: type 'student travel insurance' into your search engine and a host of names will come up. Be warned: read the small print before committing yourself. You don't want to be stranded on the other side of the world with a broken leg because of a legal loophole.

Table 39 Most popular full-time first degree courses with students starting in 2009

Degree subject	Number of students
Law (by area)	17,527
Design Studies	16,912
Psychology	15,314
Computer Science	11,461
Business Studies	10,991
Management Studies	10,969
English Studies	10,379
Combined Business and Administration	10,371
Sports Science	9,224
Combined Social Studies/Business/Law with arts/humanities subjects	8,671

Note: If the figures for Pre-clinical Medicine (7,977) and Pre-clinical Dentistry (1,215) had been combined, as in past years, they would have come in at number ten
Source: UCAS student returns 2009

Sponsorship

This chapter is a brief guide to getting sponsorship, and what to expect from it. The major topics covered here are:

Sponsors and sponsorship

Probably the best and most comprehensive way of raising extra finance to help you through higher education is sponsorship. It gives you money during term time and paid work during the vacations.

In this chapter we look at sponsorship, the changes to the sponsorship market that have been taking place recently and some of the companies most likely to offer sponsorship. But you have to face the fact that sponsorship is getting harder and harder to find in the current economic climate.

What is sponsorship?

You've heard of big companies sponsoring events such as the London Marathon, the FA Cup and cricket test matches – it means that they back the event with money. In the same way, an organisation could sponsor you through university.

Who gives sponsorship?

▶ Employers – mainly large companies, banks, accountancy firms etc. (see also the Power Academy, page 186).

Fast Facts on Sponsorship

Who gives it?
▶ Major companies

When?
▶ For a full course
▶ After first year of study
▶ After industrial placement
▶ For final study year

To whom?
▶ Degree and HND students

Most sponsored subject
▶ Engineering

Most likely sponsors
▶ Manufacturing and production companies

What it's worth
▶ £2,000 p.a. approx. bursary
▶ £1,208 per month approx. for work periods

Other plus points
▶ Work experience – industrial placement, additional skills

Will it secure a job?
▶ Helpful, but no guarantee

- The three armed forces (see page 198).
- Ministry of Defence – Defence Engineering and Science Group (DESG) www.desg. mod.uk (see page 188).
- Professional bodies e.g. IMechE (see page 208).
- Universities, on behalf of employers.

Sponsorship of university students has been going on for many years. It was originally started to attract more young people into engineering. Even today, engineering is the major area where sponsorship can be found.

Why do companies give sponsorship?

The reasons most often given by employers are: to have access to high-quality students before they graduate, with the hope of future employment; to assess students over a longer period as potential employees; to develop a student's skills and have an input into their training; and to publicise the company as a potential employer among other students. Or in their own words:

'The opportunity to see trainees in work situations before graduation.'

'Input of fresh ideas into the company.'

'Gives students a chance to look at us and us a chance to look at them before job offer made.'

How does sponsorship work?

There are no hard-and-fast rules – every company devises its own scheme. In principle it works like this.

As a sponsored student you would get training, work experience and financial help while at college – to varying extents, depending on the company scheme. You might be asked to work for a whole year in the company either before or during your course; or you might only be expected to work during the summer vacations.

In return, the sponsor gets the opportunity to develop close ties with 'a potentially good employee' and influence your development. There is generally no commitment on either side to employment after the sponsorship. However, since the company has invested a considerable amount of money in you as a student, it is unlikely not to offer you a job.

Check out the Power Academy

The Power Academy is an engineering scholarship fund launched in 2004 for students studying an Institution of Engineering and Technology (IET)-accredited degree course at a partner university. It is backed by the IET, seven universities and 16 companies in the power industry.

There are over 60 scholarships available in 2010 to students studying at the University of Bath, University of Cardiff, Imperial College London, University of Strathclyde, University of Manchester, University of Southampton and Queen's University Belfast for the full length of their courses.

The sponsorship offers:

► £2,200 annual bursary

► payment towards university fees

► £220 book allowance

► summer vacation work

► free membership of the IET

► annual seminar for all Academy-sponsored students.

Why such generosity? The Power Academy was set up because there is a shortage of good power graduates coming out of our universities and the industry could be facing a crisis. It is anticipated that 25% of the power industry's current engineering workforce will retire over the next 15 years, and there are not enough good people around to fill the vacancies. So it looks as if there could be some good jobs available in the future.

The companies involved include CE Electric, E.ON, EDF Energy, National Grid, Scottish and Southern Energy, Scottish Power, Western Power Distribution, EA Technology, Siemens, ABB, AREVA T&D, Atkins Power, RWE npower, Rolls-Royce, UKAEA and NIE. To find out more, visit www.theiet.org/poweracademy.

What would sponsorship mean to me?

There are many types of sponsorship. Generally, it will include a bursary given while you are studying and paid work experience, which is usually at the going rate for somebody of your age. In financial terms, it would probably mean that you would be around £40–£80 a week better off than your contemporaries during term time, with guaranteed work for at least eight weeks during the summer. But it's not just about money – the work experience and training are valuable assets, too.

The question of cash

Looking at it purely in cash terms sponsorship could provide:

▶ £1,500–£3,500 annual bursary, average £2,000 approx, given during academic study. For manufacturing and production students it could be higher. The armed forces give higher rates still, but they have a different kind of arrangement.

▶ Salary £1,200–£1,500 monthly, but could be more. This is what you could expect to earn when working for your sponsor. However, salaries are generally age-related, so a third-year student would earn appreciably more than a pre-university student.

Employers' additional costs

From the employer's point of view, the costs don't stop there. Generally sponsorship includes training, which may well mean several weeks at their training centre. Some companies provide a personal tutor for students. There are also courses and meetings to arrange work experience. All this takes time, and time costs money. Every time somebody stops to tell you how to do something, it's work time lost to the employer.

Will my sponsorship bursary affect what I get as my financial support package?

Any scholarship or sponsorship you receive should not be included when calculating how much loan, grant and uni bursary you can have. Money earned during vacations is also not included. So for a normal sponsorship, the answer is probably no.

Application for sponsorship

How do I get sponsored?

There are various possibilities.

▶ You apply to a company that offers sponsorships. These are generally offered to students doing specific subjects.

▶ You are offered sponsorship after a period of work experience.

▶ Your university has contacts with employers.

What subjects are most likely to attract sponsorship?

Engineering outstrips any other subject, with the largest number of sponsorships being found in the manufacturing and production sector. However, there are opportunities for civil engineers in the construction industry.

Many employers look for subjects with a close link to their own business activities. Good examples are food science, quantity surveying and polymer technology. So if you feel you are studying a degree relevant to a company's business it is worth a try.

A few organisations, especially in the financial sector, will sponsor people on any degree course, but you have to have an interest in finance.

Ministry of Defence: DESG Sponsorship Scheme

▶ The aim of the DESG student sponsorship scheme is to help you explore the variety of careers available in the Ministry of Defence (MoD) while gaining valuable work experience.

▶ There is no commitment to work for the MoD on graduation, but obviously they hope that you will.

▶ A bursary of £1,500 p.a. will be given while studying.

▶ You get guaranteed work experience at an MoD establishment in the UK during summer vacations; competitive rates of pay (salary review in August).

▶ Work placements are designed to give valuable experience to

engineers and scientists, so expect a challenging project that will make a real difference to the team you are working with.

▶ All students will be assigned a mentor who will help them select summer placements and provide advice on professional development.

▶ The scheme is open to those studying an approved engineering or science degree in a UK university and who are likely to achieve a 2:2 degree or better. (See www.desg.mod.uk for subject list.)

▶ Check www.desg.mod.uk/downloads/sponsorship_fact_sheet.pdf for more details and www.desg.mod.uk for an online application form and to go through the exercises.

When could I get sponsorship?

- ▶ After A levels or BTEC for a full degree or HND course.
- ▶ After a gap year spent with a company between A levels and HE.
- ▶ After your first year of study.
- ▶ After a successful period of work experience or an industrial placement year.
- ▶ For your final year of study.

While sponsorships are still given to A level students for their full three to four years of academic study, more and more companies are choosing to sponsor students later in their degree course when they have established a commitment to the subject. Work placements and sponsorships are now considered to be one of the best graduate recruitment tools by large employers.

'The sponsorship market has changed. Companies have certainly cut back on numbers and many offer only a final-year sponsorship, but I think it has reached its trough. Many of the smaller organisations that only want one or two sponsorship students are now going straight to the universities of their choice and asking for who they want. This is largely to avoid having to deal with the thousands of applications which advertising in our publication would engender. There are some good sponsorships around which are well worth going after.'

The University Schools Liaison Officer of ImechE

What to expect when applying for sponsorship

The application form

These are more likely to be online than paper forms, and you need to think carefully when filling them in because you only get one chance. Mess it up and your application will go no further. Employers are – quite naturally – looking for the brightest and best students to sponsor; they want to have the pick of the potential high-flyers at an early stage. If you are applying for sponsorship before you start university, you may only have GCSE results, possibly some AS level results and a head teacher's report to show what you are capable of. This can be tough on those who wake up academically after GCSE or who really excel only in their one chosen subject. But good employers are more aware than you might expect; selection is not on academic qualifications alone.

Sponsors are looking for signs of those additional qualities needed to succeed in your chosen career: leadership potential, the ability to grasp ideas quickly and to work in a team. They want ambitious, innovative people with get-up-

and-go who can think for themselves and get things done. So if your GCSE grades slipped a bit – or, as one student we interviewed put it, 'you look like Mr Average on paper' – think through what else you have been doing. Playing in the football or hockey team, helping out at the local club, hiking across Europe, getting a pop group together … it could help to redress the balance. Remember: the application form is the first weeding-out process and you are up against stiff competition. This is no time for false modesty – you've got to sell yourself for all you're worth.

The interview

Interviews vary enormously. Some companies give a full-scale assessment with psychometric testing and tricky questioning and watch how you respond to certain situations. Others are much more laid back and go for a straight interview. Whatever the process, if you are an A level student it will probably be something quite new to you. Don't worry. The company will be fully aware of this and will not ask you to do something you are not capable of. Remember, too, that your competitors will be in much the same position. Still, don't expect an easy time at an interview.

How Alex got her sponsorship

Alex is 22 and has just graduated from Manchester University. This is her story.

'Out of the blue, a letter arrived from Manchester University saying Procter & Gamble were offering sponsorships and would I like to apply? Would I!

'I had applied to Manchester to study Chemical Engineering with Chemistry; I had a provisional place, but A levels were still several months away. If I was interested, I had to apply direct to Procter & Gamble – online. Having filled in my application form, I was then asked to complete a "personality test", again online.

'Next, I went to Manchester to take yet another test, this time "critical thinking". This was in two parts – an English section and a lateral thinking section. I was told it was the same test given to graduates wanting to join the company. It was not exactly difficult, but certainly challenging. I think if you didn't have an engineer's mind you might struggle. We were told the results right away.

'Two weeks later I was back in Manchester for an interview. I was very nervous and a bit scared. By now I had learnt this was a new sponsorship programme being set up and that there were just two or possibly three sponsorships available – 25 students had applied. My chances of success were slim.

'I had never done anything like this before. It was a one-to-one interview with the head of the sponsorship programme. Most of the questions were based on how you would cope in difficult situations and leading a team – and they wanted examples. Fortunately, I had been on the Duke of Edinburgh's Award Scheme, so I had plenty of examples of leadership. But it was tough. You had to think on your feet and concentrate hard.'

Alex was successful. In her first year, she received a bursary for her academic year and then worked for Procter & Gamble at a plant in Essex for around 11 weeks during the summer. She was engaged on the environmental side and undertook her own project. Having paid for her accommodation in Essex, she used some of the money she earned, about £4,200, to pay off her university debts of around £2,000.

Of her work experience, she says: 'It was brilliant, the Procter & Gamble people were very welcoming and supportive. I learnt a lot about day-to-day life and issues of working in a process plant as well as developing my technical knowledge. I also made some good friends.'

The following summer, Alex worked at Procter & Gamble's Manchester plant. She undertook two projects: one involved looking at new equipment and the other gave her experience in day-to-day production on the plant. The highlight of her internship was a business trip with another employee to Poland where she had a fantastic few days in Warsaw.

The internship lasted ten weeks and she earned £1,650 a month. She used the money to have a good time, go on holiday and pay off her overdraft. With the offer of a job at Procter & Gamble when she graduated firmly in the bag, the firm gave her the option to have her final summer vacation off and not do an internship. She took this up and travelled in India and

Spain. She graduated last summer and has now joined Procter & Gamble in process engineering management, all as a result of her sponsorship.

What Alex received

First year

- ▶ Bursary of £1,500 p.a. (she used this to cover her fees and books)
- ▶ Ten weeks' guaranteed work experience during the summer (she did 11 weeks)
- ▶ Pay of £1,650 a month – £4,200 in total
- ▶ Entrée to the Procter & Gamble staff shop – 'Anyone fancy a Pringle?'

Second year

- ▶ Bursary of £1,500 p.a.
- ▶ Ten weeks' guaranteed work during the summer at £1,650 a month

Third year

- ▶ Bursary of £2,000 p.a.

Fourth year

- ▶ Bursary of £2,000 p.a.

Estimated total: £16,500.

Work experience

Students gain amazing experience during placements – but you should make sure it is the right experience for you. It is important not to be so mesmerised by the bursary money that you don't consider what the company offering sponsorship does and whether it can provide experience that will help your career. The down side to a sponsorship is that during your degree all your work experience will be in one company and, because of this, it can shape the direction of your future career. When you go for your interview, ask about the experience and training you can expect and the skills you will acquire.

Terms and conditions

How much time do I have to spend with my sponsor?

Some sponsors demand you spend a year working with them either during your course or for a gap year before university. Others give you the choice.

Most stipulate summer vacation work of six to eight weeks. Students often ask for more and may do Easter vacation work as well. Engineering firms are generally more demanding and the sponsorship is more likely to be geared to a sandwich course, so you could be looking at a full year in industry plus two summer vacation placements.

Planned vacation work

Some companies will hold special vacation planning sessions. These are usually during the Easter vacation and can last anything up to a week. During these sessions, you might plan with your sponsor how you want to spend your summer vacation time.

Sponsors occasionally allow their sponsored students to gain experience in other companies during vacations, as they feel that it will help to broaden their mind and knowledge. But most are loath to do so, for obvious reasons.

Thrift Tips

'Get a bike.'
First-year Geography student, St Andrews

'Swap socialising for work so you don't drink.'
Second-year Politics/Philosophy student, Durham

Am I obliged to join my sponsor after graduating? Are they obliged to employ me?

No, you are not obliged to join your sponsoring company after graduating, unless it says so in your contract. Equally, they are not obliged to offer you a job. But there is no doubt that companies are taking a tougher stand these days, and seeking value for money from their sponsorships. For example:

▶ some companies will stop your bursary payment for the final year if you don't agree to join them after graduating

▶ a few companies demand reimbursement of their sponsorship money if you don't join them. You would have been informed of this before you agreed to a sponsorship

It's a Fact

Employers recruit from students who undertake work experience with them. Employers offer work experience or sponsorship as part of their recruitment strategy.

► some companies only give sponsorship for the final year after a job offer has been accepted.

Can my sponsor terminate my sponsorship?

Sponsorship is a legal contract. Look at the terms carefully. Most agreements will have a clause that allows the employer to withdraw if your academic performance is unsatisfactory. There may be other clauses you should watch out for.

What exactly is meant by academic performance?

If you fail the odd exam, you're probably all right, but if your end-of-year results are so bad that you have to repeat the year, you may find that your sponsor is no longer interested.

Other aspects to consider

How do I choose a sponsor?

'Be practical – go for the cash' was one student's advice on selecting a sponsor. Certainly cash is something to bear in mind, but there are many other factors to consider.

advice note *i*

The armed forces are slightly different from other employers; they have always included service as part of their sponsorship schemes.

► Compare salaries for work experience and bursaries: the plus on one might cancel out the minus on the other.

► Check out the training for engineers – is the training accredited by the appropriate institution? And the experience: is it a well-organised programme of development or are you just another pair of hands?

► Talk to students on the scheme: find out about projects undertaken; how many sponsored students joined the company as graduates?

► Where would you be located? Do they provide accommodation if away from home? Are there opportunities to gain experience abroad?

► Finally, ask yourself – is it the kind of company where you would want to make your career?

When should I apply for sponsorship?

► Full degree course sponsorship: some companies offer sponsorship for your full degree course. Applications for these schemes should be made early in your final school year, and at least by the time you submit your UCAS form.

► Second-year degree course sponsorship: some sponsors like to see a commitment to your course before offering sponsorship. Applications should be made early in your first year at university. Ask your head of department for likely sponsors.

► Final-year degree course sponsorship: increasingly, employers are offering sponsorship to students for just the final year of their degree course. Often this will be offered after a successful industrial placement year or summer vacation period. Employers offering sponsorship at this stage will expect students to agree to join them after graduation.

advice note *i*

► Make sure any literature you are reading on sponsorship is up to date – school and college careers libraries are notorious for displaying last year's information.

► Look at your contract in detail and, above all, check the small print.

► Question your sponsor; they will respect you for that.

What's the competition for sponsorship?

Phenomenal. All sponsors say that applications outstrip sponsorships available, and it is getting worse – so get in early. The earlier you apply the better. Applications for full course sponsorship should have been made by the time you submit your UCAS form.

What is a sponsor looking for?

A straw poll of sponsors suggested that sponsors favour students with:

► good A level (or equivalent) grades

► maturity

► potential

► ambition

► evident team skills

► sense of humour

► hard-working attitude

► ability to get a good second-class degree

► interest in their degree topic

► ability to assimilate information and learn quickly

► a spark that sets you apart from the rest

► business awareness

► interpersonal skills.

Which comes first: UCAS or sponsorship?

They both come at once, which makes for complications. However, both sides are aware of this, so a system has been worked out. First, you should discover whether a sponsor you are interested in requires you to gain a place on a particular course – if so, you should name that course on your UCAS form.

However, it could happen that an employer you had not originally been very interested in offers you a sponsorship with the proviso that you gain a place on a course not named in your selection on your application form. While UCAS does not generally allow students to make alterations to their original application, in the case of sponsorship they usually relax this rule.

What about deferred entry?

Another complication is whether you want deferred entry or not. If you get sponsorship, your sponsor may require you to do a pre-degree year in industry, but at application time you may not know this. If in doubt, apply for the current year. It is always easier to ask a university to defer your entry rather than bring it forward. On some courses, especially popular courses such as law, deferment may be more difficult to arrange.

Will my university find me sponsorship?

If you are accepted on to a course either conditionally or unconditionally, it is always a good idea to ask the course director if they know of any sponsoring companies. Often they will have a list. Some students will find that they are automatically offered sponsors to apply to, and on some courses that are actually sponsored by employers the sponsors are involved in the selection procedure. College prospectuses may give you some guidance. A number of universities advertise sponsored courses in *Engineering Opportunities for School Leavers, Students and Graduates* – for details see 'What to read' at the end of this chapter.

Not all sponsors advertise

If you look down the list of sponsors in most sponsorship books, you will be surprised how many large companies appear not to offer sponsorship or work experience. Yet in fact they do. Many companies just don't bother to advertise – the requests flood in anyway. Others have special relationships with selected schools or universities. So just because a company doesn't advertise sponsorship, that shouldn't stop you from asking.

Don't forget the smaller companies

If you're thinking in terms of your CV, it must be admitted that a well-known name will carry more weight than a smaller company. But with a smaller, little-known company there is less competition. Perhaps more important, you are likely to be treated as an individual. You may well be the only sponsored student they have and you can develop your own training and experience package. Of course, if they have no experience of sponsored students, they may not know what you are capable of and what experience you should be getting. So you could find you have to stand up for yourself.

Is it best to apply to local companies?

It is always best to apply to a company that interests you. Nevertheless, some companies do prefer to take on local people. From their point of view, there is no accommodation problem when it comes to work experience, and statistics show that many students want to return to their home town to work when they complete their studies. So the company is more likely to keep the sponsored student as an employee.

Will sponsorship be good for my CV?

Yes, but with reservations – 73% of the companies we asked said sponsorship was a plus point. The others felt that it made little difference. A careers adviser at the University of Bath said that, while sponsorship shows that you have been 'selected', it was the work experience that would be seen as the important element on a CV.

Of course, prospective employers will probably ask why you didn't join the company that sponsored you, so you will need to have a well-phrased answer. Most employers realise that a decision made at the age of 18 may not look so right when you are 22. It's always worth remembering that a would-be employer may write to your sponsor for a reference, so it's important to leave your sponsoring company on good terms.

Should I try the armed forces?

The three armed forces offer very generous sponsorships, which can cover fees and full living costs. But their Cadetship and Bursary schemes are not open-ended. There is a service commitment involved and those taking them up should think very carefully about what they are getting involved in. Full details are available from:

▶ Army Officer Entry, Freepost LON15 445, Bristol BS38 7UE, tel: 0845 730 0111 or websites: www.army.mod.uk or www.armyjobs.mod.uk

▶ Royal Air Force, Officer Careers, Freepost 4335, Bristol BS1 3YX, tel: 0845 605 5555 or website: www.raf.mod.uk/careers

▶ Royal Navy and Royal Marines Careers Service, Department BR211, Freepost GL672, Cirencester GL7 1BR, tel: 0845 607 5555 or website: www.royalnavy.mod.uk/careers.

Will I pay tax on my bursary?

You do not have to pay tax on a bursary. But if your annual earned income is above the tax threshold – currently £6,475 (2010–2011) – you would have to pay tax. So in theory, a year's placement would not be tax-free.

However, since your year's work probably falls into two tax years you may find you pay very little or none at all.

Can I get sponsorship once I've started my degree?

Yes. As we said in the 'When should I apply for sponsorship?' section, more and more companies are giving sponsorship just for the final year or from the second year of a course. These sponsorships often develop from a successful period of work experience during the summer vacations or through an industrial placement during a sandwich course.

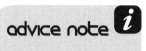

advice note

Were you unlucky in securing sponsorship? Try the back door.

When you're looking for a summer vacation job, seek out companies that you feel could be interested in sponsoring your particular skills. You may be lucky, and there's no harm in asking.

Should sponsorship determine which course I choose?

In theory, no. First you should decide on the course that best suits you. You're going to spend at least three solid years – and possibly more – studying, so make sure you're going to enjoy it, otherwise the results could be at best disappointing and at worst disastrous.

I'm a sponsored student, but find I don't like the course I'm studying: what can I do?

This happens. You choose a course in something that you may never have studied before, and after a term or so you discover that you and the subject just don't get along together. A sponsorship is not a life sentence, and neither is a degree course. Talk first to your college tutor. It may be just one aspect of the course you don't like. Then talk to your sponsor. You will probably be able to change your degree course, but it may be more difficult – or impossible – for your sponsor to put you on an appropriate sponsorship scheme. Don't despair.

Whatever you do, be frank about your change of heart – and the sooner the better, before too much time or money is wasted.

To sum up

What do I gain from being sponsored?

- ► Money – probably an annual bursary plus good rates of pay when working.
- ► Training – most sponsorships will involve some form of training.
- ► Meaningful work experience.
- ► Guaranteed employment for the summer in an area that will assist you with your studies.
- ► Chance of future employment – but no guarantee.
- ► Help with final-year project work – possibly.
- ► Opportunity to gain first-hand knowledge of the working environment where you might possibly start your career.
- ► Understanding of what it means to work in industry.
- ► Chance to gain new skills.
- ► Plus-point to put in your CV.

What do I lose?

- ► Your holiday time is not your own. So, for example, you would not be able to spend the whole summer abroad going InterRailing.
- ► You have the chance to see only one industry or company during work experience.
- ► You make a career choice at 18 that may not be what you want at 21.
- ► You may be obliged to work for a company whether you want to or not because of a payback clause.

▶ You may be asked to work in locations that are not very appealing and possibly a long way from home.

Further information

Who to contact

▶ The Year in Industry (YINI – see page 157).

▶ Local employers that interest you – many employers prefer to sponsor local students.

▶ Don't forget the smaller companies. Some may never have thought of offering sponsorship before, so it can be a matter of making yourself sound like a good bet.

▶ Your course director.

▶ Your university or college may well have a list of sponsors who are interested in sponsoring students on your particular course. Some universities advertise in the books listed below.

▶ Black and Asian high-flyers can also try the Windsor Fellowship Undergraduate personal and professional development programmes, which include summer work placements and community work. Application forms and further information can be downloaded from www.windsorfellowship.org/leadership.

What to read

▶ *Everything You Wanted to Know about Sponsorship, Placements and Graduate Opportunities*, regularly updated and published by Amoeba Publications – see the website: www.everythingyouwantedtoknow.com.

▶ *Engineering Opportunities for School Leavers, Students and Graduates*, published by the IMechE on behalf of the engineering profession. It lists sponsors, universities with sponsored courses and companies offering industrial placements and internships. The book is available free from IMechE c/o Marketing & Communications Department, 1 Birdcage Walk, London SW1H 9JJ or email: education@imeche.org.uk.

▶ *University Scholarships, Awards & Bursaries*, published by Trotman, website: www.trotman.co.uk.

CHAPTER 9

Other sources to tap

In this chapter we investigate all the other legitimate sources of finance you could tap to raise extra cash, and how to set about approaching them. They include trusts, charitable awards, scholarships, grants, bursaries (from sources other than Student Finance England, your local authority or university) and competitions. The topics covered in this chapter are:

Other sources of finance: a reality or a vain hope?

You'd be right to be a little sceptical. If there were a prodigious number of organisations all eager to hand out money to students, you wouldn't have seen so many student demonstrations highlighting their financial plight or stories in the press about the difficulties students face. But there are a surprising number of educational charities, trust funds and foundations, professional bodies and benevolent funds in this country that offer financial help to students. This may take the form of a scholarship or charitable award. One directory of grant-making trusts we consulted listed over 1,500 organisations under the broad heading of 'Education'. But before you get too excited and think you've found the route to a crock of gold, be aware that when you start sifting through the many restrictions by which trusts generally have to abide, you soon realise there are relatively few – if any – that could meet your exact needs.

What is a scholarship?

Scholarships differ from sponsorships in that they provide money while you study but without the industrial training. They can, of course, be for a specific purpose such as travel, to fund some special area of research or possibly to study abroad. They are usually, though not always, given by an institution – this could be your university, a professional institute or a charitable trust – rather than by individual companies.

Competition is keen. Awards can be made on grounds of academic achievement or need. Whatever the criteria, they are not going to come your way without considerable effort and often disappointment, so be prepared. Nobody gives money away easily.

it's a fact

Who gives bursaries and scholarships?
Charitable trusts, universities and colleges, professional bodies and institutions.

How much?
From £12 to £4,000 and everything in between.

What is the success rate?
Low.

How does a scholarship differ from a bursary?

It doesn't, really. Look up 'scholarship' in the dictionary and you'll find the definition is 'award of money towards education'. Look up 'bursary' and it says 'scholarship or grant awarded to students'. Sometimes, a bursary is awarded if you meet certain criteria. For example, bursaries are given to low-income students under certain funding arrangements – English students should see Chapter 2, Scottish, Welsh and Northern Irish students should look at Chapter 4, and all other students, including nurses and midwives, for whom the bursary isn't means-tested, turn to Chapter 5. To win a scholarship there is more likely to be an element of achievement (for example, academic, musical or sporting).

What is a charitable award?

The difference between a scholarship and a charitable award is, again, very indistinct, and you could say there is no difference at all, as charitable awards can often be scholarships. Charitable awards are always paid out by a charitable organisation, which must abide by the terms and conditions of the original endowment. So, however good and reasonable your case may be, if the money has to be paid out to a student from Gloucester studying Chemistry, it is no good being an arts student from Leeds (or even from Gloucester). To claim an award, both you and your financial predicament must fit the charity's help profile.

What kind of awards are available?

Often the payments are small – to buy books or equipment – but they can be quite substantial and cover fees or maintenance. So the amount of money available could range from a few hundred pounds to a few thousand. They can be one-off payments, or given each year for the duration of your course.

Who gives scholarships and charitable awards?

Universities, schools, trust funds, professional institutions.

Finding out about scholarships and charitable awards

Can my school help me?

Yes. Most schools will have a list of local charities that offer help to students. The fact that you have been to the school could be a condition of receiving a grant. Also try your primary school. It is a good idea to find out whether such scholarships, grants and charitable awards are available before you send off your UCAS application, as these sometimes stipulate a certain HE establishment.

Can my local authority (LA) help?

Your LA should have details of any local charities offering help to students in higher education. Also try the following.

► The Welsh Assembly, which offers bursaries to Welsh-born students attending Welsh universities.

► The Carnegie Trust for the Universities of Scotland, which provides financial assistance to students of Scottish birth or who have at least one parent born in Scotland or who have completed at least two years' secondary education in Scotland and who want to attend a Scottish university to study for a first degree. They also offer vacation scholarships to enable undergraduates at Scottish universities to undertake a research project during the long vacation. Scholarships are also given to graduates from Scottish universities with a first-class honours degree for three years' postgraduate research at a university in the UK, usually in Scotland. Contact the Carnegie Trust for the Universities of Scotland, Andrew Carnegie House, Pittencrief Street, Dunfermline, Fife KY12 8AW, tel: 01383 724 990, fax: 01383 749 799, email: jgray@carnegie-trust.org or website: www. carnegie-trust.org.

► SAAS, which maintains a register of educational endowments of Scottish trusts, many of which are local and open only to Scottish-born students who want to attend Scottish universities and colleges. The agency will search the register on behalf of any student who submits an enquiry form. Forms are available from SAAS, Gyleview House, 3 Redheughs Rigg, South Gyle, Edinburgh EH12 9HH, tel: 0131 476 8212, email: saas.geu@scotland.gsi.gov.uk or website: www.saas.gov.uk. See also 'What to read', page 218, for directories and registers of trusts.

Check out your parents' employers!

… or at least get your parents to. A surprising number of companies and large employers have special trusts set up to help with the education of their employees' or former employees' children. Typical examples are:

► the National Police Fund, which helps the children of people who are serving in or have served in the police force

► the Royal Medical Benevolent Fund, which helps the children of medical graduates, and the Dain Fund Charities Committee (contact the British Medical Association – www.bma.org.uk), which helps the children of registered members of the medical profession

► the Royal Pinner School Foundation, which helps the children of sales representatives.

Do universities and colleges give scholarships?

Some HE institutions are endowed by generous benefactors and can award scholarships and bursaries to selected students who meet the required criteria. Usually an institution will have a very mixed bag of awards that bear very little relation to its academic strengths and interests. Most establishments don't give many awards, and competition in the past has been keen.

But with the advent of top-up fees, universities are having to provide bursaries for students to offset the high cost of university education (see page 55). Many of the university scholarships on offer have a subject or location condition attached, which does considerably limit those eligible to apply. *University Scholarships, Awards & Bursaries*, published by Trotman, supplies full information on the bursaries given by universities, especially to students from low-income families, and lists over 100 institutions offering scholarships or awards.

These are largely for people studying specific subjects, or are travel awards. Subjects range from the more usual (engineering, history, geography, languages, law and the sciences) to the distinctly unusual, such as cultural criticism studies, paper science, rural studies, retail studies, leisure, town planning, textiles – and a great deal in between.

Sports scholarships and bursaries are increasingly commonly available. These cover areas such as rugby, cricket, netball and even golf. A sports scholarship is a boon for any student who plays in a national team and needs to take time out and coaching to train for an international event. You can be studying any subject to get a sports scholarship.

A number of universities and colleges give music or choral awards. Many of these are from old foundations and the award may include a commitment to take part in services in the college chapel or local church or cathedral. Then there are awards with geographical restrictions. For example, students at Bangor University might get an award of £300 if they live in Criccieth or, better still, £1,500 if they were born in one of the counties of Anglesey, Conwy or Gwynedd, while Exeter University students whose parents have resided in Devon for at least three years could be in line for a scholarship ranging from £12 to £80 p.a.

Your university may also give travel awards to undertake special projects during the vacation, for certain subjects. Ask your university for details of possible awards, and check their prospectus or website (see also *University Scholarships, Awards & Bursaries*, published by Trotman). For English universities, try http://bursarymap.direct.gov.uk.

Are there awards for foreign students?

Yes. Overseas students are eligible to apply for many of the awards offered by universities. In some universities, there are awards specifically for foreign students – for example, Engineering and Applied Sciences at Aston (£1,500–£3,000), Law at City University (£1,500 approx.) and a number of scholarships for students from Japan, Malaysia, Singapore, Thailand and the USA at Edinburgh. For further information, contact the British Council or British Embassy in your own country, the British Council in the UK (www.britishcouncil.org) or the university where you will be studying.

How much would a college scholarship be worth?

Awards vary tremendously: some are given annually for the length of the course, others are a one-off payment. The highest award we found for undergraduates was £5,000, while the lowest we found, at Exeter, was £12 – this is because the foundation was made in the 19th century when £12 was a lot of money, and its status cannot be changed.

Thrift Tips

'Get a meeting with a bank to find the best options for getting interest on savings.'
First-year History and Politics student, Aberdeen

'Borrow from your parents: they are interest-free loans.'
Third-year Applied Psychology student, Liverpool John Moores

'Get the free overdraft and put it in a high-interest account, bond or ISA.'
Business Studies student, Staffordshire

How would I go about getting a college scholarship?

Scholarship distribution methods differ from institution to institution and, of course, according to the terms of the foundation. Aberystwyth, for example, holds formal examinations during February, which can be taken at the student's own school or college. It gives some 50 Entrance Scholarships worth £1,200 for each year of study and 250 Merit Awards worth £1,000 for the first year only. Applications must be made by 15 January; see www.aber.ac.uk/en/scholarships/entrance-scholarships. Aberystwyth offers other bursaries – in Music, for example, available to experienced players of instruments who can make an active contribution to the university's wide range of orchestras and bands. Closing date for applications for these is mid-April; see www.aber. ac.uk.

The ancient Scottish universities all offer a range of bursaries. Those at Glasgow are awarded once students have begun their courses. However, at Aberdeen, Edinburgh and St Andrews, bursaries are available to entrants. Traditionally, awards were made on the basis of exam performance, but at Aberdeen and Edinburgh in particular, the bursary schemes have developed to include a significant number of awards that take into account applicants' financial and personal circumstances. Application forms are available from the universities concerned; increasingly, bursary information and application forms can be found on university websites. Most of these scholarships are worth £1,000 for each year of degree study (in total, £4,000 for a Scottish honours degree or £5,000 for a degree in Clinical Medicine).

First, look at the college prospectus or its website – it should either list the awards available, or give you an address to write to for details. This should be done early in the autumn term of your final school year and before or about the time you are filling in your UCAS form. Obviously at this stage you do not know which university you are likely to go to, and any exam can be held early in the academic year before you have made your final decision.

Professional institutions

Do professional institutions give scholarships?

Some do, some don't. The engineering institutions are among the most generous. Awards are made to students studying accredited degree courses.

Institution of Engineering and Technology (IET)

Through its scholarships and awards, the IET promotes engineering as a career, rewards achievement and assists with postgraduate research. In 2010, the IET will award a number of scholarships of £1,000 per annum for the duration of an IET-accredited MEng degree course. There are also grants of £1,000 (one year only) available for final-year undergraduate students. For postgraduates, there are scholarships ranging from £1,250 to £10,000. To find out more, contact the

It's a fact

Remember, scholarships and bursaries are not necessarily for students from low-income families and are totally different from those offered by universities now that top-up fees have been introduced.

IET, Michael Faraday House, Six Hills Way, Stevenage SG1 2AY, email: awards@
theiet.org or website: www.theiet.org/ambition; see also information on
sponsorship through the Power Academy, page 186.

Institution of Civil Engineers (ICE)

The Queen's Jubilee Scholarship Trust (QUEST) runs an undergraduate
scholarship for civil engineering students embarking on a degree accredited
by the ICE. The scholarship is up to the value of £3,000 p.a. for the duration
of the course, with a maximum total value of £12,000. QUEST scholars are
partnered with top civil engineering and construction companies that provide
paid summer work placements, a head start on becoming professionally
qualified and possible employment on graduation. Contact the ICE, 1 Great
George Street, London SW1P 3AA, tel: 020 7665 2193, email: quest.awards@
ice.org.uk or website: www.ice.org.uk/quest.

Institution of Mechanical Engineers (IMechE)

The institution gives undergraduate scholarship awards of £1,000 p.a. for a
maximum of four years (students must be or become an affiliate member of
the Institution and have a place on an IMechE-accredited degree course),
postgraduate research scholarships, postgraduate Master's scholarships, awards
of up to £750 for students studying or taking a work placement overseas
and awards of up to £1,000 for overseas voluntary or project work. Contact
IMechE Prizes and Awards Department, ASK House, Northgate Avenue,
Bury St Edmunds IP32 6BB, tel: 01284 717 887 or 717 882 or website: www.
imeche.org/industries/prizeaward.

IMechE also handles the awarding of up to 10 Whitworth Scholarships
for undergraduate degree-level courses (including MEng and MSc) valued
at £4,500 p.a. (full-time study) and £3,000 p.a. (part-time study). These
scholarships are for outstanding engineers who have served at least a two-year
hands-on engineering apprenticeship before commencing their undergraduate
studies (see 'How Paul got a Whitworth Scholarship' on page 209). Whitworth
Senior Scholarships of £7,500 are also awarded to postgraduate students
who go on to study for a PhD or EngD. Whitworth Scholarships are open to
engineers of any discipline, not just mechanical engineers. Applicants must be
British, Commonwealth or European Union citizens normally resident in the
UK for at least three years prior to commencing their degree-level course.

Institute of Marine Engineering, Science and Technology (IMarEST)

Up to four scholarships of £1,000 are awarded each year to undergraduate
students attending approved, accredited courses leading to registration for
chartered status – Chartered Engineer (CEng), Chartered Marine Scientist
(CMarSci) or Chartered Marine Technologist (CMarTech) – and who
demonstrate a commitment to marine engineering, marine science or

marine technology by spending at least two years in the industry or in study. The institute also offers awards to postgraduates through the Stanley Gray Fellowship scheme and prizes to students through various industry schemes. More information is available from IMarEST, 80 Coleman Street, London EC2R 5BJ, tel: 020 7382 2600 or website: www.imarest.org.

How Paul got a Whitworth Scholarship

Paul Tuohy left school at 16 with 11 GCSEs and then started to study for his A levels. But illness meant that he would have to repeat a year and he decided to begin a Modern Apprenticeship instead. Having scored excellent marks in a BTEC Ordinary and Higher National Certificate through day release, he wanted to continue studying. This is his story.

'I liked learning something new, I had the study bug; so when the personnel officer at the company where I was working said the firm would sponsor me if I wanted to take a degree part time, I jumped at the chance. However, there was one proviso: I needed the permission of my boss, the chief engineer. It seemed like just a formality, but to my horror he said categorically "No!" I could not believe it. Nor could anyone else. A few months later I left the company.

'To be honest, he probably did me a favour. I decided to study for a degree anyway, but to do it full time. It was to be a BEng (Hons) in Mechatronics with Industrial Experience. Fortunately, I lived in Manchester and the course being offered at Manchester University was much better than the part-time course I had considered. Even though I had no A levels, the university said they would give me a chance. "You may struggle with the maths," they said, and they were right, but other topics came more easily and I was prepared to work hard.

'I was used to having plenty of money to spend – I'd been on a salary of over £20,000 – and wondered how I would cope as a student. I had some money saved. I took out a student loan. My parents said I could live at home free while I studied and I bought a bicycle to save on travel fares.

'In my first semester my results averaged 76%. In my second semester I did even better, and with an average of 81% was awarded the Mechatronic Student of the Year Prize. It was then that our Industrial Liaison Manager, Eddie Welch, suggested I should apply for a Sir Joseph Whitworth Scholarship given by IMechE.

'There were around 40 applicants that year and only 10 scholarships to be awarded. Having filled in an application form, I attended an interview with a panel of five lecturers and engineers down at the IMechE in London. It was tough. Two days later, they phoned to say I had been awarded a scholarship valued at £3,000 a year. That certainly helped with my finances.

'The next year I spent in industry, at Rolls-Royce. When I returned to uni for my final year I received another award under the Whitworth Scholarship scheme – this time £4,000.'

Paul graduated with a first-class honours degree in Mechatronic Engineering. As a Whitworth Scholar, he can put the prestigious letters BEng WhSch after his name. He then went on to do a PhD at Manchester, developing a new type of marine propulsion engine in collaboration with Rolls-Royce, and received a stipend of around £12,940 to live on as well as being awarded a Whitworth Senior Scholarship worth another £7,500.

Charities and trusts

Which charities and trusts give help to students?

You may be surprised to learn that it would take a book several times the size of this one to list them all. For example, the *Educational Grants Directory* (see 'What to read' at the end of this chapter) lists more than 1,600 charities that between them give away more than £60 million a year – and this is by no means an exhaustive list.

But before you get too excited, most charities have restrictions on how much they can give away, to whom and for what reasons. Also, most charities and trusts will only consider you after you have exhausted all the more conventional avenues such as loans and Access funds.

Trusts and charities fall largely into four major groups.

▶ Need – e.g. charities for people with disabilities. Well-known organisations such as the RNIB and the RNID fall into this category, along with less familiar organisations such as the Shaftesbury Society and Scope.

▶ Subject – charities that will give help to students studying certain subjects. For example, the Company of Actuaries Charitable Trust Fund helps those studying to be actuaries; the Chartered Surveyors Company Charitable Trust and Mr Sidney A. Smith's Fund help those studying surveying; the Honourable Society of Gray's Inn is just one of a number of charities helping would-be lawyers; and there are quite a few charitable organisations set up to help those studying medicine, for example the Charity of Miss Alice Gertrude Hewitt, which helps some 40 students aged under 25.

▶ Parents' occupation – this can be a great source of additional income. If one of your parents is an airline pilot, artist, banker, barrister, coal-miner, gardener, in the clergy, in the precious metals industry, you name it, there could be some help. Some trusts stipulate that your parent should be dead, but fortunately not all.

▶ Geographical location – where you study and also where you live can really make a difference. Take, for example, the lucky students living in the parishes of Patrington and Rimswell in East Yorkshire, in Oadby in the Midlands or in Yeovil in Somerset – they could be in line for help towards books, fees, living expenses or travel abroad.

There are literally hundreds of these trusts covering many areas of the country. It has to be said that pay-outs can be small – under £100 – but they can be substantially more – say £1,000.

'My income was extremely low, so I applied for as many bursaries (in and outside college) as possible. The effort paid off: I got a bursary from college for around £2,000 and another from a company trust of £1,000.'

First-year Law student, Cambridge

What sort of help do trusts give?

Help with fees, maintenance, books, equipment, travel either to and from your college or abroad, special sports activities, child-minding and special projects.

They all vary in what they will offer, and to whom.

Is there anybody who could advise me on applying to charitable trusts?

The Education Grants Advisory Service (EGAS), which is part of Family Action, is an independent organisation that offers a range of services providing information on funding for those in post-16 education in England. EGAS specialises in funding from charitable trusts and maintains a database of 120 trusts and charities that assist students. You will need to put your information into their online database, which will then match you to the charities and trusts that are most likely to help you. The criteria for eligibility are set by the individual trusts and charities or by the people who bequeathed the legacy, not EGAS, and are therefore extremely diverse. Trusts can seldom help in an immediate financial crisis. The more time you have to raise the funds, the more likely you are to succeed.

To find out more and carry out your own search of trusts, the quickest route is to visit Family Action's website: www.family-action.org.uk/educationalgrantssearch. Alternatively, you can request that a search is carried out for you by downloading a questionnaire from Family Action's website or sending a large stamped addressed envelope to EGAS, 501–505 Kingsland Road, London E8 4AU, requesting a questionnaire. Please note, however, that it can take up to six weeks to receive an initial response, so wherever possible, students are encouraged to carry out their own search online.

For further assistance you can phone the EGAS helpline on 020 7241 7459, open Tuesday, Wednesday and Thursday 2–4p.m.

Can EGAS help overseas students and those wanting to study abroad?

It is very difficult to find trusts willing to fund overseas students who are already studying in the UK, and EGAS cannot assist students wishing to study outside the UK. However, there are trusts that give funding for travel, and these should be contacted directly. See 'What to read' at the end of this chapter for help if you would like to winkle them out.

What are my chances of hitting the jackpot?

advice note

Before making an application to a charity, it is important to be clear in your own mind exactly what kind of student they are likely to help, and what kind of financial assistance you are after, otherwise you could be wasting both your time and theirs.

Your chances are slim, although the odds are certainly better than the likelihood of winning the national lottery. Competition is fierce. Last year, EGAS received nearly 2,000 written applications, and over 60,000 online trust fund searches were completed. Family Action administers over 30 educational trusts, providing small grants principally to families and individuals on low incomes, particularly those living on benefits. Applicants must be studying at a college or university affiliated to EGAS. Funds are not available for items already covered by statutory funding, private school fees, repayment of loans, childcare costs or daily living expenses.

Last year Family Action gave some 1,157 grants totalling around £252,825 to HE and further education students. However, any funding it does offer is usually small, around £150, for something specific like books, equipment or travel. It handles about 350 grant applications a month and most grants are given to help students in their final year.

Typical examples of why money might be given are:

► for books or equipment
► if a parent is suddenly made redundant and can't continue to finance your college course fees
► to a student who has been paying their way through part-time work but feels they need to give up their job to concentrate on that final two-month push.

Additionally, Family Action delivers the Horizons Education Fund. Funded by Barclaycard, this fund aims to support lone parents who have the motivation, determination and ability to improve their employment prospects. The fund operates until summer 2011. Further details can be found at www.family-action.org.uk/educationalgrantsprogramme.

Is there any other way to find out about charities and trusts?

Search the net. The web has a fund of information on sources for finding charities and trusts. Type 'educational grants charities and trusts' into your favourite search engine and follow the leads. Sites such as www. londonmet.ac.uk should come up for a start. Refugees could strike lucky if they visit www.lasa.org.uk. Another helpful site is www.careersadvice.direct.gov.uk.

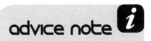

advice note

The last word: be realistic when contacting EGAS. Don't expect miracles – they can rarely be worked.

One excellent site is Hotcourses – go to www.scholarship-search.org.uk, where you'll find an extensive database of just what's available and, more importantly, whether you are eligible for an award.

When should I contact a trust?

Most trusts have an application deadline. This is usually given along with the general information in the trusts and grants directories. Check out each entry carefully; they are all different. Trusts are not the answer for a fast financial fix. Like all bodies, they tend to move exceedingly slowly. Your case will be scrutinised along with many others, so it could be months before you get an answer.

Could I get through higher education funded only by a charitable trust?

It could be done, but don't depend on it. Many charities won't consider you until you have tried all the usual channels available to students, and they do tend to give help towards the end of a course rather than at the beginning.

If I get help from a charity, will it affect my loan and fees?

It shouldn't. Charitable awards, scholarships and sponsorships are not generally taken into consideration when calculating your grant and loan package.

Can I apply to more than one charity?

Yes, but blanket application is not advisable. Limit your applications to organisations that are really likely to give you funds.

How do I go about applying to a charity?

There are no set rules. What one charitable trust wants, another won't. The usual procedure is as follows.

- ▶ Put together a list of suitable charities by consulting either EGAS or directories in the library.
- ▶ Find out exactly what each charity is offering and whether you meet their criteria.
- ▶ Check if there is a final entry date for applications.
- ▶ Write a brief note to selected charities, explaining your need and asking for an application form.
- ▶ Fill in the application form. Make sure answers are clear, concise and truthful. You may be questioned on them later. Bear the trust's criteria in mind.
- ▶ Photocopy the completed form before you send it back.
- ▶ Wait patiently. These things can take many weeks to process.

Do students actually get help?

'As an engineering student I needed a computer, but couldn't afford one. Were there any charities that could help? I searched around, and discovered the Earls Colne Educational Trust, which assisted students living within 10 miles of Earls Colne

in Essex. I lived in Halstead, just within the limits – it was worth a try. I wrote to them explaining my needs; they sent me a form; I filled it in; I waited; I went for an interview. The result: £500 – easy money. It cost just two sides of A4!'
Jonathan, who applied when studying Electronic Engineering
at Loughborough University

If all else fails

A few tips from *Student Money*'s student contacts on other ways of earning money.

'Work for the course team, and as a note-taker for deaf students.'
Second-year Photography student, Falmouth

'Psychology and economical experiments.'
Third-year English and Religious Studies student, Aberdeen

'Online surveys, eBay.'
First-year Philosophy student, Aberdeen

'Be an ambassador (for university).'
First-year Photography student, Falmouth

'Televisual supporting artist.'
Second-year Media Practice student, UWE

'Poker.'
Third-year Economics student, UWE

'Youth work.'
First-year Social Work student, UWE

'Questionnaires, and write for a journal.'
Fourth-year Maths student, St Andrews

'Sign up with a website that lists all the psychology experiments available at the university.'
First year Theology, Imagination and the Arts student, St Andrews (see also www.
markosweb.com/tag/earn+money)

'Surveys, and dooyoo.co.uk review site for cash.'
Third-year Sustainable Development student, St Andrews

Competitions

Are they worth it?

The world is full of competition addicts. There are magazines devoted solely to the topic, steering readers to the next give-away bonanza. Whole families eat crazy diets just to get the labels off the right tins and jars. People do win – holidays in exotic places, new cars, toasters, DVD players, washing machines and cuddly toys. It's always worth having a go, if it only means the cost of a stamp and perhaps writing a catchy slogan. While most competitions cannot be seen as a serious means of raising finance, if it's a competition set by your university with prizes for excellence, in a subject area you know well, you're in with a real chance – and winning could be a useful addition to your CV.

Try www. prizefinder.com, http://uk competitions.com or even www.studentstuff.com, or type 'competitions' into your search engine. This will give you information on all the competitions that are available on the web at the moment – best of luck!

A little icing on the cake is the best you can hope for, and even that is quite a hope. But don't dismiss competitions altogether. If it's aimed specifically at students, it very often involves writing an essay, but students, being the overworked (or lazy?) lot they are tend to give them a miss ... so the number of entries can be low. All the more reason to give it a try. How does this grab you?

Win £700

All you have to do is write a 900-word essay about your industrial placement and you could win a cash prize. The latest winner was Lucy Armstrong from the University of Bath who wrote about her placement at Macquarie University, Sydney, Australia, in the Anxiety Research Unit. A commendation and special runner-up prize of £150 went to Christopher Pagett from Liverpool John Moores University, who worked at Cheshire Police Headquarters in the Forensic Footwear Unit. Next time it could be you. The competition is run by ASET, the Work-Based and Placement Learning Association. Entries should be in by the beginning of December, and the results are announced in February.

To find out more about the competition, visit the ASET website: www. asetonline.org/comps, email: aset@asetonline or tel: 0114 221 2902. Best of luck!

Who won the *Guide to Student Money* £100?

Any student who filled in the *Guide to Student Money* questionnaire this year was automatically included in our £100 prize draw. This year's winner is Alison, a second-year Geography student at the University of St Andrews – and a very altruistic winner she turned out to be.

Alison has decided to donate her £100 to a Christian charity where she helps out. Called Solid Rock, it provides a £1 a meal lunch bar for students and local people once a week. Between 90 and 100 people generally turn up for the tea, coffee, doughnuts, ham and salad.

'I have budgeted for the year and I didn't need anything,' Alison says. 'I have food, clothes, a house what more do I need?'

Three £1,000 Green Cheese Scholarships to be won

Every year, BUNAC awards three scholarships of up to £1,000 each to help applicants cover the costs of taking part in a BUNAC Work Abroad Programme in the USA or Canada. To enter the Green Cheese Scholarships, all you need to do is submit a humorous piece of original creative writing based on a travel-related topic. You're free to write about anything at all – whether it's a trip to the other side of the world or a journey you made closer to home. Entries should be no more than 1,500 words. Contact your university or college, or BUNAC, 16 Bowling Green Lane, London EC1R 0QH, tel: 020 7251 3472, fax: 020 7251 0215, email: enquiries@bunac.org.uk or website: www.bunac.org.

Lotteries

Then, of course, there's the lottery. Not strictly a competition, but an option. This book is not in the business of advocating gambling, and at £1 a go, or at least £104 a year depending on how addictive it becomes, is it worth it? The odds on winning the jackpot are 14 million to one, and if you did win, what would happen to your studies?

The web

Finally, students have been writing in with news of competitions on the web and in the media. Here are a couple of their stories.

advice note

The litmus test with any competition has to be: 'Is it worth it?' Look at the hassle involved, the cost, the time factor, the number of cans of baked beans or cat food you have got to get through and, above all, the odds – and then make your decision. The drawback with any competition is that the winner takes all, and the also-rans get nothing. Still, it doesn't hurt to keep your eyes open.

'Enter internet competitions using uni computers, since the web is free. I did, and won a round-the-world trip, a TV, a video, a computer and £1,000 in cash.'

Third-year Economics student, York

'Whatever the prize, have a go. You can always sell it. I won a scooter worth £1,000 in a radio competition. It was a life-saver. I sold it immediately, and was able to solve my financial problems, which were dire. I still have a student loan, of course, but no overdraft.'

Second-year student, Lancaster

Facts and Figures

Most voluble students and their weekly spend on phone calls:

- Cambridge: £12.18
- Dundee: £11.49
- Brighton: £11.46
- Leicester: £10.96
- Birmingham: £10.91
- Liverpool: £10.84
- Glasgow: £10.50
- Oxford: £10.48
- Leeds: £10.06
- Manchester/Plymouth: £9.57

Source: *NatWest Student Living Index Survey* 2009

Further information

Where to look

- On your college noticeboard.
- In the careers office.
- National newspapers.
- Student newspapers.
- The web.

Who to contact

- EGAS helpline, tel: 020 7241 7459 or website: www.egas-online.org.uk.
- Scholarship Search UK, website: www.scholarship-search.org.uk.

What to read

- *The Grants Register*, published by Macmillan, lists over 3,500 awards. It's available from tel: 01256 329 242 or email: macdir@macmillan.co.uk – but it's very expensive (£195 for the 2010 edition), so try your local library.
- *Directory of Grant-Making Trusts*, published by the Charities Aid Foundation; website: www.cafonline.org or also try www.grantsonline.org.uk.
- *University Scholarships, Awards & Bursaries*, published by Trotman; website: www.trotman.co.uk.
- *Educational Grants Directory*; website: www.dsc.org.uk/Publications.

CHAPTER 10

Postgraduate study: where to find funding

The number of postgraduate students in the UK keeps increasing, almost doubling in the last ten years. How are they managing to pay for their studies? Has funding kept pace with the demand? In this chapter, we look at the main sources of finance for postgraduates.

Is it worth obtaining a postgraduate qualification?

If you are going to enter a career in which you will need extra qualifications, such as the legal profession, or if you are seeking a post in academia or teaching then of course further study is worth every penny. But otherwise, will it actually earn you extra cash? Employers don't always agree on this one. Some value additional qualifications, others ignore them. However ...

A report published by Universities UK some three years ago suggested that holders of postgraduate degrees earn more than their graduate counterparts – on average £70,000–£80,000 over a lifetime, but less if you hold a postgraduate certificate, on average £30,000–£40,000 over a lifetime.

More up-to-date information from the AGR *Winter Graduate Recruitment Review 2010* suggests that further qualifications are worth a premium of £3,000 for a PhD (median figure), £1,125 for a postgraduate qualification such as an MA or MSc (median figure) and £1,000 for relevant experience. Around a third of AGR members who provided information said they would give premiums.

How much will it cost?

Tuition fees

For UK residents and EU nationals:

- most subjects: £3,440-plus (research councils' fee level) – average figure. Certain courses may cost more. Part-time students: about half the full-time rate
- law: (approx. rates) Graduate Diploma in Law (GDL)/Common Professional Examination (CPE) course £3,000–£7,000; LPC £6,000–£12,500 and possibly more
- Master of Business Administration (MBA): general range £10,000–£16,000 (£12,400 median, but could be more than double that at top schools).

Fees for overseas students studying in the UK are shown in Table 40.

Maintenance

The results of the research shown in Chapter 1 will give you some idea of how much it is going to cost you to live. Just for basic costs, including rent, that's

Table 40 Students from abroad: average fees for 2009–2010

	Taught	Research
Classroom	£9,700	£9,800
Laboratory/workshops	£11,700	£11,900
Clinical	£23,100	£23,400
Medicine/Dentistry	£24,500	£23,400

around £275 a week (*NatWest Student Living Index Survey*). The NUS reckon much the same, with figures of £11,865 if you're living in London and £10,863 everywhere else for a 39-week academic year based on figures for 2009–2010. And remember, none of these figures includes fees.

It's a fact

The online postgraduate applications system enables postgraduate students in the UK and overseas to apply electronically to HE institutions. Access it via www.prospects.ac.uk, which hosts the national postgraduate database, or through a participating institution's website.

Sources of funding

Will I get funding?

Don't bank on it. Competition for postgraduate funding is phenomenal. There is no all-embracing funding system as for first degrees, and students generally have to search around to get help. It is much easier to get a place on a course than it is to get the money to pay for it. Many postgraduates have to finance themselves with loans and other means, which is probably why part-time study for postgraduates is increasing in popularity. If you are offered funding, make sure it covers both tuition fees and maintenance.

What are the possible sources of funding?

► Government funding from research councils – these are by far the largest sources of funding in the UK. Some 7,000 new awards are made each year. Each 'awarding body' funds different courses and there is little overlap, so it is important to identify the appropriate body for your needs (see page 223; for Scotland and Northern Ireland see also pages 236 and 237).

► Erasmus (often known as Socrates–Erasmus) is a programme developed by the European Commission to provide funds for the mobility of students and staff in universities throughout the EU member states and the countries of the European Free Trade Association (EFTA). See page 125 for full details and information on Erasmus and other similar programmes, such as the Leonardo da Vinci scheme.

► Employers will occasionally sponsor employees through courses, especially MBAs.

- Companies may sponsor students on a research project. This could be as the result of a work experience association during a first degree, or in co-operation with one of the research councils.

- Trusts and charities are more likely to award small amounts of money than full financial support, but they are certainly worth considering (see Chapter 9). Your local authority awards officer would have details of any local charities. Otherwise contact EGAS (see page 211 for details) or look in the published charities and grant-making trusts' directories and registers. Apply early: processing can be inordinately slow.

Facts and Figures

The latest figures show 536,815 postgraduate students are enrolled on postgraduate courses in the UK – 268,000 full time, and 268,815 part time.

Source: HESA figures 2008–2009

- Local authorities (LAs) – except in the case of teacher training, LAs are not required by law to fund postgraduates. Funding is discretionary, is given mainly for vocational courses that lead to certificates or diplomas, is means-tested and is subject to different criteria according to the local authority. Likely subjects are accountancy, journalism, law, music, secretarial work, youth work and computing. If you are tapping your local authority, it is essential to apply early because their funds are limited and you'll need to present a good case for yourself. But because there are no set rules for funding, it is always worth a try.

- Universities' own postgraduate studentship awards – many institutions have a small number of studentships available for specific courses. Aberystwyth, for example, gives around 12 awards each year to UK/EU students for research degrees. Awards generally cover fees and maintenance. Closing dates vary. For the Aberystwyth competition, the date is 1 March. Check your university of choice for details.

- University departments – they may have nothing, and probably won't advertise. But if they particularly want you, or there's something they are interested in doing, they may have sources they can tap. You could find that they stipulate you have to take on some tutorial work or assist the department.

cash crisis

London is a lot more expensive than you think: just a two-zone day pass on the Tube is over a fiver, and landlords can ask for up to two months' rent as a deposit. But did you know: you can put your 16–25 Railcard discount on your Oyster Card in London?

- Research assistantships are salaried posts in academic departments, which provide the opportunity to study for a higher degree. Salaries vary and opportunities can become available throughout the year. Watch the relevant press for adverts – the *Guardian, The Times, New Scientist, Nature* or *Prospects* – and the web.

- Loans from banks – see later in this chapter, page 248.

Can I get a student loan?

Only if you are taking a PGCE. Even though it's generally only a one-year course, you will be classed as a first rather than a final-year student, so you can take out the maximum loan offered.

You can also take out a loan to cover fees (see page 240 for full details of special funding arrangements for PGCE). Or you could try a bank loan (see page 248).

Funding from research councils

The research councils are the main sources of government funding for postgraduates. There are eight major award-making bodies in the UK, and each one operates independently; the awards they offer are all slightly different, as are their regulations. The information given here should therefore be seen as a general guide to what you could expect to get. All the award-making bodies issue information about their own awards, which you can get by writing to them or calling them (contact details are given later in this chapter) or by looking on the internet.

The areas of study covered by individual research councils can change, so make sure any information you get is up to date.

What kind of award could I get?

There are essentially four kinds of awards for postgraduate students.

1. Research Studentships are generally a three-year award leading to a doctorate (PhD or DPhil).

2. Collaborative Research Studentships are when the research project is part-funded by an external industrial organisation and may well give the student some experience outside the academic environment. The collaborating company generally gives the student extra cash on top of the studentship award. The awarding body may also give an additional award on top of the basic studentship. This is certainly so with Co-operative Awards in Science and Engineering (CASEs).

Thrift Tip

Tip from Aberystwyth: 'We say to graduates it's always worth a try; all it needs is the right phone call just at the right time.'

From a student who knows: 'You always need double the money you think you need when you are moving to a new location to study. There are always hidden costs.'

3. Advanced Course Studentships are given for taught courses that must be of at least six months' duration, but are generally for one or possibly two years, often leading to a Master's degree (MSc, MA) or other qualification.

4. Bursaries are allocated by the Central Social Care Council for courses in social work; the amounts offered are much lower.

Not all awarding bodies give all types of award. And some give additional awards and fellowships.

Is the award means-tested?

Only maintenance grants for training in social work are means-tested.

What could an award cover?

► Payment of approved fees to the institution.

► Maintenance allowance.

► Dependants' and other allowances.

► Assistance with additional travel and subsistence expenses for something like fieldwork.

Do I have to get a 2:1 to take a postgraduate course?

Each course will set its own requirements. If you are thinking of specialising in your degree subject, a first or 2:1 is probably what you will need. For a vocational course, you'll need to show real commitment and interest in the subject. If, however, you are seeking funding from a government funding council, they will generally demand:

► a first or upper second-class honours degree, or a lower second with a further qualification such as an MA for a Research Studentship

► at least a lower second-class honours degree for a taught/one-year course (this does not apply to social work courses).

How do I go about getting funding?

Start with the university careers office where you want to study. Most are clued up when it comes to tapping the scarce resources available to postgraduates. They may even publish a special leaflet on sources of funding for postgraduate study. Many of the publications listed in this chapter, which we suggest you consult, should also be in the university careers library. Talk to the tutors in your department, especially if you want to undertake a research degree, as they will know what projects are likely to gain funding. Consult university prospectuses.

When should I approach the award-making bodies?

If you want general information on their award scheme – any time. It is important to read thoroughly the individual information produced by the different award-making bodies, because closing dates, methods of application and what is on offer will vary. In most cases, application for awards is through the institution you hope to join. Check the information for procedures.

How do I apply for funding?

In the case of most research councils – the Biotechnology and Biological Sciences Research Council (BBSRC), the Engineering and Physical Sciences Research Council (EPSRC), the Economic and Social Research Council (ESRC), Medical Research Council (MRC), the Natural Environment Research Council (NERC) and the Science and Technology Facilities Council (STFC) – funding for students is funnelled through university departments and courses. They select the students for their courses or projects and submit their names to the awarding body. Application forms are obtained from the department where you intend to study, and must be returned well in advance of the end of July, when the department will submit them to the appropriate awarding council.

The Arts and Humanities Research Council (AHRC) has a different allocation mechanism with two ways you can be asked to apply. There is the Block Grant, which is awarded to an institution that then nominates students to each funded place. Alternatively, there is the Studentship Competition, where the student applies to the institution and their application is forwarded to the AHRC with attachments from referees and the institution. Either way, your first port of call is the institution where you want to study.

The General Social Care Council is different again and bursaries are administered by the NHS Business Services Authority.

Will it make a difference where I choose to study?

Yes. Not all courses or departments attract funding. It is important to find out the situation when you apply. And just because a course is eligible for studentships and you have a place on that course, it still doesn't mean you will necessarily get one. It is very competitive. And remember, if you don't get funding it could mean you have to pay not only your own maintenance but also your course fees. In that case, a university close to your own home might be the answer, or studying part time (e.g. by day release, evening course or distance learning).

When and how can I find out what projects have funding?

From April onwards, your university should have a list of departments that have been given funding by the awarding bodies. Under the scheme, universities are committed to attracting the very best students for the awards so they must advertise for candidates outside as well as within their own university. These are typically publicised in media such as *New Scientist*, *Nature*, the *Guardian* or university magazines, depending on the topic.

A Fresh Approach to Flexible Work

Need to earn while you study? FreshMinds could be the answer.

FreshMinds is an award-winning research and recruitment consultancy that allows some of the brightest brains in the UK to flex their intellectual muscles while working at big-name clients in every sector from banking to government. Among the pool of Minds are top graduates, postgraduates and business analysts drawn from the world's leading universities, business schools and companies. If you're in between periods of study or looking for a job, FreshMinds can help you find the perfect way to while away the time and bring home some much-needed money.

Research ranges from information and data-gathering to more complex analysis, including market research, company profiling and competitor benchmarking. Depending on where the wind takes you, you could be working in the heart of FreshMinds' Holborn office or on placements with clients for anything from three days to six months. FreshMinds only works with the best – graduates who not only have a 2:1 degree or better from a top university, but who have revelled in excelling among their peers. If you are a glowing example of a fresh, young Mind take a look at www. freshminds.co.uk or give them a ring on 020 7692 4300 to find out more.

If you want a list of which courses and projects throughout the country have received funding, contact the appropriate awarding body after 1 April. Information may also be available on their websites.

Can I approach more than one awarding body?

No. There is generally no overlap between the awarding research councils: they each have their own designated areas, so it is important to identify which body to apply to, as you can only approach one. In the case of the AHRC, there does appear to be some overlap between its three different arms. However, a course that attracts bursaries from one will not generally gain funding from other state sources.

Levels of award from the different bodies are given in Table 41.

Table 41 Awards available (2010–2011 figures)

Awarding body		In London	Elsewhere	Any location
BBSRC		£15,590	£13,590	Vet £20,970
ESRC		£15,590	£13,590	
MRC[1]		£15,510	£13,290	
STFC		£15,590	£13,590	
AHRC	Research Master's[2]	£11,040	£9,040	
	Professional Master's[2]	£10,420	£8,420	
	Doctoral award[1]	£15,290	£13,290	
EPSRC	PhD studies			£13,590
NERC	PhD studies	£15,590	£13,590	
	Advanced course	£10,712	£8,712	
GSCC[3]		£3,762.50	£3,362.50	

1. 2009–2010 figures
2. 2008–2009 figures
3. Non-income assessed

The award-making bodies

Subjects given for each body have been selected to give a broad view of topics covered, and are by no means exhaustive. Candidates should check with the appropriate organisation, or on the appropriate website. (Note that research councils increase their fee and stipend levels in line with inflation. Provisional values for 2010–2011 are likely to see an increase of 1.5% on the 2009–2010 levels.)

Arts and Humanities Research Council (AHRC)

Awards are available for Master's degree courses and doctoral study across a number of subject panels and these are continually evolving. Typical subjects are:

- ► classics, ancient history and archaeology
- ► English language and literature
- ► medieval and modern history
- ► modern languages and linguistics
- ► librarianship, information and museum studies
- ► music and performing arts
- ► philosophy, religious studies and law.

The AHRC offers studentships through four different competitions:

- ► Block Grant Partnerships (BGPs)
- ► Studentship Competition (SC)
- ► Collaborative Doctoral Awards (CDAs)
- ► Research grants with Project Studentships (PS) attached.

Within these competitions, the AHRC operates three separate schemes:

- ► Doctoral Awards (DA)
- ► Research Preparation Master's (RPM)
- ► Professional Preparation Master's (PPM).

For more details, see the AHRC's website, www.ahrc.ac.uk.

Research Preparation Master's Scheme

Type of award:
Support for students undertaking Master's degree courses that focus on advanced study and research training, which provides a foundation for further research at doctoral level. Awards will normally be for one year's full-time study or two years' part-time study.

Amount (2009–2010 figures):

- ► studying in London: £11,280
- ► elsewhere: £9,280
- ► part-time study: £4,640 (London £5,640)
- ► tuition fees: £3,390 full time/£1,695 part time.

Professional Preparation Master's Scheme
Type of award:
Support for Master's degrees or postgraduate diploma courses that focus on developing high-level skills and competencies for professional practice. Awards will normally be for one year's full-time study or two years' part-time study.

Amount (2009–2010 figures):

▶ studying in London: £10,650

▶ elsewhere: £8,650

▶ part-time study: £4,330 (London £5,330)

▶ tuition fees: £3,390 full time/£1,695 part time.

Doctoral Scheme
Type of award:
Support for up to three years of full-time study or up to five years' part-time study leading to a doctoral degree.

Amount (2009–2010 figures):

▶ studying in London: £15,290

▶ elsewhere: £13,290

▶ part-time study: £7,970 (London: £9,170)

▶ tuition fees: £3,390 full time/£1,695 part time.

Contact details
Programmes Division
AHRC
Whitefriars
Lewins Mead
Bristol BS1 2AE
tel: 0117 987 6543
fax: 0117 987 6544
email: pgenquiries@ahrc.ac.uk
website: www.ahrc.ac.uk

Biotechnology and Biological Sciences Research Council (BBSRC)

Typical subject areas covered include the biological sciences and associated technologies:

▶ agriculture and food sciences

▶ animal sciences

- ► biochemistry and cell biology
- ► biomolecular sciences
- ► engineering and biological systems
- ► genes and development biology
- ► plant and microbial sciences.

Type of award:

- ► Research Studentship
- ► Master's Studentship.

Amount (2010–2011 figures):

- ► study in London: £15,590
- ► elsewhere: £13,590
- ► doctoral Training Account minimum stipend can be higher.

Students with a recognised veterinary degree can get £20,970, while students holding a first degree who wish to intercalate a PhD during their veterinary training receive an annual supplement of £2,000 p.a. from BBSRC. With CASE, there is an additional minimum £2,500 by collaborator.

Contact details
BBSRC
Polaris House
North Star Avenue
Swindon SN2 1UH
tel: 01793 413 200
email: postgrad.studentships@bbsrc.ac.uk
website: www.bbsrc.ac.uk

Engineering and Physical Sciences Research Council (EPSRC)

Subject areas include:

- ► engineering
- ► chemistry
- ► mathematics
- ► physics
- ► information and computer technologies
- ► materials science and the life sciences interface.

Types of support:
EPSRC supports all of its postgraduate training through packages of funding provided to the universities. It is the responsibility of the university to assess student eligibility for and select students to receive funding. Prospective students should contact universities or departments direct.

Funding is provided for:

▶ Standard Research Studentships

▶ Industrial CAS Studentships

▶ Centres for Doctoral Training.

Amount (2010–2011 figure):
Amounts may vary, depending on university, but EPSRC requires that PhD students receive a stipend of at least the national minimum rate.

▶ PhD students: £13,590

Contact details
EPSRC
Polaris House
North Star Avenue
Swindon SN2 1ET
tel: 01793 444 000
website: www.epsrc.ac.uk

Economic and Social Research Council (ESRC)

Typical subject areas include the following:

▶ area studies

▶ economic and social history

▶ economics

▶ education

▶ human geography

▶ linguistics

▶ management and business studies (accounting, finance, industrial relations and other specialist management courses)

▶ planning

▶ politics and international relations

▶ science technology and innovation studies

▶ psychology

▶ social anthropology

▶ social policy

▶ socio-legal studies

▶ sociology

▶ sports

▶ statistics

▶ research methods and computing as applied to the social sciences.

Type of award:

- Annual Studentship Competition (1+3 and +3)
- 113 Quota awards.
- Joint ESRC/NERC Studentships
- Joint ESRC/MRC Studentships
- Joint ESRC/Department for Transport Studentships
- Joint ESRC/Scottish Executive Studentships
- Joint ESRC/Department for National Statistics Studentships
- GLC Grants Research Studentships
- GLC Grants, one-year Master's
- Welsh Assembly Research Studentships
- CASE Studentships
- Centre Linked Studentships
- Language-Based Area Studies
- Project Linked Studentships
- Capacity Building Cluster CASE studentships.

Amount (2010–2011 figures):

- studying in London: £15,590
- elsewhere: £13,590
- enhanced stipends given by the Welsh Assembly and Scottish Executive of £2,000; if studying Economics or Quantitative Methods an additional £3,000.

Contact details
ESRC
Research, Training & Development Directorate
Polaris House
North Star Avenue
Swindon SN2 1UJ
tel: 01793 413 150
email: ptd@esrc.ac.uk
website: www.esrc.ac.uk

General Social Care Council (GSCC)

The GSCC covers the subject area of social work.

Type of award:
The social work bursary for students in full-time postgraduate study is available to those normally resident in England taking an approved course. Students must also meet certain other eligibility criteria. The bursary consists of a non-income-assessed basic grant including a fixed contribution towards practice learning, opportunity-related expenses and tuition fee support. It also includes an income-assessed maintenance grant and income-assessed allowances to assist with certain costs of living as recipients of the postgraduate bursary will not ordinarily be entitled to LA funding. Financial awards are dependent on individual circumstances.

Amount (2010–2011 figures):
The basic full-time grant (non-income assessed) is:

▶ London: up to £3,762.50 (52 weeks)

▶ elsewhere: up to £3,362.50 (52 weeks).

Contact details
Social Work Bursary
NHS Business Services Authority
Sandyford House
Archbold Terrace
Newcastle-upon-Tyne NE2 1DB
tel: 0845 610 1122
email: swb@ppa.nhs.uk
website: www.ppa.org.uk/swb

Medical Research Council (MRC)

Subject areas covered by the MRC include:

▶ medicine (including tropical medicine)

▶ areas of biology including cancer

▶ clinical neurosciences and mental health

▶ clinical psychology

▶ cognitive science

▶ neurobiology

▶ imaging

▶ epidemiology

▶ population health

▶ medical statistics

▶ quantitative biology

▶ infections and immunity (including HIV and Aids)

▶ molecules, cells and genetics

▶ toxicology and pharmacology

▶ stem cell and regenerative medicine

▶ ageing

▶ reproduction and child health

▶ nutrition

▶ systems medicine.

Types of support:
The MRC supports much of its postgraduate training through packages of funding provided to universities as Doctoral Training Accounts. Funding is not supplied directly from the MRC to individual students. Prospective students should contact universities or heads of department directly to see whether there is funding available.

Funding is provided for the following areas:

▶ Research PhDs for up to four years' duration

▶ Integrated Research Master's within PhDs (1+3 year studentships)

- ► Advanced Course Master's Studentships (MRes and MSc)
- ► Capacity Building Area (Priority Area) Studentships
- ► Industrial CASE Studentships
- ► Interdisciplinary Studentships in collaboration with the ESRC
- ► Clinical Research Training Fellowships for students with a clinical background.

Amount (2009–2010 figures):
Minimum values set by Research Councils UK each year; a PhD student starting an MRC studentship in 2009 would expect to receive a minimum stipend according to where they lived:

- ► studying in London: £15,510
- ► elsewhere: £13,290.

Contact details
MRC
20 Park Crescent
London W1B 1AL
tel: 020 7636 5422
fax: 020 7436 6179
email: students@headoffice.mrc.ac.uk
website: www.mrc.ac.uk

Natural Environment Research Council (NERC)

NERC cover the following subject areas:

- ► atmospheric chemistry
- ► earth observation and associated science
- ► freshwater ecology
- ► geology
- ► geophysics
- ► hydrology

- ► marine ecology
- ► organic pollution
- ► physical oceanography
- ► science-based archaeology
- ► soil sciences
- ► terrestrial ecology.

Type of award:

- ► PhD (three-year Research Studentship): can be a straight research award, CASE or an OPEN CASE (these studentships are awarded to the universities in competition – approx. 25 a year)
- ► MSc and MRes (one-year Advanced Course Studentships).

Amount (2010–2011 figures):

- PhD stipend: £13,590 p.a. (£15,590 in London)
- Advanced Course stipend: £8,712 (£10,712 in London)
- extra PhD allowances: conference allowance – £450
- Research Training Support Grant (RTSG): £3,000 (CASE – minimum of £1,000 p.a. by collaborator)
- London weighting: £2,000 for PhD, MSc and MRes students.

Contact details
NERC
Polaris House
North Star Avenue
Swindon SN2 1EU
tel: 01793 411 500
website: www.nerc.ac.uk

Science and Technology Facilities Council (STFC)*

Subject areas covered by the STFC include:

- astronomy
- astrophysics
- nuclear physics
- particle physics
- solar system science.

Type of award:

- Research Studentship – 260 allocated
- CASE – ten allocated.

Amount (2010–2011 figures):

- studying in London: £15,590 p.a.
- elsewhere: £13,590 p.a.
- CASE – additional £615 p.a. given plus minimum of £2,760 p.a. by collaborating company.

---

*The STFC was formerly the Particle Physics and Astronomy Research Council (PPARC).

Contact details
STFC
Polaris House
North Star Avenue
Swindon SN2 1ET
tel: 01793 442 000
email: studentships@stfc.ac.uk
website: www.stfc.ac.uk

See Table 41 on page 227 for a quick reference guide to postgraduate awards. Those taking postgraduate teaching courses should turn to page 240.

Wales

Graduates are eligible for funding from the research councils listed above. Those taking postgraduate teaching courses should see page 241.

Scotland

Graduates seeking funding for science-based subjects are eligible for studentship awards from most of the research councils mentioned above. Funding for postgraduate vocational courses, mostly at diploma level (usually for one year), may be available through the Postgraduate Student Allowance Scheme (PSAS) – not all postgraduate courses are supported. Students taking PGCE or PGDipCE will be funded in the same way as undergraduates. Tuition fees up to a maximum of £3,400 will be paid for eligible students. All funding is means-tested. Contact SAAS on 0845 111 0244 for postgraduate enquiries.

Northern Ireland

Postgraduate students can compete for funding from the award-making bodies already listed. Additional options include the following.

▶ The Department for Employment and Learning (DEL) offers two types of award: for research (MPhil, DPhil, PhD) and for approved courses of advanced study (Master's degrees) in the fields of humanities, science and technology and the social sciences. Awards are not means-tested.

▶ For studentships to pursue postgraduate study in Northern Ireland (at either Queen's University Belfast or the University of Ulster), contact the institution for an application form. The offer of a place does not mean that funding will be provided.

- The Northern Ireland Department of Agriculture and Rural Development provides funds for agricultural study in Northern Ireland, including horticulture and related sciences such as agricultural economics, engineering science and food science. The closing date is the last Friday in February.
- Medicine – see the MRC details on page 233.
- The basic rate of maintenance grant for 2010–2011 is £13,489. Additional allowances may also be paid for dependants and students with special needs.
- Co-operative Awards in Science and Technology (CAST) support research projects at Northern Irish universities for one year or three years in collaboration with industry. The maintenance grant is £13,489 p.a. and should be supplemented by a payment from the collaborating body.
- Johns Hopkins Fellowship Award – a one-year fellowship award, covering fees only, is given for the Johns Hopkins University's School of Advanced International Studies in Bologna.
- One student is funded by DEL to take a one-year course in Administration, Economics and Law at the College of Europe, Bruges. For further information, tel: 028 9025 7699, email: studentfinance@delni.gov.uk or website: www.delni.gov.uk/studentfinance.

Channel Islands/Isle of Man

Apply direct to the appropriate education department. For an idea of fees, go to www.universitiesuk.ac.uk/PolicyAndResearch/Statistics/Island-Fees.

David's story

How I got an income of £26,260 tax-free to study for an EngD

'I was in my final year at Manchester and thinking of going on to take a PhD when an advert came through for an engineering research doctorate working in collaboration with the engineering firm NIS Ltd. The project involved RF (radio-frequency) imaging for industrial processes, just up my street.

'It was actually for an EngD, which I preferred since it included a management element, and was sponsored by the EPSRC, who would pay my fees and provide a stipend of £13,800 p.a. What's more, by working with a company, I not only received another £3,500 p.a. but would gain valuable work experience. Everything was falling into place.

'Then, for the first time, the Whitworth organisation decided to give Whitworth Senior Scholarships to postgraduate engineers doing a PhD or EngD – £7,000 a year for the length of your course – so I applied.

'To be eligible for a Whitworth Scholarship you have to be an "outstanding student" – their words, not mine – who has done a "hands-on" engineering apprenticeship before taking your degree – which I had.

'Whitworth Scholarships are open to engineers from any discipline, but as they are awarded through the Institution of Mechanical Engineers, I had no idea that an electrical engineer like me was eligible. If I had, I would have applied during my first degree – now that would certainly have helped the finances and debt.'

Table 42 shows David's income over the course of his four years. And all tax-free.

Table 42 David's income

	1st year	2nd year	3rd year	4th year
Stipend from EPSRC	£13,800	£14,100	£14,400	£14,760
Allowance from sponsoring company	£4,000	£4,000	£4,000	£4,000
Senior Whitworth Scholarship	£7,000	£7,500	£7,500	£7,500
Fees paid by EPSRC				
Total	£24,800	£25,600	£25,900	£26,260

I want to study abroad: can I get funding?

There are a number of routes you can take.

If you are thinking of taking up postgraduate studies at the European Union Institute (EUI) in Florence, the College of Europe in Bruges or Warsaw or the Bologna Centre in Bologna, you may be eligible for an award from the Department for Business, Innovation and Skills in England, SAAS in Scotland or DEL in Northern Ireland.

Information on Socrates–Erasmus, generally known as Erasmus (the European Community Action Scheme for the Mobility of University Students), and the Leonardo da Vinci programme, which covers vocational training, is on page 125.

The UNESCO publication *Study Abroad* has over 2,570 entries and provides information on courses, international scholarships and financial assistance available in countries and territories worldwide. It should be available at your local library or careers office (see information at the end of Chapter 5, page 132).

I want to study in the United States

It's not cheap. Tuition for one nine-month academic year in state universities ranges from $4,000 to $13,000 and in private universities from $8,000 to $35,000. On top of that you will have living expenses, which vary tremendously, from $7,000 to $20,000. Last year, over 2,500 UK students chose to go to the US for postgraduate study. Don't automatically rule out the more costly courses, as the university may offer financial help through:

▶ scholarships or fellowships

▶ teaching/research assistantships

▶ a loan.

US universities spend $47 billion on research and development, which they pass along to students in the form of fellowships (grants) and assistantship packages. Awards from bi-national exchange programmes, foundations, corporations etc. may also be available. See the appendix in the *Fulbright Commission Guide to Postgraduate Study in the US*, available from the Fulbright Commission (details below), or log on to www.fulbright.co.uk and find out about USA grad school days, postgraduate study seminars and Fulbright awards for postgraduate study.

Studying abroad: what to read, who to contact

▶ Directory of Study Abroad Programmes: website: www.studyabroaddirectory.com.

▶ German Academic Exchange Service, 17 Bloomsbury Square, London WC1A 2LP, tel: 020 7235 1736. See also www.daad.de/deutschland/foerderung/ stipendiendatenbank.

▶ *Education US Guide to Getting Started with US Postgraduate Study*: information on applying, tuition fees etc. Available from the Educational Advisory Service, Fulbright Commission, Fulbright House, 62 Doughty Street, London WC1N 2JZ (write enclosing an A4 SAE with 48p stamp), tel: 020 7404 6994, email: education@ fulbright.co.uk or website: www.fulbright.co.uk.

▶ Try the UK Embassy or High Commission of the country where you are interested in studying: they may well have guides on awards and assistance offered.

▶ See also www.intstudy.com and www.studyoverseas.com.

Hot Tips on Funding from an Edinburgh Postgraduate

▶ Many departments provide opportunities for undergraduate teaching and demonstration work. Pay varies – it may only be a few pounds a term (e.g. £500 a year) or it could amount to several thousand.

▶ Work as a research assistant. Many staff secure a funding award that they must spend on their project, which includes assistants.

▶ Don't aim to fund tuition and living costs by taking a job. It is possible for Master's students to maintain a part-time job – and many do. But it is rare for a full-time PhD student to do so: a PhD is a job in itself. A few hours' work a week can ease the financial burden and provide useful respite from academic work – but only that.

▶ Try raising funding for individual experiments. Start with your department and funding sources for your individual subject. Success is more likely with experimental

degrees than bog-standards like French literature.

▶ Don't underestimate the time your PhD will take. Practically all PhDs overrun. It can easily take four or more years to complete. Research Council funding lasts for three years only and they won't help you for the fourth year. Budget for this. There is a good chance there'll be decent money coming in once you qualify. In the meantime have a contingency plan – it would be dreadful to give up on the last lap.

▶ Money, or perhaps one should say lack of it, is a major stress factor for many postgraduates. Excellent students quit because they can't afford to be a student any longer. Unrealistic budgeting undoes many: while rent and food are generally factored in, things such as holidays, contents insurance etc. are not. These all add up.

What help can I get if I want to train as a teacher?

England

Up to £9,000 just to train. This is the package of incentives available for students beginning a postgraduate course of initial teacher training (ITT) in England.

- Training bursary of £9,000 (non-repayable, tax-free) for students training to teach the following secondary shortage subjects: design and technology, information and communications technology (ICT), maths, physics, chemistry and engineering/ manufacturing; or teaching diplomas in information technology, engineering, construction and the built environment, environment and land-based studies and manufacturing and product design.

- Training bursary of £6,000 (non-repayable, tax-free) for students training to teach biology, combined/general science, other sciences, music, religious education (RE), English, geography and modern languages.

- Training bursary of £4,000 (non-repayable, tax-free) for students training to teach art and design, business studies, citizenship, health and social care, history, leisure and tourism, classics, dance, drama, media studies, social sciences, physical education and psychology; or diplomas in business, administration and finance, creative and media, society, health and personal development, and travel and tourism; or for primary education.

- A non-means-tested loan to cover the cost of fees – up to £3,290.*

- In addition, you may be eligible for a means-tested grant, which is non-repayable.

- Student loan based on the full-year allowance for students (up to £6,928 in London and £4,950 elsewhere, or £3,838 if you're living in your parents' home), 28% of which is means-tested (see Chapter 2).*

- Postgraduate students taking a subject enhancement course prior to an ITT course leading to qualified teacher status will receive £200 per week and fees will be paid.

- 'Golden hello' paid to secondary shortage-subject teachers on completion of their induction year: £5,000 to those teaching maths, science and applied science and £2,500, to those teaching ICT, applied ICT, design and technology, modern languages, music and RE.

The training bursary will be given in nine monthly instalments (18 monthly instalments if you are studying part time). It is not means-tested and is not a loan. Tax and National Insurance will have to be paid on any golden hello. For more details see www.tda.gov.uk.

Wales

The package of incentives on offer in Wales for 2010–2011 has changed and moved more in line with that in England to ensure that Welsh-domiciled students receive a level of support comparable with their English counterparts.

---

*Note: maintenance loan and tuition fee loan to be repaid in line with income after students have left their courses and are earning over £15,000 per annum.

Domiciled and training in Wales

▶ Training grant of £9,000 (non-repayable) for postgraduate students training to teach secondary priority subjects, which include: design and technology, ICT, maths, physics, chemistry and Welsh.

▶ Training grant of £6,000 (non-repayable) for postgraduate students training to teach secondary priority subjects of music, RE, modern languages, biology, combined or general science, English and geography.

▶ Training grant of £4,000 (non-repayable) for students on all other secondary postgraduate ITT courses and on primary postgraduate ITT courses.

▶ A means-tested Assembly Learning Grant (ALG) of up to £5,000 if studying for ten weeks or more.

▶ A means-tested student loan for maintenance (see page 241).

▶ A teaching grant for eligible trainees who go on to complete at least four months as a qualified teacher in a maintained school in a secondary priority subject, following completion of their induction period: £5,000 for those teaching mathematics, physics and chemistry; £2,500 to those teaching ICT, design and technology and Welsh.

▶ Trainees taking secondary ITT postgraduate courses through the medium of Welsh may be eligible for the £1,500 Welsh medium improvement supplement while those taking mathematics and science courses may get £1,800. This is to provide extra help to raise students' confidence in their ability to teach in Welsh.

▶ Finally, employment-based funding is available to institutions to pay discretionary grants to support students.

To find out more about teacher training in Wales, phone 0845 600 0991 (or 0845 600 0992 for a Welsh-speaking consultant) or visit www.tda.gov.uk/Recruit.aspx.

Welsh-domiciled but studying in another part of the UK

If you are domiciled in Wales but choose to study in another part of the UK, i.e. England, Scotland or Northern Ireland, you should contact Student Finance Wales (website: www.studentfinancewales.co.uk) for information on the full range of available student support. Also, contact the ITT provider with which you are hoping to study to check your entitlement to any other grants – you may be in for a surprise.

Teaching in Scotland

To train as a teacher in Scotland you can apply for support if your course qualifies you for a Scottish Studentship or other studentship award from a research council or government department.

There is no training bursary or secondary shortage subject scheme in Scotland. Scotland does not suffer from the same shortage of teachers as some parts of England. In Scotland, teachers are employed by one of the 32 LAs, but some of the more rural LAs find it hard to attract the number of teachers they would like. A pilot scheme was introduced for teachers trained in Scotland who are eligible for the teacher induction scheme.

If you're prepared to be placed anywhere in Scotland for your first year, you could get a golden hello of £8,000 for secondary school teaching and £6,000 for primary teaching. This is given in three instalments. If you are allocated to a Scottish island, you may also qualify for the Distant Islands Allowance, which would give you an additional £1,728 p.a. The success of the 'preference waiver' scheme is assessed each year.

To find out more, phone 0845 345 4745, or visit www.infoscotland.com/teaching. The preference waiver payment is only available for teachers trained in Scotland. If you have trained as a teacher in another part of the UK, you will not receive the funding offered.

Teaching in Northern Ireland

In contrast to England, there are no shortage or priority subjects in Northern Ireland. In fact, competition for teaching posts is extremely high. So while teaching students will receive the same general funding as undergraduates in Northern Ireland (see Chapter 4), no additional incentives are available.

However, if you train in England you will receive the incentive package offered to students there. See the section on teaching in England on page 240.

Further information for trainee teachers

▶ In England, call the Teaching Information Line: 0845 600 0991 or visit the website: www.tda.gov.uk.

▶ In Wales, call the Teaching Information Line: 0845 600 0991 (English) or 0845 6000 992 (Welsh), or visit the website: www.tda.gov.uk/recruit/thetrainingprocess/fundinginwales.

▶ In Scotland, tel: 0845 345 4745 or visit the websites: www.teachinginscotland.com or www.saas.gov.uk.

▶ In Northern Ireland, contact the Department of Education, tel: 028 9127 1272, email: mail@frni.hob.uk or visit the website: www.deni.gov.uk/index/teachers-pg.

What do Graduates Do?

A Higher Education Careers Services Unit (HECSU) survey looked at what graduates who qualified in 2008 were doing six months later at the start of 2009. This was a time when the economic downturn was beginning to bite.

▶ 14.1% went on to do further study.

▶ 8.1% were combining work with study.

▶ 7.9% were unemployed – that's up on the previous year's figures of 5.5%.

▶ 61.4% had entered employment.

▶ The most popular destination was still health and associated professions.

▶ Unsurprisingly, financial occupations were down on the year before from 8.7% to 7.5%.

▶ Also on the downward trend were:
  ▶ legal executives and paralegals – down 31%
  ▶ mechanical engineers – down 21%
  ▶ chartered and certified accountants – down 17%
  ▶ IT consultants and software professionals – down 18%.

▶ On the upward trend:
  ▶ teaching – up 14%
  ▶ social work – up an outstanding 55%
  ▶ sports and fitness instructors/coaches – up 17%.

Source: *What Graduates Do 2010*, HECSU survey based on 2008 graduating cohort six months after leaving university

Is there any help if I want to study medicine?

There is a special deal for graduates domiciled in England and Wales who are on the four-year fast-track medical programme.

In year one, you can apply for the same support as undergraduates – student loans for fees and maintenance.

From year two onwards you are eligible for:

▶   help with tuition fees
▶   a means-tested NHS bursary
▶   50% of student loan.

I want to study law: what help is there?

With full-time course fees for the GDL/CPE at about £3,150–£8,730, and the LPC running at an average of £7,070–£12,500 (the lowest and highest figures we found), most students are going to need some help.

▶ Training contract: this is the best route financially. A firm providing a training contract will generally provide sponsorship for one or two years while you are at law school, which could involve paying your fees and providing a maintenance allowance. But sponsorship is competitive, and even the best students can find it difficult to get. There are an increasing number of good candidates in the market. Those who do secure sponsorship would normally expect to complete their training contract with that firm. Occasionally a longer commitment to employment is demanded.

Clifford Chance, a leading international law firm, recruits around 100 trainee lawyers each year from the law and non-law populations. The firm will cover the cost of tuition fees for its future trainees on the GDL and LPC and will provide a maintenance grant during this period. This is also a valuable time for building up your network of contacts before commencing your actual training contract.

For sponsorship information see the Careers Service Unit (CSU) publication *Prospects Legal*, available from your university.

▶ Vacation placement programmes: a number of firms run programmes for second-year undergraduates (or in your final year if you are a non-lawyer), when they will size you up for a training contract. To get accepted for a placement programme is in itself an achievement, but it is certainly no guarantee of success.

▶ Law Society Bursary Scheme: this scheme is funded through a number of trusts established to support the development of individuals who can demonstrate academic ability and potential. Applications must have a confirmed place on an LPC before applying. Applications for awards – see below.

▶ Law Society Diversity Access Scheme: this aims to provide support to those with talent who will have to overcome particular obstacles to qualify as a solicitor. These could relate to social, educational, financial or family circumstances or to disability. Applications for awards for 2010–2011 for both the above schemes were invited in March 2010. More information and application forms for next year are available from the Law Society's JLD hotline; tel: 08000 856 131 or email: juniorlawyers@lawsociety.org.uk. See also www.lawsociety.org.uk/bursaries.

▶ Local authority grants: LAs are not obliged to fund GDL or LPC students and rarely do, but they do have discretionary funds available for a wide range of courses and, providing you meet their criteria for awards, you could strike it lucky. There are no set rules as every LA has its own policy. Your LA may well issue a leaflet giving information on study areas eligible for financial support. Enquire at your local education authority. Failing that, contact the Law Society (see website above).

▶ Loans: if all other lines of attack have failed there is always a loan (see page 250).

Laura's story

Laura is studying at the College of Law (London). 'Most of the top law firms recruit for training contracts two years in advance, i.e. in the third year of uni or at the beginning of the GDL,' she says. 'This can lead to the bizarre situation I found myself in where you get a job in a law firm before you have even started studying law!

'Competition for places at the top firms is extremely stiff: applicants are all expected to have at least a 2:1 degree, As and Bs at A level and a lot more besides – they must have something extra to make them stand out.

'Despite maintenance grants and the funding of fees by law firms, it is quite usual for students to finish law college with up to £30,000 of debt. Many take professional studies loans of up to £20,000 because the maintenance grant usually only covers rent in London and little else!

'It can be quite stressful to be in so much debt, but I think most people view it as an investment – in themselves. The debt repayments can be quite crippling when you are a trainee, but are less significant on qualification as there is usually a big pay rise. The debt is manageable, but it may not be great if you suddenly decide after law college or the training contract that law is not for you!

'For the top law firms, the recruitment process is long and laborious, involving testing application forms. If your application is successful, there are usually up to three interview stages, which include verbal reasoning tests, a team exercise, a written exercise and interviews with partners.

'The careers department in my college was fantastic and gave one-on-one advice and guidance about firms, how to tailor application forms to present yourself in the best way, and they also provided mock interviews and feedback from other students.'

Further information for law students

▶ For the most comprehensive information about firms offering sponsorship, see www.prospects. ac.uk or ask your university for details.

▶ *Lawyer 2B* is a dedicated magazine for law students and those considering a career in or around the legal profession. A sister publication of *The Lawyer*, it provides news, comment, features and careers advice in an informal yet informative style. It is published five times a year and is available free from most UK law schools. In addition to the magazine, *Lawyer 2B* has launched a new website, www.lawyer2b. com (or http://l2b.thelawyer.com) which offers breaking news, features, comment and advice to reinforce the information in the magazine.

▶ For vacation placements and mini-pupillages look at the Prospects website, www. prospects.ac.uk.

▶ For general information, see www.lawsociety.org.uk.

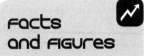

Facts and Figures

Fees at the BPP Law School:

▶ Leeds: £6,832 GDL; £9,995 LPC

▶ London: £8,730 GDL; £12,500 LPC

▶ Manchester: £6,830 GDL; £9,995 LPC.

Other professional qualifications

Accountants, engineers, actuaries – all usually join firms that specialise in that kind of work. The firm will pay for your training and pay you while you are being trained.

Extra funding

Are there any other funds I can apply for?

There may be, but not all councils and funding bodies give them, and these are under review.

advice note *i*

Seeking a career in the legal profession? Check out *Graduate Prospects Law Directory* for training contracts and law course vacancies. It's published annually in September. See www.prospects.ac.uk.

Child Tax Credit

This is available to students with dependent children and paid by the Inland Revenue. The amount you get will depend on circumstances. Call 0845 300 3900 8a.m. to 8p.m. for more details, or visit www.taxcredits.inlandrevenue.gov. uk and check out how much you could get.

Access to Learning Fund

Usually given as a grant to students with higher-than-expected costs and according to need; part-time students can apply if studying at least 50% of a full-time course. Contact your university.

Help for students with disabilities

The Disabled Students' Allowance for postgraduate study offers up to £10,260 p.a. for full- or part-time students on a course that requires first-degree entry. See *Bridging the Gap*, available free from the Department for Business, Innovation and Skills Publications Department.

Are funding arrangements the same for all parts of the UK?

No. For residents of Scotland, Wales, Northern Ireland, the Channel Islands and the Isle of Man, funding arrangements are slightly different.

Loans

OK, so nobody is going to fund me: can I get a loan?

Yes, but not the student loan. There are four excellent alternative schemes.

1. Professional and Career Development Loan

These are available only to those taking vocational training of up to two years. You can borrow up to £10,000 and not less than £300. The loan is designed to cover course fees (although only 80% is given if you are in full employment) plus books, materials and living expenses where applicable. The loan is provided by three banks only: Barclays, the Co-operative and the Royal Bank of Scotland. Loans can be for a full-time, part-time or distance learning course. Interest on the loan is paid by the government while you are studying and for one month after your course has finished (or up to six months if you are unemployed when repayment should start); call 0800 585 505 for a free booklet on Professional and Career Development Loans (the line is open seven days a week 8a.m.–10p.m.) or contact the banks directly. It is worth talking to all three banks as payback arrangements may differ.

See page 250 for other loans from banks.

What Do (Full-time) Master's Graduates Do?

Six months after graduation:

▶ commercial, industrial and public sector managers: 19.4%

▶ teaching professionals: 11.5%

▶ business and financial professionals: 11.5%

▶ marketing, sales and media professionals: 8.3%

▶ health professionals: 7.9%

▶ numerical clerks, cashiers, clerical, retail and bar staff: 7.1%

▶ information technology professionals: 3.5%

▶ engineering professionals: 3.2%

▶ scientific professionals: 3.1%

▶ other professionals: 19.9%.

Source: HECSU, *What do Master's Graduates do?* 2007–2008

2. Business School Loan Scheme

If you want to take a Master of Business Administration course, the Association of MBAs (AMBA) should be able to help. It runs a special scheme to assist graduates and other suitable applicants to study for an MBA. The scheme is run in conjunction with NatWest. To take advantage of the scheme you need to have a Bachelor's degree or other suitable professional qualification, a minimum of two years' relevant work experience or five years' experience in industry or commerce, and to have secured yourself a place on an MBA course at a business school that is on the association's approved list.

cash crisis

If you have just graduated and already have a loan to pay off, think twice before getting even further into debt.

Maximum loan

▶ Full-time students: two-thirds of present or last gross salary, plus tuition fees for each year of study; no repayments required while studying.

▶ Distance learning students: tuition fees plus study equipment to a value of £10,000.

See www.mbaworld.com for more details. Table 43 shows which of the UK's business schools are the most internationally renowned.

Table 43 International Business School Ranking: where the top UK business schools come in the world top 100

School name	2010 rank	2009 rank
London Business School	1	1 (joint)
University of Oxford: Said	16	20
University of Cambridge: Judge	21	11
Lancaster University Management School	24	27
Cranfield School of Management	26	35
Imperial College London Business School	32	39
Manchester Business School	40	32
City University: Cass	41	41
Warwick Business School	42	37
University of Strathclyde Business School	51	41
Aston Business School	73	77
Durham Business School	74	80
Birmingham Business School	75	83
University of Bath School of Management	87	83
University of Edinburgh Business School	89	–
Bradford School of Management/TiasNimbas Business School	89	87/–
Hult International Business School	94	–

Source: *Financial Times* Business School Ranking 11 March 2010

3. Law school loans

Assisted by the Law Society, a number of major banks run a special scheme to help students fund law school courses. The loan, which currently stands at up to £25,000, is given at very favourable rates. For more details and an application form, contact the banks directly.

4. Postgraduate loan

What loans do banks offer to postgraduates? Table 44 gives the breakdown of what's on offer.

Table 44 Postgraduate loans available by bank and course area

Bank	Course area	Amount offered
Barclays	Professional and Career Development Loan (for vocational training lasting at least one week)	£300–£10,000
Co-operative	Professional and Career Development Loan	£300–£10,000
HSBC	Graduate Loan: only available to existing customers	£1,000–£25,000; available up to five years after graduation

Bank	Course area	Amount offered
Lloyds TSB	Further Education Loan: only available to existing current account customers studying full time for a professional qualification: architect, barrister, chartered engineer, dentist, doctor, optometrist/optician, pharmacist, solicitor, surveyor or veterinary surgeon	£1,000–£10,000 at a preferential rate; can delay repayments for 48 months and can take up to five years to repay; must be permanent UK resident studying at a recognised UK institution
	Graduate Loan	£1,000–£10,000
NatWest	Professional Trainee Loan: available for those studying to be barrister, solicitor, doctor, dentist, pharmacist, vet, chiropractor, optometrist, osteopath or physiotherapist	Up to £20,000 for full-time students; full-time trainee solicitors and barristers can borrow up to £25,000
	MBA Loan	Full-time students can borrow up to two-thirds gross pre-course salary plus course fees up to 80% (less any grants); repayment holiday for three months on completion of course; tranche draw-down option available
	Graduate Loan: NatWest current account holders only	£1,000–£15,000 if graduated in last three years and have full-time job or job offer
	Interest-free Graduate Overdraft Repayment Plan	Interest-free loan to repay your student overdraft – up to £2,000 in the first year, £1,000 in the second year, £500 in the third year after graduation; whole sum must be repaid within three years of graduation
Royal Bank of Scotland	Law Student Loan (GDL/LPC full time or part time)	Up to £15,000 repayable over seven years; conversion courses limited to £5,000
	Healthcare, Chiropractic, Dentistry, Veterinary, Osteopathy, Medicine	Up to £15,000 repayable over seven years; no capital repayments will be made during the course (normally one year) or for 12 months after, with interest rolling up during that time

(Continued)

Bank	Course area	Amount offered
	Professional and Career Development Loan (for vocational training lasting at least one week)	£300–£10,000
	Graduate Loan: RBS current account holders only	£1,000–£15,000 for those who have graduated in the last three years and who have a full-time job or job offer
	Interest-free Graduate Repayment Loan	Up to £2,000 in the first year after graduation, £1,500 in the second year and £1,000 in the third year; whole sum must be repaid within three years of graduation

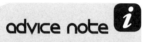

advice note

Want to know more about the cost and routes available to fund postgraduates? Visit www.prospects.ac.uk and search for 'Funding my further study'. The guide is designed to cater to the needs of the whole range of people who might consider participating in further study. Information on how to secure employer sponsorship makes it as relevant to those returning to study as to those going straight from university, and it also offers specific advice for both international students and those with disabilities.

For more details on Professional and Career Development Loans, see page 248.

Overseas students

What help is there for students coming to the UK from abroad?

There are scholarships specifically for overseas students, but there aren't very many, so apply early. The best source for finance is your own home government. Failing that, try the British Government through the British Council, the Foreign and Commonwealth Office or the Overseas Development Agency schemes.

International Students House provides accommodation bursaries for postgraduates from developing countries who are studying in London. Students should already have won a scholarship to cover fees. It also administers the Mary Trevelyan Fund, a hardship fund that will give up to £1,000 to London-based final-year postgraduates and undergraduates from developing countries who are facing financial difficulties. Last year this scheme was under-subscribed.

For more details, contact: International Students House, 229 Great Portland Street, London W1W 5PN, tel: 020 7631 8300 (or 020 7631 8310 for accommodation). See also www.ish.org.uk, which includes details of accommodation (see also *Sources of Funding for International Students* in the book list below).

There are also the Commonwealth Scholarship Plan, the UN and other international organisations. Some universities give awards and scholarships especially to students from abroad – but each university needs to be contacted individually. Some charitable trusts also cater for foreign students. EGAS (see details on page 211) might be able to help you winkle them out, or check for yourself in appropriate directories (see further information below). EU students can compete for UK postgraduate awards already listed in this chapter, but on a fees basis only.

As a student from abroad, what is it really going to cost?

Fees

There is no set rate of fees for postgraduate courses. In the past a minimum has been recommended, but each institution can charge what it wants. Fees for overseas students are generally substantially more than those for home students.

EU nationals are generally eligible for UK home student rates. Science courses are usually more expensive than arts courses. For average overseas postgraduate fees in 2009–2010, see page 220.

Living expenses

International Students House recommend that you will need at least £10,000 (excluding fees) to live in London per year. Our research in Chapter 1 will give you some idea of what living in Britain is likely to cost.

Further information for foreign students studying in the UK

► *Sources of Funding for International Students*, free from the British Council Information Centre, Bridgewater House, 58 Whitworth Street, Manchester M1 6BB, tel: 0161 957 7755 or email: generalenquiries@britishcouncil.org.

Facts and Figures

Top ten book-buying/ course equipment universities and their weekly spend.

► Plymouth: £13.87
► Leicester: £13.41
► Edinburgh: £11.97
► Newcastle: £11.80
► Brighton: £11.21
► Reading: £10.52
► Liverpool: £10.36
► Birmingham: £10.27
► Bristol: £9.97
► UEA: £9.73

Source: *NatWest Student Living Index Survey* 2009

- ▸ *The International Student's A–Z* is a guide to studying and living in England, Wales or Scotland (three editions) and published annually by International Students House, 229 Great Portland Street, London W1W 5PN, tel: 020 7631 8369.
- ▸ Association of Commonwealth Universities scholarships: www.acu.ac.uk.

Who to contact/what to read

- ▸ *Postgraduate Directory*: this is available free from your careers service.
- ▸ *Prospects* postgraduate magazine: options for further study and research, available free from your careers service.
- ▸ Prospects website: it's massive – see www.prospects.ac.uk.

CHAPTER 11

Making the money go round

In this final chapter, we look at banking and budgeting and try to give you some advice on how to manage your money, with the help of students and a bank student adviser who has first-hand knowledge of some of the difficulties students get themselves into, and how best to help them. With no increase in grants and loans in England for this year, but with fees still increasing, perhaps this chapter is more important than ever before. The main topics covered in this chapter are:

Problems and predicaments

'My rent is over £70 a week. There's gas and electricity and telephone on top of that; I'm not making ends meet.'

'I've got an overdraft of £3,500 and the bank is charging interest; if I've got an overdraft how can I pay the interest charges?'

'I thought: "£1,500, wow!" at the beginning of the term and blew the lot in the first few weeks. I haven't even got the money for my train fare home.'

'I'm a Geography student and have to go on a compulsory trip. Where on earth am I going to find £120?'

'I know now that I shouldn't have bought the car and spent all that money on booze, but ...'

Budgeting: what it is and how you do it

The principles are incredibly simple. But putting them into practice is, for many people, incredibly hard. It is a matter of working out what your income and expenses are and making sure the latter don't exceed the former. It may sound rather boring, but it's a lot better than being in debt. The students quoted earlier obviously didn't budget.

A bank student adviser's view

'A student loan of over £4,900! It certainly sounds a lot, but is it really? If all you are receiving is the standard funding for students then you haven't got wealth beyond your dreams, just the absolute minimum for survival. Bear that in mind right from the start and every time temptation looms, you shouldn't go far wrong. There will always be those who like to live on the edge – spend now and cope with debt and disaster later. Most students who get into debt are genuinely surprised at how easily the money "just slipped through" their bank account. Debt has a way of just creeping up on you if you let it. So be warned.'

Student views

Where to keep your money: bank, building society or under the mattress?

Before you can start budgeting you need to choose somewhere to keep your money. In fact, the Student Loan Company won't pay out your loan unless you have an account.

We would recommend either a bank or a building society. They are generally quite keen to attract students' accounts because they see students as potential high-earners – as you'll see on page 261, where we look at the enticing freebies they offer. These are worth looking at, but they shouldn't be the deciding factor.

It is more important to choose a bank or building society that is located close to your home or place of study. While these days you can use the cash-dispensing machines in most branches of most banks and building societies, it's a good idea to be able to speak to someone face to face.

Beware the private enterprise **cash crisis** cash machines; they generally charge for withdrawals, sometimes as much as £2. Not a good deal if you are only drawing out £10. Most banks' cash machines are free to users whether you are a customer of that bank or not. The machine will always tell you if it is making a charge, so always check.

What type of account?

There are a number of different types of account. At the bank you'll need to open what's called a current account so you can draw money out at any time. Many banks offer accounts specially designed for students, so it's worth checking with them what they have. Some current accounts give interest – not as much as a savings account, but every little helps. Check your bank for interest rates. A building society current account is very similar to a bank account. They, too, give instant access to your money, and also pay interest on any money in your account. How much depends on the going rate and your building society. Look for 'free banking' – this means that you don't pay charges when in credit or within your interest-free overdraft.

Sharia-compliant accounts

There are a number of banks that offer Sharia-compliant accounts, including HSBC, Lloyds TSB and the Islamic Bank of Britain. However, you would not be entitled to the special student incentives mentioned later in this chapter – at the moment. But things could change!

Shop around

If you are looking for a bank account, shop around and compare the banks and what they can offer you in terms of overdrafts, etc. If you want an overdraft, the simplest way to compare charges is to ask for the EAR – the effective annual rate. This is a standardised way of expressing the total cost of borrowing if you were continually overdrawn for a year.

It is, banks advise, also worthwhile asking the following questions.

- How much interest will I earn if I am in credit?
- Do I get a free overdraft facility? If so, how much?
- If I want to arrange a larger overdraft, will I be charged an arrangement fee?
- What will the interest rate be on my overdraft?
- If I am overdrawn without consent, how much will I be charged for:
  - the unauthorised balance?
  - the bounced cheques?
- How easy is it to get an overdraft?
- What are the rates of interest charged if my overdraft goes beyond its limit, and how easy is it to extend it?
- What are the interest rates on graduate loans? (Some are much better than others.)
- What happens to my overdraft once I graduate?
- How close is the local branch to my university/lodgings?
- Are there reciprocal cash-dispensing facilities close to my institution? (Otherwise you could be charged for making withdrawals.)

What will you get when you open an account?

When you open an account you may receive some or all of these services and facilities.

► Chequebook, which you can use to pay big bills and for large purchases.

► Cheque guarantee card, which could be for up to £100. Some banks limit it to £50 for students. This states that the bank will guarantee your cheque up to the amount shown on the card, so the shop where you are making your purchase will let you take the goods away there and then. This is often incorporated into your cash card.

► Cash card, which enables you to withdraw cash from a cash machine, and may offer additional payment functions.

► Debit card (SOLO, Switch, Maestro or Delta), which will automatically debit your account for goods bought when passed through a terminal at the point of sale.

► The three-in-one card. Most banks and building societies combine the facilities listed above into multifunctional cards, which act as cheque guarantee cards, give access to cash machines and can be used as debit cards so you can purchase goods and services without writing a cheque.

► Account number, which you will need for any correspondence with your bank.

► PIN – this is your personal identification number, which you will need to remember and use when getting money from the cash dispenser.

► Paying-in book containing paying-in slips, probably with your branch name printed on them, which you can use when paying in cheques and cash. Just fill in the slip and pass it to your bank. Most banks provide pre-printed envelopes, which you can pick up in your branch and then post through a letter box in the banking hall. You can also pay in cheques through some cash machines.

► Statements sent to you at regular intervals (we would advise you to ask for them monthly). The statement will give details of the money going in and out of your account – an essential factor in budgeting properly.

► Internet banking.

► 24-hour telephone banking, which allows you to keep in touch with your student account and credit card account day and night.

advice note ⓘ

► Don't keep your cheque guarantee card and chequebook together. If they're stolen, somebody could clean out your account.

► Keep your personal identification number (PIN) secret. Never write it down or tell it to anyone else.

► Cheques take three days to clear from an account – so don't go on a mad spending spree if you find you have more money in your account than you thought. The read-out on the cash machine may not be up to date.

▶ Student contents insurance.

▶ You may also be able to apply for a credit card, but think about it seriously before doing so – it could mean more debt.

▶ Freebies (see below).

Overdrafts, loans and freebies

Which bank should I choose? What's the carrot? What will they do for me?

So what's on offer?

Overdraft

The most useful offer made by banks to students is the interest-free overdraft. As you will see from Table 45 (page 262), it could add between £1,000–£3,000 to your spending power. Is it used? Our research with students showed that around 50% of students thought they would be overdrawn this year. But it eventually has to be paid back. And don't assume it is yours as a right: you must ask first.

Most banks also offer special arrangements for paying the overdraft off once you graduate (see Table 45, page 262). But check with your bank what the arrangements are before you step on the slippery slope to debt. How long will they give you to pay it off? What will the charges be then? How long does the interest-free loan last? These are the questions to ask.

Banks are the Student's Friend

Despite all the talk of students and their financial difficulties (our research shows that most students are likely to be in debt of anything up to £20,000 or even £50,000 by the time they qualify), banks are still falling over themselves in an effort to gain your custom. Nearly all offer students some kind of carrot to get them to open an account, and promise some kind of interest-free loan which, for most students, is an essential part of their funding package. 'How generous,' you might think. But banks aren't charities. Their reasoning isn't difficult to fathom: they are in the business of long-term investments. Students are the country's potential high-earners. Statistics show that people are more likely to change their marriage partner than their bank. The strategy is: get 'em young and you've got 'em for life.

Freebies

Most banks keep their new student offer under wraps right until the very last minute – largely so that their competitors can't top it with a better inducement.

This means the new offer is on the table from around June or July. Some banks have a closing date for their main offers, which could be as early as November, when the first loan cheques have been happily banked. The offer is generally open only to first-year students. Before giving you the benefit of their freebies, the bank of your choice will ask for some proof of your student status, such as your loan award letter or your first term's loan cheque.

To give you some idea of what you can expect and to check the next round of offers, we looked at the options students were given in 2009–2010 (see Table 45 on page 262). When comparing the facilities offered, if an interest-free overdraft facility of £3,000 sounds like an attractive inducement, and well it might, remember it could also be a temptation and will add to your overall debt.

What's the best banking buy?

Compare the current facilities offered by some of the major banks. Remember, student packages are usually revised each summer, so check with the banks for the latest information.

Graduates

There are other benefits to be considered once you graduate, such as covering your student bank overdraft and terms for paying it back and finding the money to tide you over while you get started in work. If you are thinking of undertaking further study, the banks may be able to help. But should you be bribed into choosing a bank?

Forward-thinking students may well decide that interest-free overdraft facilities carry more weight in making the choice than a paltry one-off cash offer. You would do well to look carefully at the small print before making a decision. Some banks offer more in the second and third years. But do you want that kind of temptation?

'I went for the freebies – rather than the most sympathetic bank manager – bad move when debt loomed.'

Third-year student, Glasgow

Table 45 Student facilities offered by some of the major UK banks in 2009–2010

	Santander	Bank of Scotland	Barclays	Halifax	HSBC	Lloyds TSB	NatWest	Royal Bank of Scotland
Free banking	Yes	Yes	Yes	Yes	Yes	Yes	Yes	Yes
Interest on current account	Yes, paid monthly 3%	Yes, paid monthly	Yes, paid quarterly	Yes, paid monthly	Yes, paid monthly	Yes	Yes, paid monthly	Yes
Free overdraft	1st year: £1,000 2nd year: £1,250 3rd year: £1,500 4th year: £1,800 5th year £2,000	1st–5th year and 1 year postgraduates: £3,000	Up to: 1st–5th year £2,000	Up to: 1st–5th year and one-year postgraduates: £3,000	Up to: 1st year: £1,000 2nd year: £1,250 3rd year: £1,500 4th year: £1,750 5th year: £2,000	1st–3rd year: £1,500 (tiered in 1st year); 4th–6th year: up to £2,000	1st year: tiered up to £1,250 2nd year: £1,400 3rd year: £1,600 4th year: £1,800 5th year: £2,000	Up to: 1st–5th year: £2,750
Student adviser	Yes, in all university campus branches	All branch advisers can help	Dedicated relationship managers	All branch advisers can help	Yes	Call-centre advisers available 24 hrs + branch advisers	Yes, in/near campus branches	Yes, on/near campus branches

Student insurance	No special package	See freebies	Student possession insurance	See freebies	Four levels of possessions cover from £2,000 to £5,000	No special package	Student essentials insurance	Yes – student essentials insurance
Freebies (often only available in the first few months)	£50 cash gift welcome for opening an account	Commission-free travellers' cheques and foreign currency, 25% off AA membership for one year, 20% discount on Card Care insurance	Mobile broadband offer through Orange, giving 25% off the monthly cost and a free USB modem	Commission-free travellers' cheques and foreign currency, 25% off AA membership for one year, 20% discount card on Card Care insurance	Two yrs free worldwide travel insurance, free Talkmobile SIM card with £5 pre-loaded credit, 24/7 internet banking, graduate service, 25% off *Lonely Planet* travel guides, savings with Dell and on CDs	Free NUS Extra Card giving discounts at 60+ retailers, free mobile banking until August 2010, AA learning to drive offer worth up to £75.99, free YHA membership for a year and 35 free eMusic downloads	Free five-yr 16–25 Railcard worth £130, student discounts for high-street and online retailers	Scotland only – three-yr 16–25 Railcard and bus pass in Edinburgh, Glasgow or Aberdeen
Paying off undergraduate overdraft	Interest-free advance overdraft of up to £2,000 decreasing to £500 p.a. over three yrs	Can keep student account for a year after graduating	Initial £200 interest-free, up to £1,500 – Yr 1: up to £1,500	Can keep student account for a year after graduating	Interest-free overdraft – Yr 1: £1,500	Interest-free overdraft – Yr 1: £2,000	Interest-free overdraft – Yr 1: £2,000	Interest-free overdraft – Yr 1: £2,000

(Continued)

	Santander	Bank of Scotland	Barclays	Halifax	HSBC	Lloyds TSB	NatWest	Royal Bank of Scotland
			Yr 2: up to £1,000		Yr 2: £1,000	Yr 2: £1,500	Yr 2: £1,000	Yr 2: £1,500
			Final yr with further interest-free limits available up to £3,000			Yr 3: £1,000	Yr 3: £500	Yr 3 £1,000
Low-cost graduate loan	Up to £10,000 (minus any interest-free overdraft)	No		No	Up to £25,000 at preferential rate. Range of repayment periods	Up to £10,000 with up to five yrs to repay	Up to £15,000 at preferential rate over seven yrs (five yrs for loans of £10,000 or more)	£1,000–£15,000 at preferential rate over base rate with seven years to pay if amount £10,000 or over
Professional study loan e.g. for Medicine, Dentistry, Optometry, Veterinary Science or Law		No		No	Considered on an individual basis	Further Education Loan up to £10,000 for existing Lloyds TSB current account holders	Up to £20,000 (trainee barristers/solicitors up to £25,000) MBA Loan available	Up to £15,000
Career development loan	No	No	Yes up to £10,000	No.				Yes up to £8,000

Can I open two student bank accounts?

The banks don't like it, but the fact is you can and there isn't much they can do about it. However, two overdrafts to pay off are not to be recommended, especially if you are also paying off student and fee loans.

What is a bank student adviser?

A student adviser is somebody in the campus branch of the bank or the branch closest to your college who deals with student problems. They are usually fairly young, and they are always well versed in the financial issues students face. Certainly you will find them sympathetic and full of good advice on how to solve your particular problems. But you won't find them a soft touch, as one student adviser pointed out: 'It's no good us handing out money like confetti – it just builds up greater problems for the student later on.'

What is a low-cost graduate personal loan?

This can be a life-saver for the newly qualified graduate. It is a special personal loan scheme offered by some banks to graduates to help tide them over the first few months while they get settled into a job. Most banks offer anything up to £10,000, some up to £25,000 or more, and others up to 20% of your starting salary. A graduate loan can be individually negotiated. The loan could be used to pay for suitable clothes for work, a car, advance rent – whatever you need. But remember: nothing is for free. You will have to pay interest, and if you already have a student loan and a substantial overdraft, this might be just too much debt. The graduate loan should not be confused with the many other types of loan banks offer to postgraduates to assist with study (see Chapter 10).

Banks' websites

Check out the banks' websites for the latest information and offers.

- Bank of Scotland – www.bankofscotland.co.uk
- Barclays – www.barclays.co.uk
- HSBC – www.hsbc.co.uk
- Lloyds TSB – www.lloydstsb.co.uk
- NatWest – www.natwest.com
- Royal Bank of Scotland – www.rbs.co.uk.
- Santander (formerly Abbey) – www.santander.com

> Never run up an overdraft without asking the bank first. They are much more sympathetic if you put them fully in the picture. And unless they know you are a student, you could find you miss out on the interest-free loan. Talk to your bank's student adviser – ideally before you hit a problem.
>
> **cash crisis**

'I ended my first term at uni £300 overdrawn. What a shock! How did it happen? It's only too easy if you don't keep a close watch on your account. I now bank online so can check-up all the time. Okay, so I do have an overdraft, but at least I know.'

Second-year Languages student, Durham

'Create a spreadsheet with all your outgoings and income – unless you see it written down it's very hard to see how much you're spending.'

Fourth-year Medicine student, St George's

'Have a budget – only way to really keep track of things. Helps you realise how much you do spend. Good way to do this is to take out cash at the beginning of the week and never use cards.'

Fourth-year Classics student, St Andrews

Your income: how much?

It's all very well to have an official piggy bank in which to keep your money, but where is the money going to come from and how much is it likely to be? If you have read the rest of this book, you should by now have some idea how much you are likely to have as a student. We have listed some of the likely sources in our budgeting plan. With a little ingenuity, you may have discovered others.

A step-by-step budgeting plan

1. Take a piece of paper and divide it into four columns (see Figure 1). On the left-hand side, write down your likely income sources and how much they will provide, for example:

    ▶   maintenance grant

    ▶   bursary

    ▶   parental contribution

    ▶   fee loan

    ▶   student loan

    ▶   sponsorship

    ▶   money earned from holiday job

    ▶   money earned from term-time job

    ▶   money from Access to Learning Fund

Figure 1 Sample budgeting plan

Income		Outgoings	Predicted	Actual
Grant	£	Fees	£	£
Bursary	£	Rent/college board	£	£
Parental contribution	£	Gas	£	£
Fee loan	£	Electricity	£	£
Student loan	£	Telephone	£	£
Sponsorship	£	Launderette/cleaning	£	£
Job	£	Food	£	£
Access to Learning Fund	£	Fares – term time	£	£
		Fares – to college/home	£	£
		Car expenses	£	£
		Books/equipment	£	£
		TV licence	£	£
		Student rail/bus card	£	£
		Broadband	£	£
Total:	**£**	**Total:**	**£**	**£**
		Socialising	£	£
		Hobbies	£	£
		Entertainment	£	£
		Clothes	£	£
		Presents	£	£
		Holidays	£	£

- ▶ interest-free overdraft
- ▶ other (including additional help, trust funds, scholarships etc.).

2. The trouble with budgeting, especially for students, is that money generally comes in at one time, often in large chunks at the beginning of a term, and your outgoings are needed at other times. When you work you will probably find it easiest to budget on a monthly basis, but as a student you may have to do it either termly or yearly, depending on how the money comes in.

3. In the second column, write down what your fixed expenses will be – things that you have to pay out – like rent, gas, electricity, telephone, food etc. Don't forget to include travel fares. Now total them up in the third column.

4. Subtract your fixed expenses from your income and you will see just how much you have, or haven't, got left over to spend. Draw a line under the list and below it list your incidental expenses – things like socialising, clothes, the cinema, hobbies, birthdays etc. This is your 'do without' list: the area where you can juggle your expenses to make ends meet.

5.   Apportion what's left over to the things in this list, making sure you've got at least something left over for emergencies. Do the figures add up?

6.   Seems simple enough and logical on paper. But of course, it doesn't work quite as easily as that. There's always the unexpected. You can't get a job. Your car needs a new battery. People use more gas than expected. Did you really talk for that long on the phone?

7.   Having worked out your budget, use the final column on your budget sheet to fill in exactly how much your bills *actually* come to. In this way, you can keep a check on your outgoings and how accurate your predictions were and do something before the money runs out.

If you are having difficulty putting together a budget, look at the student examples at the end of Chapter 1, page 35.

Hot tip from a burnt student

'There are so many hidden costs at uni – expenses pop up all the time. It's impossible to budget at the beginning of term, which makes financial management a nightmare – sports levies, balls, tours, travel, books – and that's just for starters.'

Second-year Music student, Durham

What is a standing order?

Regular payments such as rent can be paid automatically from your bank account through a standing order. You just tell the bank how much to pay out and to whom, and they will do the rest. The system is ideal for people who are bad at getting round to paying their bills. Oops – forget to pay the electricity and you'll soon know.

Standing orders are not so easy to organise when you are in shared accommodation with everyone chipping in to pay the bill. However, we did discover one student household in Durham which had a special bank account, just for bills, which they all paid into.

What is a direct debit?

With a direct debit set up on your account, the bill is again paid automatically, but it works in a different way. The bank of the organisation you are paying the money to will collect the money directly from your account. This is an ideal way of paying when the amount being paid out is likely to vary.

Cards and the catches

Credit cards

These are an easy way to pay for things but they can also be an easy way to get into debt. When you have a card such as Mastercard or Visa, you are given a credit limit. This means you can make purchases up to that sum. Each month, you receive a statement of how much you owe. If you pay back the whole lot immediately there are no interest charges. If you don't, you will pay interest on the balance. There can be an annual charge for credit cards.

You can use your card in the UK and abroad at most shops and many restaurants. They are a way of getting short-term credit but are an expensive way of borrowing long term. On the plus side, they are a way to spread payments or ease temporary cash flow problems. If you live, as most students do, at two addresses (college and home), make sure you don't miss a monthly bill that needs to be paid.

Store cards

Many stores offer credit cards that operate in much the same way as described above, but can only be used in that particular store or chain of stores. Although most stores will check your credit rating before issuing you with a card, they are still too easy to come by – get a stack of them and you could find you're seriously in debt. A store card is quite different from a store loyalty card – the type issued by Boots, Tesco and many other companies. These give you points for everything you buy in that store, which you can save up and use to purchase products – a good thing to have if you are a regular customer.

Debit cards

You've probably seen the Switch/Maestro card in action, as most stores and garages have the system installed. By simply passing your debit card through a Switch/Maestro terminal, the price of the purchase you are making is automatically deducted from your account. What could be easier? Details of the transaction will show up on your next statement. Some stores will offer you cashback on a debit card, which could save you a trip to the bank.

While most big stores and pubs will not charge for giving cashback, some of the smaller stores may. Always check.

cash crisis

Safety check

Most banks and building societies will not send plastic cards or personal identification numbers to customers living in halls of residence or multiple-occupancy lodgings, because they could go astray or sit unclaimed in the hallway for days. All too easy to steal. You may have to collect them from a branch nearby.

What if the money runs out?

Help, I'm in debt!

Don't panic, but don't sweep the matter under the carpet and try to ignore it because it won't go away; in fact, it will just get worse. Get in touch with the student welfare officer at your university, the student adviser at your local university branch or your bank manager – or all three. They will have plenty of experience of helping students in debt and will be able to give the best advice and help. Impoverished and imprudent students are not a new phenomenon.

'I needed £200 to put down as my deposit for renting a house next year, but I hadn't got it, so I went round to my bank and they extended my overdraft.'

Getting an overdraft

If you are struggling, don't turn your back on the interest-free overdraft facilities that most banks offer students – they are considered by many students to be an essential part of their income, helping to fill that financial black hole between loan payments. As you can see from Table 45 on page 262, free overdraft facilities vary enormously, as do the amounts you can borrow – up to £3,000 in your first year.

If you go over your overdraft limit, get on the phone or call in to your bank immediately. Many of the clearing banks have campus branches or at least a branch in the town geared to dealing with students (see page 265). They'll probably be sympathetic and come up with a helpful solution.

'Don't borrow from a lot of places. If you've got an overdraft and a student loan, that's probably enough.'

First-year Urban Planning Studies student, Sheffield

A planned overdraft

'I'm going for an interview and need something to wear.'

This is not an unusual request from students in their final year – jeans and a scruffy T-shirt rarely make a good impression. Banks are very good at coming up with a plan to help you out with an obvious or specific need. After all, an interview success could mean you'll clear your overdraft that much more quickly.

An overdraft is often the cheapest way of borrowing, even if it is not part of the special student package. There are charges and interest rates, and these need to be checked out. The advantage of an overdraft is that you don't have to pay it back in fixed amounts, although the bank has the right to ask for its money back at any time.

Borrowing on credit

'Haven't got the money at the moment so I'll buy it on Mastercard.'

Easily done, but be warned – although Mastercard/Visa is excellent as a payment card, credit can cause problems. If you don't pay off your bill by the date given on your statement, you will have to pay interest and, compared with other sources of borrowing, the rate is very high. Unlike your friendly bank, credit card companies are not the sort of people you can negotiate with, and are very likely to sue. Don't see them as another source of income.

Personal loan

This is quite different from an overdraft. It is usually used when you want to borrow a much larger sum, over a longer period – say several years. It differs from an overdraft in that you borrow an agreed amount over a set period of time and the repayments are a fixed amount, generally monthly. You might take out a loan to pay for your course fees, but not for short-term credit to tide you over until your next grant cheque arrives.

What students did when in financial difficulties

Most students told the *Guide to Student Money* survey that they either borrowed from their parents, went to the financial or accommodation adviser at their university or cut down on their social life. Some also cut down on food. Getting a job was a popular course of action, but not always successful. All of this is good advice. A lot of students just said things were 'unresolved'. There were also some original thoughts:

'Worked too much, and neglected my social life for about a month.'
Second-year Genetics and Immunology student, Abderdeen

'Was forced to withdraw my entire poker winnings and start from scratch again.'
Third-year Economics student, UWE

'Ate less. Seriously.'
Second-year International Relations and Biblical Studies student, St Andrews

'Buy a lottery ticket and hope.'
Second-year Applied Genetics student, UWE

'Grow your own vegetables.'
Third-year Music student, Dartington

A bank manager's view

'The problems students have are very real. As a bank manager, all too often we find we are just picking up the pieces when things have gone too far. Debt brings stress, and that will affect your ability to study. Come sooner rather than later.'

Don'ts

… which unfortunately some students do!

▶ Don't fall into the hands of a loan shark. Any loan offered to students, except from a recognised student-friendly source e.g. banks, building societies, parents or the Student Loans Company, should be treated with the utmost caution and suspicion. It's bound to cost you an arm and a leg, and lead to trouble.

▶ Don't run up an overdraft with your bank without asking first – even the much-vaunted interest-free overdraft offered by most banks to students should be checked out first, otherwise you might find you are being charged. They need to know you are a student.

▶ Don't forget to pay your gas and electricity bills. Make them top priority. A week or two on bread and (cheap) jam is better than having to pay court costs.

▶ Don't pawn your guitar, only to find you can't afford to get it out to play at the next gig.

Thrift Tips

Leeds University Union Welfare Service suggests these ways of managing your money.

► Get value for money – use markets or large supermarkets for fresh fruit and vegetables. Your local corner shop may be convenient, but is often more expensive.
► Make the most of student discounts for coach and rail travel, clubs, restaurants and hairdressers.
► Use the library rather than buying books – has your uni got a second-hand bookshop?
► Withdraw only the amount of cash you actually need on a weekly basis from the bank – otherwise it will disappear.
► Don't try 'kiting'. The banks have got wind of what's been going on, and you're bound to be found out and get into real trouble. For the uninitiated (like this author), 'kiting' is the dishonest practice of making the most of the time lapse between people reporting that their credit card is missing and it being recorded as stolen. Be warned: it is a criminal offence, and could end up increasing your debts – or even worse.
► Don't get blacklisted with the bank. 'Kiting' is a sure way of getting a bad record. Running up an overdraft you can't pay off is another.
► Don't see credit cards as another source of income.

A final word of advice from a student

'Before starting a degree, students don't realise just how tough it's going to be. You think, how on earth can anybody be so irresponsible as to get into £22,000 worth of debt? But once you are into university life, you know only too well. Despite the hardship, don't be put off; university is excellent – an incredible experience not to be missed!'

Savings?

Most books on budgeting give lengthy advice on saving. We think it unlikely that students will do more than just make ends meet, and even that will be a struggle. However, if you do find that you have some surplus cash, or are in the lucky position of being able to do without the student loan and decide to take it out as an investment, you could put it in an ISA or open a savings account at a bank, building society or the Post Office. Check out the interest rates and the terms and conditions. Many high-interest accounts give limited access to your money – so watch out.

Barclays' Money Managing Tips

Most banks close to universities have student advisers. Barclays has a national network of over 200, whose full-time job is to advise students on how best to manage their money while at university. This is their list of top tips on managing your money. (Some have already been suggested by students elsewhere in this book, but repetition can't hurt if it keeps you out of debt.)

▶ Don't wait until you get to college to open an account. Open one at your local branch. You will need it in order to apply for a student loan.

▶ Once you know how much you will have to live on per term, ask your bank for advice on budgeting. Don't be worried about going back for further guidance if you're finding it hard to cope.

▶ Limit your borrowing to a few sources. Spreading debts around too much makes it difficult to keep track of them and can only create problems later.

▶ Be cautious about how much money you borrow on your overdraft, even if it is interest-free.

▶ Arrange to have your monthly statements sent to your term-time address to help you monitor your budget.

▶ Try to limit your trips to the cash machine to once a week, otherwise you could easily lose track of how much you are spending.

▶ Insurance is vitally important, but check with your parents first if you can be included on their house insurance.

▶ Wait until you arrive at university before buying expensive books and equipment, then you will know what you really need. Ask around for places offering the best deals such as your university bookshop, or buy second-hand textbooks from students in the years above you.

▶ As your loan comes termly, it is often a good idea to get the money paid into your savings account and then transfer money over perhaps every week or every month. This will help you budget and spend within your means.

▶ Familiarise yourself with the student services available to you at your university. Student support centres are in place to help you with all aspects of student life, including your finances.

▶ Keep checking your account to ensure all payments are made.

- Always deal with bills and statements as they arrive – try to avoid putting them to one side or forgetting to pay them. We recommend paying by direct debit if possible.

- If you've got problems, remember that your bank's student adviser is there to offer advice and support. Don't ignore a problem, hoping it will go away by itself – because it won't.

University is a great experience. Enjoy every minute of it. Be concerned about money, but don't get stressed out. Most students do find a way of making the financial sums add up and having a good time.

Index

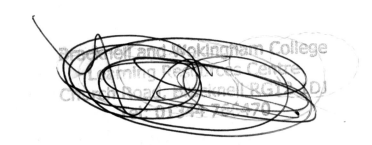